Binghamton Babylon

THE SUNY SERIES

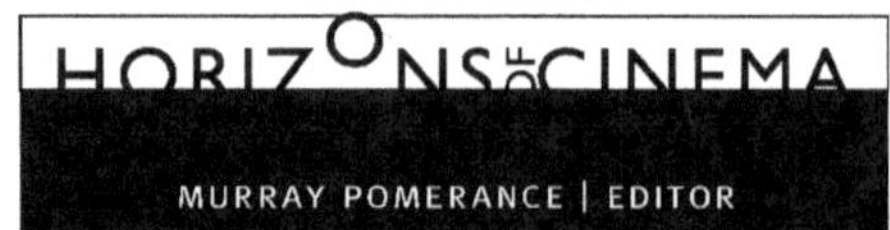

Also in the series

William Rothman, editor, *Cavell on Film*

J. David Slocum, editor, *Rebel Without a Cause*

Joe McElhaney, *The Death of Classical Cinema*

Kirsten Moana Thompson, *Apocalyptic Dread*

Frances Gateward, editor, *Seoul Searching*

Michael Atkinson, editor, *Exile Cinema*

Paul S. Moore, *Now Playing*

Robin L. Murray and Joseph K. Heumann, *Ecology and Popular Film*

William Rothman, editor, *Three Documentary Filmmakers*

Sean Griffin, editor, *Hetero*

Jean-Michel Frodon, editor, *Cinema and the Shoah*

Carolyn Jess-Cooke and Constantine Verevis, editors, *Second Takes*

Matthew Solomon, editor, *Fantastic Voyages of the Cinematic Imagination*

R. Barton Palmer and David Boyd, editors, *Hitchcock at the Source*

William Rothman, *Hitchcock, Second Edition*

Joanna Hearne, *Native Recognition*

Marc Raymond, *Hollywood's New Yorker*

Steven Rybin and Will Scheibel, editors, *Lonely Places, Dangerous Ground*

Claire Perkins and Constantine Verevis, editors, *B Is for Bad Cinema*

Dominic Lennard, *Bad Seeds and Holy Terrors*

Rosie Thomas, *Bombay before Bollywood*

Binghamton Babylon

Voices from the Cinema Department, 1967–1977

(a non-fiction novel)

❧

Scott M. MacDonald

Foreword by

J. Hoberman

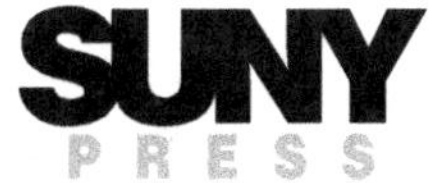

Cover: Frames from the film *Serene Velocity* courtesy of Ernie Gehr.

Published by State University of New York Press, Albany

Printed in the United States of America

For information, contact State University of New York Press, Albany, NY
www.sunypress.edu

Production, Ryan Morris
Marketing, Anne M. Valentine

Library of Congress Cataloging-in-Publication Data

MacDonald, Scott M.
Binghamton Babylon : voices from the cinema department, 1967–1977 / Scott M. MacDonald ; foreword by J. Hoberman.
pages cm. — (SUNY series, horizons of cinema)
Includes bibliographical references and index.
ISBN 978-1-4384-5889-2 (hardcover : alk. paper)
ISBN 978-1-4384-5888-5 (pbk. : alk. paper)
ISBN 978-1-4384-5890-8 (e-book)
1. State University of New York at Binghamton. Cinema Department. 2. Motion pictures—Study and teaching (Higher)—New York (State)—Binghamton. I. Hoberman, J. II. Title.

PN1993.8.U5S75 2015
791.43071'174775—dc23 2015001355

10 9 8 7 6 5 4 3 2 1

With the recovery of Babylonian independence, a new era of architectural activity ensued, and . . . Nebuchadnezzar II (604–561 BC) made Babylon into one of the wonders of the ancient world. Nebuchadnezzar ordered the complete reconstruction of the imperial grounds, including rebuilding the Etemenanki ziggurat and the construction of the Ishtar Gate—the most spectacular of eight gates that ringed the perimeter of Babylon. . . . All that was ever found of the original Ishtar gate was the foundation and scattered bricks.

—From a 2013 Wikipedia entry on Babylon

Contents

Foreword by J. Hoberman ix

Preface xi

BINGHAMTON BABYLON (a nonfiction novel)

Introduction 3

The Voices 11

The Weave 21

1. Emergence 21
2. First Flush 45
3. Maelstrom 69
4. Collision 97
5. New Directions 117
6. Younger Colleagues and More Visitors 143
7. Politics 163
8. Denouement 183

Appendix 1: "A Pedagogical Cinema" 197

Appendix 2: *Ken Jacobs* by Art Spiegelman 239

Acknowledgments 243

Index 245

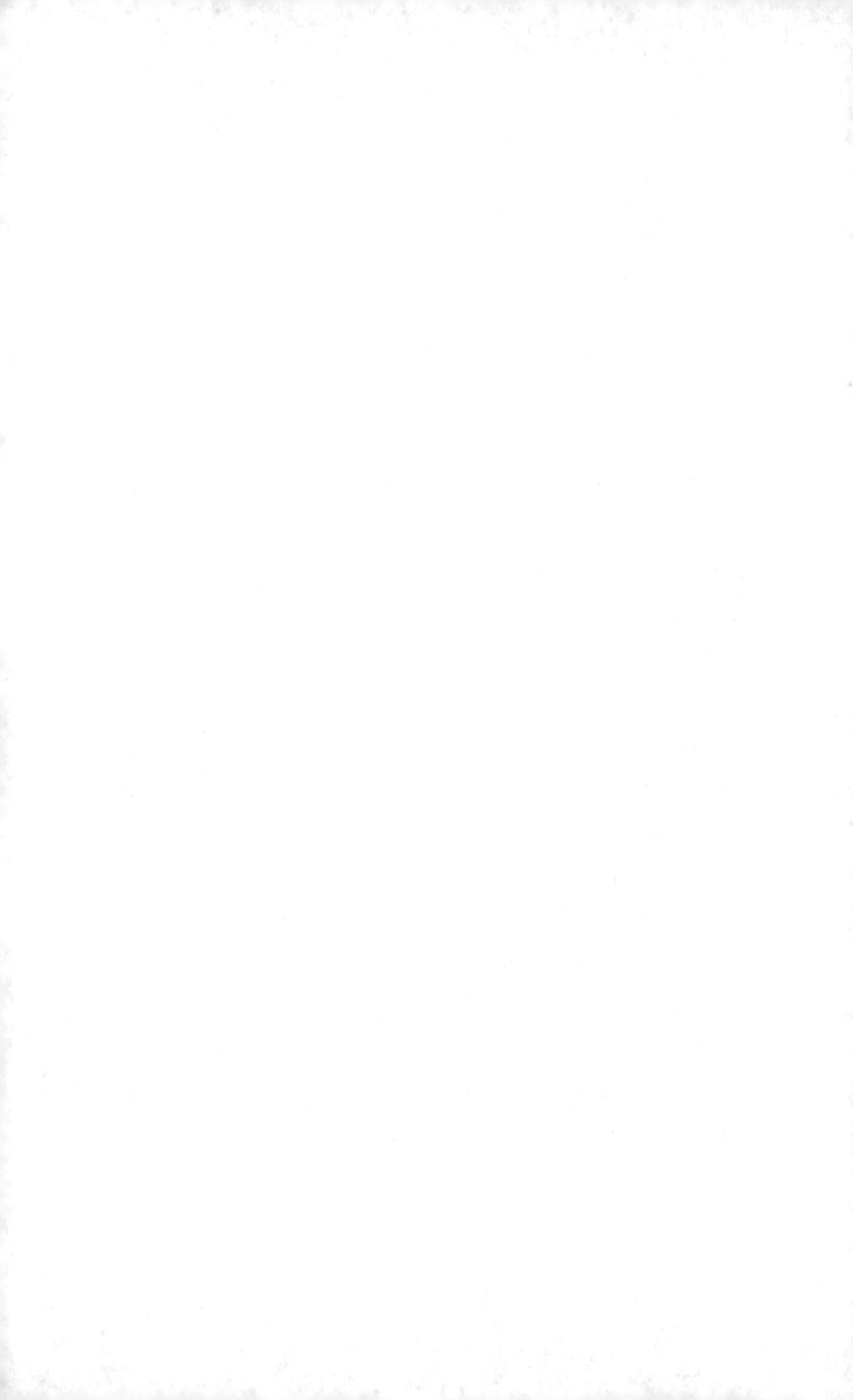

Foreword

J. Hoberman

Binghamton Babylon; Binghamton, My India; Binghamton Confidential: For me, the State University of New York at Binghamton aka Harpur College was the High Sixties (sex, drugs, confusion), culminating in the life-changing creation of the Cinema Department orchestrated by lit-prof-turned-filmmaker Larry Gottheim and the Big Bang arrival of the film artist Ken Jacobs.

I came to Binghamton in the fall of 1966, because, like many kids who might otherwise have gone to one of New York City's then free colleges, I had won a Regents Scholarship—tuition cost but $200 a semester—and because a girl I dated in high school was there as well. If the institutional red brick Harpur campus looked a bit like a housing development to this son of Queens, there was nothing familiar about the Triple Cities of Binghamton, Endicott, and Johnson City, and the surrounding Southern Tier. To call this place exotic was to say the least.

Binghamton was the back of beyond, the end of the world. We heard that Senator Robert F. Kennedy had obtained federal aid by making it the northernmost part of Appalachia, and that in the 1930s, when the Communist Party wanted to exile someone they sent them up here to organize the Endicott Johnson shoe factories. It was only a few miles from campus to the site of the 1957 Mafia summit called the Apalachin Meeting and less than an hour's drive to the remote Pennsylvania farmhouse where the fugitive Patty Hearst would later lie low during the summer of 1974. So many legends! But mainly, as Scott MacDonald makes clear, Binghamton was a unique environment for the study of cinema, the avant-garde American Film Institute of an alternative universe. Professor

MacDonald's understanding of what he has most astutely identified as "pedagogical film" and the way that it developed on the Southern Tier is lucid and illuminating.

Not that I can be objective. Reading Scott's book I was moved, chastened, startled, and intensely grateful. A huge chunk of my life flashed (or perhaps erupted) before my eyes. I relived my own youthful enthusiasm, idiocy, and emotional tumult. It was a revelation to learn what other people had been thinking then and what they remembered of it now—not to mention the amazing stuff that happened after I left Binghamton (under a cloud) and returned to New York in the spring of 1971, the semester before Nicholas Ray appeared on the scene. In the tapestry of voices, gathered and tightly woven by Scott, I reexperienced epic events that I had seen and heard and almost forgotten—the epochal screening of Shirley Clarke's *Portrait of Jason*, the appearance of Hermann Nitsch's *Orgien Mysterien Theater*, the stormy world premiere of Hollis Frampton's *Critical Mass*, the indescribable adventures of "Mr. Radio Man," the gestation of the Collective for Living Cinema, and more.

Binghamton Babylon brought Binghamton back to me but, in a sense, I never left the place. I am still friendly with Ken and Flo Jacobs, with Steve Anker and Ernie Gehr and a half-dozen other Harpur veterans. I am still married to Shelley Katowitz, whom I met there. I am still writing film notes and still (though a senior citizen) trying to understand just what it was that I experienced as a twenty-year-old projectionist in Lecture Hall 6.

—New York City, May 2014

Preface

The cover of the Summer 2007 *Binghamton University Magazine* touts caricatures (by Bill Cigliano) of Binghamton graduates writer/producer/director Marc Lawrence, class of 1981 (whose writing credits include *Miss Congeniality*, 2000; and *Miss Congeniality 2*, 2005); the actor/comedian Paul Reiser '77 (star of the television series *Mad About You*, 1992–1999); and actor Billy Baldwin '85—drawing the reader's attention to "That's Entertainment," inside the issue (subtitle: "Alumni in the film field have the track records to prove it's possible to thrive in this competitive, ever-changing arena") by staff writer Tamar Morad. "That's Entertainment" includes a more elaborate set of caricatures featuring Reiser again, front and center, and in the near foreground, Marc Lawrence, Billy Baldwin, and film critic J. Hoberman '71 (holding a copy of the *Village Voice*). Toward the rear of the image, on the right, are caricatures of filmmaker Alan Berliner '77 and in the way-back, a tiny image of longtime Binghamton film professor, Ken Jacobs.[1] As one might expect, "That's Entertainment" is focused on the struggles and rewards of having a career in commercial media and implicitly suggests that a Binghamton University education must be at least adequate training for such a career. (See fig. 1.)

"That's Entertainment" also includes a sidebar, "The epicenter of experimental film": a photograph of the Collective for Living Cinema, which served the New York City cinema scene from 1973 to 1992, is accompanied by comments by Ken Jacobs, Alan Berliner, Dan Eisenberg '76, Steve Anker '72, and one of the founders of the Collective, Ken Ross '73. Morad suggests that the "novelty of experimental film waned in the late 1970s," but he quotes Steve Anker, then the Dean of the School of Film and Video at CalArts, to the effect that "independent

1. Two other caricatures are included: on the far left in the back, writer Andrew Bergman '65 (*Blazing Saddles*, 1974) and UCLA screenwriting professor, Richard Walter '65.

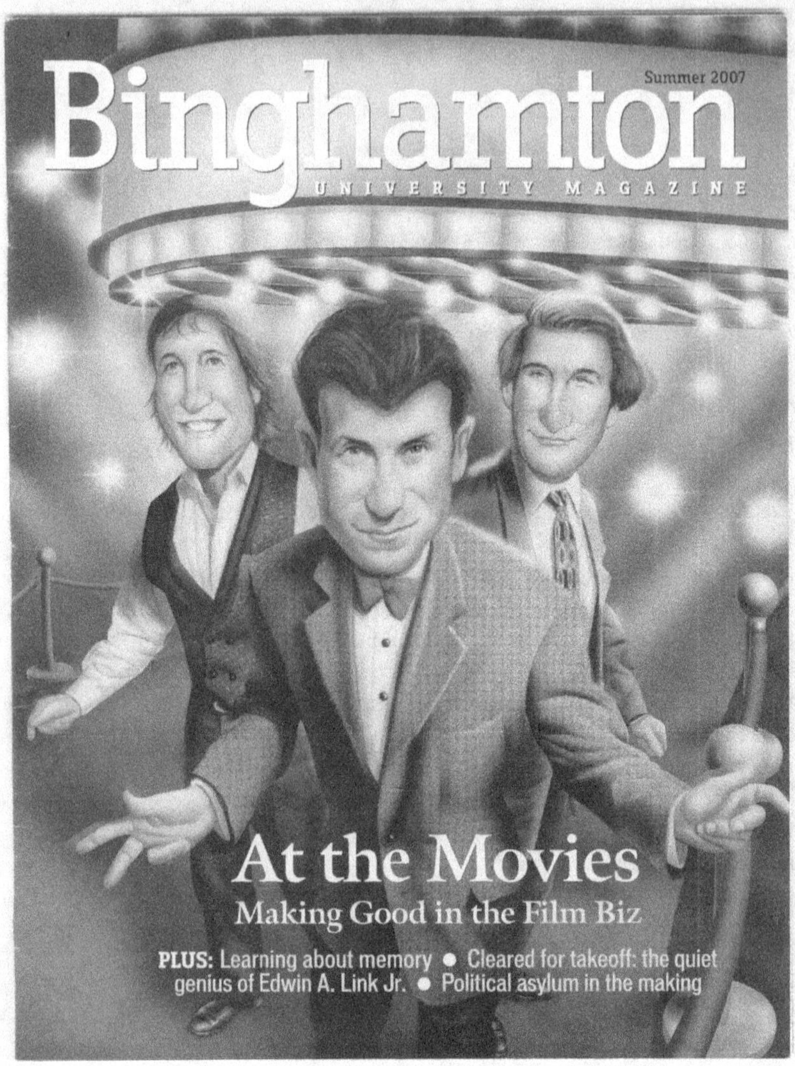

Figure 1. Cover of the Summer, 2007 issue of the *Binghamton University Magazine*. Courtesy *Binghamton University Magazine*.

film has become an accepted part of film culture." Though this brief puff piece relegates Binghamton University's contribution to the evolution of independent cinema to a sidebar, Morad can hardly be faulted, since this balance of attention is anything but unusual; indeed, given the way most colleges and universities privilege financial success, he can be congratulated for including any mention of the major thread in the tapestry of film history that has been least financially remunerative. Nevertheless, for those of us who are committed to the full range of cinematic accomplishment, "That's Entertainment" has Binghamton University's contribution to cinema history backassward; indeed, one might argue that the smaller the caricature in "That's Entertainment," the more important the person has been to the evolution of cinema and cinema studies, and further, that what is relegated to the sidebar in Morad's piece should have been the primary text.

For about ten years, between the mid-1960s and the mid-1970s, the Cinema Department at what was then the State University of New York at Binghamton (until 1965 it had been Harpur College, and in 1992 it became Binghamton University—though the undergraduate programs in fine arts and humanities, science and mathematics, and the social sciences are still called Harpur College of Arts and Sciences) created one of the most dynamic focal points for the study and production of independent cinema in the nation.[2] In a number of ways what happened at Binghamton during these years was quite special, and in large measure because of its ongoing influence, has become legendary. Graduates of the Cinema Department who experienced that moment are spread across the country, often in positions of considerable importance to the history of modern media and to the field of cinema studies.

At the same time, what happened in Binghamton, and especially the overall trajectory of events from about 1967 until 1977, was typical of the arrival of cinema into American academe during an era when traditional academic life itself was being challenged and transformed. Dana Polan has shown that the teaching of filmmaking and film studies in America had begun in a few universities by the 1920s, but the sudden excitement about studying film, especially on the part of college *students*, that welled up across America during the late 1960s was unprecedented, and indeed, has been unmatched in more recent decades.[3] In fact, during

2. I am using *cinema* to refer to all forms of moving-image media: that is, both film and video.

3. For a remarkably thorough history of the earliest American academic efforts to come to terms with cinema, see Dana Polan, *Scenes of Instruction: The Beginnings of the U.S. Study of Film* (Berkeley: University of California Press, 2007); see also Polan's "Young Art, Old Colleges: Early Episodes in the American Study of Film," in Lee Grieveson and Haidee Wasson, eds., *Inventing Film Studies* (Durham, NC: Duke University Press, 2008): 93–117. Dudley Andrew reminds us that cinema and media studies as a written discipline did not originate in the United States, indeed, that American scholars came late to film studies: his "The Core and the Flow of Film Studies" reviews the early contributions to film studies in Japan and the more recent developments in France and the UK that led to what he calls "the explosion of American film studies in the 1980s." See *Critical Inquiry* 35 (Summer 2009): 879–915.

the 1960s and early 1970s, film studies was the fastest-growing area of arts education in American universities.[4] Nowhere was this more obvious than in Binghamton.

Of course, much of this excitement was a product of the expansion of cinema history itself. During the 1960s art house cinemas proliferated and for a time films from western Europe and some other parts of the world as well, found their way to American audiences; cineastes even in smaller cities could see an Antonioni or a Buñuel or a Truffaut film in a local theater. At the beginning of the 1960s, documentary film had been energized by the arrival of the several technologies that made cinema-verite shooting (sync-sound shooting from within evolving events) possible, and new documentary genres—the rock documentary, most obviously—were attracting audiences. A substantial audience had also formed, at least within several major cities, for the forms of independent cinema that were coming to be known as Underground Film, the New American Cinema, experimental film, and avant-garde film—the proliferation of terms echoed the considerable variety of approaches. And even American commercial film was in a moment of transformation: a new level of experimentation was producing a broad range of interesting features, from *2001: A Space Odyssey* (1968) to *Night of the Living Dead* (1968) to *Easy Rider* (1969).[5]

By the end of the 1960s a multifaceted public film culture had clearly developed, and colleges and universities across the country were challenged to find faculty to minister to the many students wanting film

---

4. Michael Zryd provides useful information about this moment in "Experimental Film and the Development of Film Study in America," in Grieveson and Wasson, eds., *Inventing Film Studies*: 182–216, and reminds us of Thomas Bender's study of university enrollments during the era; Bender found that enrollments in film courses increased nearly tenfold during a period when university enrollments increased only threefold. See Thomas Bender, "Politics, Intellect, and the American University, 1945–1995," in Bender and Carl E. Schorske, eds., *American Academic Culture in Transformation: Fifty Years, Four Disciplines* (Princeton: Princeton University Press, 1998): 25.

5. Of course, *2001: A Space Odyssey* was filmed almost entirely in the UK, though it was produced by MGM. All three of these films have various connections with avant-garde filmmaking. The early sequence in *Easy Rider*, introducing the motorcycles, seems virtually an homage to Kenneth Anger's *Scorpio Rising* (1963) and *Kustom Kar Kommandos* (1965); avant-garde critic/scholar Annette Michelson's seeing *2001* over and over during its first run led to her interest in writing about cinema and her championing avant-garde film in *Artforum*; and *Night of the Living Dead* was made with a small budget, in an anti-Hollywood frame of mind and in Pittsburgh, which was becoming an important nexus for a variety of kinds of independent cinema.

courses. At SUNY-Binghamton, as at many colleges and universities, the challenge was accepted first by faculty trained in the literary arts. Larry Gottheim, a Yale PhD in what was then the new field of comparative literature, took upon himself the development of a more broad-ranging campus film culture and the establishment of a department of cinema—and transformed himself into a filmmaker. His first full-time hire was Kenneth Jacobs, an autodidact whose formal education ended in high school, but who had made a name for himself within the New York independent film scene and had, with his partner Florence Jacobs, led a fight against New York State film censorship of Jack Smith's *Flaming Creatures* (1963). Ralph Hocking, an art-education teacher who would become a video pioneer and found the Experimental Television Center; and Nicolas Ray, who had had a distinguished career in Hollywood, directing twenty-four features, including *They Live by Night* (1949) and *Rebel without a Cause* (1955), soon joined the department.

Since the teaching of cinema was new in most institutions, including at SUNY-Binghamton, the Cinema Department faculty were faced with the challenge and opportunity to design both a film curriculum and standards for what might sensibly be required of students. Not surprisingly, since Gottheim, Jacobs, Ray, and Hocking were driven largely by a passion for cinema and the new areas of moving-image study that were opening up, they assumed that their students should be passionately committed as well. Early on, courses involved three hours of class time three times a week, and, especially for those students working with Jacobs and Ray, this was just the beginning: Jacobs and Ray demanded virtually round-the-clock commitment. Indeed, what now seems most unusual about the Cinema Department in those early years is that so many students were not just willing, but *excited* to devote their lives to their studies.

Despite its many distinctive dimensions, however, the way in which Binghamton's small, dynamic department evolved during the period explored in this study was also, for better and/or worse, typical of the impact of the institutionalization of film studies during the 1970s. The euphoria around the arrival of cinema in academe resulted in several crises and conflicts that, in the end, caused a transformation in what it meant to study film and video. This transformation involved both gains and losses. In the end, the expansion of institutions to accommodate what has come to be called cinema and media studies often required that the freewheeling curricula and the open-ended commitment to learning so characteristic of the late 1960s and early 1970s be reined in, made to conform to the traditional structures of the academy.

To its credit, the first generation of formally trained film scholars created a field that is now recognized internationally. The Society for Cinema and Media Studies (SCMS), currently numbering "nearly 3,000 scholars in over 500 institutions located in 38 nations," to quote the SCMS website, has made a place for cinema and media study in educational institutions virtually worldwide. But the success of cinema's institutionalization has been accomplished at a significant loss for the vitality of film education: while, on one level, film study is alive and well across the United States, the complex public film culture that instigated cinema's arrival into academe at the end of the 1960s and the beginning of the 1970s is no longer apparent. In fact, except in a very few major urban areas, opportunities for experiencing the full range of cinematic possibility have either disappeared or have become confined to classrooms. The reasons for this are complex—though my suspicion is that this change is, at least in part, a downside of the way in which film studies made itself academically respectable.

The mantra of American academe since the 1960s has been "publish or perish," and in order to demonstrate that cinema studies was worthy of intellectual attention—to many academics in established fields, studying film seemed a fad—the first generation of film scholars focused on writing as the primary means of demonstrating their seriousness. That much of this writing, inspired by a range of mostly European theorists, turned out to be challenging, not just intellectually, but in its complicated prose (a function to some degree of the difficulty of merging a complex written discourse with a multifaceted visual art) has tended to limit the audience for "serious" film writing and study—and for many, has taken some of the pleasure out of being a cineaste.

It is also true that for many of those who see themselves as cinema and media study professionals, the glory of the field is the remarkable discourse the field continues to produce. Indeed, for the preponderance of scholar/teachers this discourse *is* film studies. In his review of the history of the field, Dudley Andrew conflates the study of cinema and media with writing about it: that is, with the literary discourse of criticism and theory that has struggled to take account of how cinema works and how it functions in the world.[6] And while few would deny the value of this understanding of the way in which film is studied, an unfortunate result is that this literary discourse has tended to limit scholarly commitment to the discourse of cinema itself.

6. Andrew, "Core and the Flow."

The field's continued, nearly exclusive reliance on published writings, at least for its evaluations of those who are, or hope to be, teaching cinema and media study, has had a cumulative tendency of exhausting energy for making sure that colleges and universities provide extensive opportunities for experiencing the full range of classic and modern cinema, not just within the classrooms of specialists but in the semipublic arena of the institution and even within the expanding world of new electronic media. One can hope that now that cinema and media studies have been integrated into the curricula of so many colleges and universities, increased attention can be paid to redeveloping a broader cinema exhibition culture within academic life and the society at large.

My considerable excitement about what seemed to be developing during the early years of the Binghamton Cinema Department, and its long-term impact on me, was precisely its foregrounding of an approach to film studies that did not rely on literary discourse. The Binghamton Cinema Department faculty assumed that the theater itself was a theoretical space and that the curating and screening of a broad range of films was a way of exploring the history and nature of cinema. Not surprisingly, the decade explored in *Binghamton Babylon* did not produce film scholars in the current sense or a notable written discourse. What it did produce was a remarkable number of men and women passionate about cinema—passionate about producing film and video, yes, but even more, about seeing that the theoretical discourse of cinema itself would continue to be available to academic and public audiences.

Further, during the extended moment when the Cinema Department established itself, those teaching within the department (and some of their students) produced a body of film and video work meant to offer in-theater experiences designed to teach audiences about the nature of moving-image media, and its accomplishments and potentials. This pedagogical cinema includes such canonical films and film projects as Ernie Gehr's *Serene Velocity* (1970), Ken Jacobs's *Tom, Tom, the Piper's Son* (1969, 1971), Larry Gottheim's *Fog Line* (1970) and *Horizons* (1973), Hollis Frampton's *Critical Mass* (1971), Tony Conrad's *Film Feedback* (1974), and Nicholas Ray's film-in-progress, *We Can't Go Home Again* (released in an unfinished version in 2013); and some of the seminal experiments in what would become known as video art, including Ralph Hocking's *The Experiment* (1969) and *Sitting by the Window* (1977). Hopefully, my documentation of the context out of which this body of work evolved adds something to our understanding of the work and expands our sense of the era within which it was produced. A number of these films and videos are discussed in the essay that forms an appendix of *Binghamton Babylon*.

The "weave" of voices that follows is based on interviews I have conducted with veterans of the Cinema Department—faculty, students, filmmakers who visited the department—over the past several years. Obviously, these voices account for only a miniscule percentage of the hundreds of students who took courses with the Cinema Department or even who majored in cinema during the period covered (the full-time faculty are more adequately represented). In making my choices, I have tended to privilege men and women who have played a demonstrable role in moving-image culture and the fine arts since leaving Binghamton. Further, I have privileged men and women who seem to have been particularly important to one another during their Binghamton years. I did not start out with a clear idea of how many interviewees I would want for the project, but as the process evolved and I began to hear many of the same memories and stories over and over, I came to feel that the essential experience of the Cinema Department during that moment was becoming reasonably clear—and began to focus on structuring the weave using the conversations I had assembled.

While most of those I was able to track down were willing to talk with me (many were enthusiastic), some were not, and I expect these absences, perhaps even some of the reasons for them, will be implicit within the weave itself. Like any research project, this one can only go so far; in order to present one interpretation of the particular history it documents, it must ignore a virtually infinite body of experience not explored. There is no escape from this, and my apologies in advance for whatever gaps seem especially problematic. Throughout my interviewing process, I urged the interviewees to be candid not only about intellectual and academic matters, but about the *life* of that extended moment, which like all real life is a combination of exhilarations and disappointments, collaboration and competition, affection and animosity, successes and failures, excesses and compromise.

One of the fascinations with memory is the way it can reflect lived experience in ways that actual documents of the remembered experiences cannot (of course, documents can often tell us what memory cannot). A fascinating example is the postscreening discussion of sections of Hollis Frampton's *Hapax Legomena* [1971–72], which took place on March 11, 1972. Thanks to Anthology Film Archives, this discussion is available at UbuWeb (http://ubu.com/sound/afa.html), but my guess is that no one who listens to that two-hour-plus discussion, without further knowledge of what particular individuals came to remember about that evening, will have any idea that this was a volatile and pivotal moment for the Cinema Department and even for the history of American independent film. The recollections within in the weave, however, make the significance of the moment quite clear.

My shaping of the interviewees' comments into a metaconversation that reflects my own sense of this extended cultural moment has led me to call Binghamton Babylon a nonfiction novel. After transcribing and editing these interviews and returning them to the interviewees to be checked for accuracy, I eliminated my interview questions and transformed the interviewees' comments into a metaconversation about the period from the mid-1960s to the mid-1970s, as they remember experiencing it. When I had decided which passages of the interviews to use, I gave the interviewees the opportunity to check the passages for accuracy again, but once they had returned this version of their comments to me with corrections, they had no further say in the weave itself: that is, all juxtapositions of speakers and whatever implications these juxtapositions may seem to create are my responsibility. Further, with only minor exceptions, I did not make the interviewees aware of what other interviewees had said. *Binghamton Babylon* is not meant to provide give-and-take within

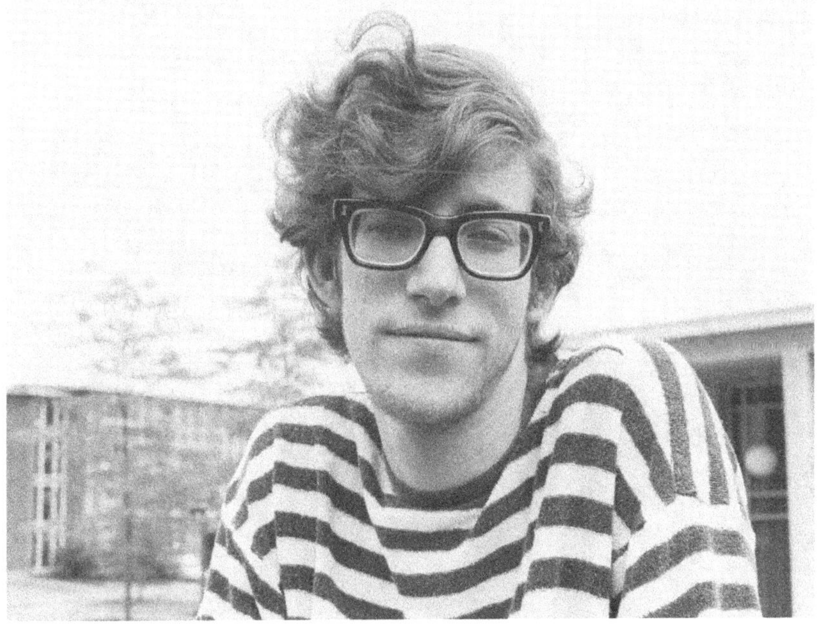

Figure 2. Mark Goldstein selfie, c. 1969. Courtesy Mark Goldstein.

a contemporary round-table discussion. I was interested in what memories those with a Binghamton connection would decide were important to recount, what has stayed with them over the decades as their personal psychic residue of the Binghamton experience.

Binghamton Babylon is illustrated with a variety of documents. As I explored the early years of the Cinema Department, I learned that one student, Mark Goldstein, had carefully documented people and events in dozens of photographs. As fully as anyone, Goldstein understood that what was happening around him might be of long-term importance. I have chosen imagery with regard to its relevance to comments made by the various voices, sometimes even when particular images do not attest to Goldstein's skills as a photographer.

Ultimately my goal has been to organize the voices so that this volume might communicate something of the experience of studying film and video during one extended and transformative moment. My hope is that this project will suggest other research projects evoking other nodal points in the history of cinema and of cinema studies, and perhaps, that it might instigate an ongoing discussion across the field of cinema and media studies about how creativity in independent filmmaking and in the study of moving-image media are best nourished, particularly within an academic context.

Binghamton Babylon

(a nonfiction novel)

Introduction

> "So we beat on, boats against the current, borne back ceaselessly into the past."
>
> —The concluding line of Nick Carroway's narration in F. Scott Fitzgerald's *The Great Gatsby*

Sometime during the spring of 1972, I received in my mailbox at Utica College of Syracuse University (where I had been hired to teach twentieth-century American literature, in which I had earned my PhD, and film, about which I knew very little), an invitation to a "University-wide Film Symposium" to be held at the State University of New York at Binghamton on Saturday and Sunday, April 29 and 30. As I hold this invitation in my hand now, it feels remarkably fancy, rather like a graduation announcement or a wedding invitation: it is printed on eighty-pound cover stock with deckle edge and felt finish and is folded horizontally so that the front page opens up, revealing the schedule of events. It is not a mailer; it must have come in an envelope specially printed for this invitation. The formality and elegance of the invitation suggests an excitement about the expanding interest in studying film history. As is clearer now, it is also evidence of a moment when the economy of New York State seemed to be booming and the SUNY system was building its reputation. (See fig. 3.)

The schedule of events begins with registration at 12:00 noon, followed by a 1:30 p.m. "screening and discussion of films by independent film artists," including *The Act of Seeing with Ones'* [*sic*] *Own Eyes* (1972) by Stan Brakhage, *Serene Velocity* (1970) by Ernie Gehr, *Nissan Ariana Window* (1969) by Ken Jacobs, *Barn Rushes* (1971) by Larry Gottheim, and a film "to be announced" by Richard Leacock. The screening is to be followed by "dinner on your own," then by a preview of "a film currently in production at Binghamton" by Nicholas Ray. Sunday events include a 10:00

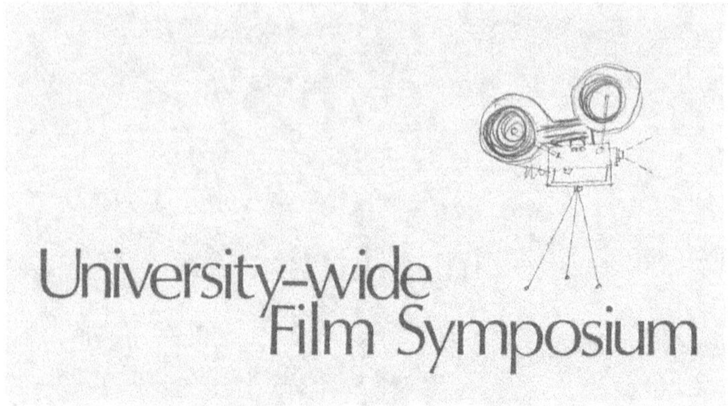

Figure 3. Cover of invitation to the first University-wide Film Symposium, April, 1972.

a.m. talk by Lawrence Alloway on "The Commercial Film," followed by a panel and discussion on "The Role of Film in the University" with Gerald O'Grady (who is mistakenly listed as a SUNY-Binghamton professor),[1] Richard Leacock (MIT), Larry Gottheim, and Kenneth Jacobs.

For a young assistant professor who had been hired to teach film history (and who was desperate to learn something about it!), this looked to be an event worth attending—even though I had not heard of any of the "independent film artists" listed in the program, and only vaguely remembered Nicholas Ray. Two local colleagues from Utica—Jerome Finklestein, who wrote movie reviews for the Utica *Observer-Dispatch*, and Joseph A. Gomez, who was teaching at Mohawk Valley Community College and researching what would become the first book on Peter Watkins (*Peter Watkins* [Boston: Twayne, 1979])—joined me, and we drove to Binghamton on the morning of the 29th. We must have decided in advance not to stay until Sunday morning—though I don't remember whether we had planned to stay for the Nicholas Ray event (I believe we drove back after the afternoon screening).

The program notes that were provided for the Saturday afternoon event announce a slightly different set of films from what is proposed in the invitation, to be presented in a different order. Two Jacobs films

1. O'Grady had begun teaching at SUNY at Buffalo in 1967, and would build a remarkable department of film and video there during the early 1970s.

2. The program notes indicate that *Adjacent Perspectives* is an excerpt from "a longer film THE RUSSIAN REVOLUTION: SON OF GOD: BINGHAMTON, MY INDIA (and other titles) being wholly shot in The Southern Tier" (the Southern Tier is that area of New York State that crosses the state just above the Pennsylvania line).

are listed—*Nissan Ariana Window* and *Adjacent Perspectives*[2]—along with Richard Leacock's *Happy Mother's Day* [co-made with Joyce Chopra, 1963]. The order of the filmmakers whose work was presented, as listed in the program notes, accords with my memory of this event—though I recall that the screening included only one Jacobs film: not one of those announced, but *Soft Rain* (1968). The screening opened with *Serene Velocity*, followed by *Soft Rain*, then apparently by *Happy Mother's Day* (ironically, despite the fact that it was already recognized as a canonical cinema-verite documentary, I have no memory of seeing this film that day), by *Barn Rushes*, and finally, by *The Act of Seeing with One's Own Eyes*. (See fig. 4.)

We tend to return, in memory and in our storytelling, to particular moments that seem pivotal to what we understand as our psychic and/or intellectual development, and I have returned to this particular screening, in my teaching and in my writing, over and over. Indeed, it has come to seem the single most transformative moment in my education—though I would not have been able to admit this on that fateful Saturday afternoon or during the drive back to Utica that evening, when I regaled my two colleagues with witticisms provoked by my outrage at the screening and what seemed the pretension of the symposium hosts' assumption that

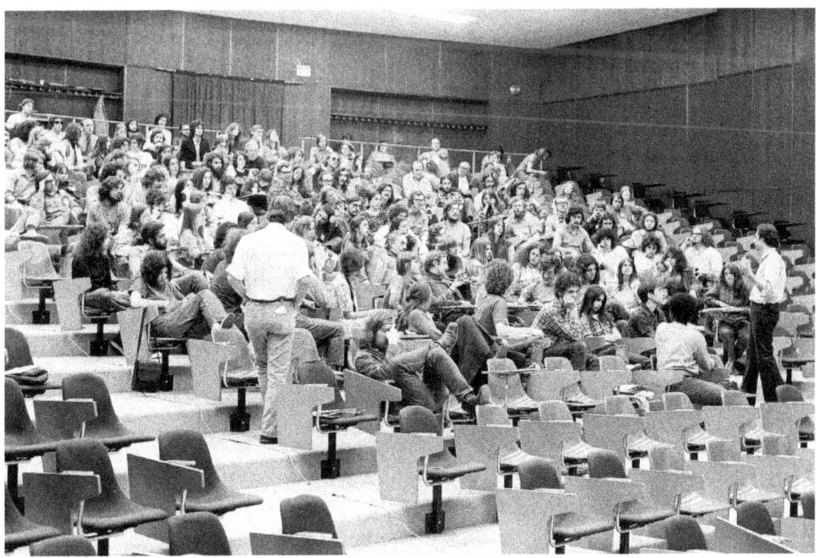

Figure 4. The audience at the University-wide Film Symposium, April, 1972; on the left, standing, Larry Gottheim; on the right, standing, Ken Jacobs. Ricky Leacock sits just to the right of Gottheim. I am visible in the top left of the image, in profile with long blond hair. Courtesy Mark Goldstein.

these were films by "independent film *artists*"—as I remember, my colleagues were a thoroughly receptive audience.

At the time, my sense of a "film artist" was someone like Luis Buñuel, or Akira Kurosawa, or François Truffaut, or even (thanks to the influence of Andrew Sarris), Buster Keaton—indeed, in 1972, I could not have told you what an "independent film artist" would have been independent from. What I saw on that afternoon in Binghamton was outside my sense of what was possible for cinema and entirely outside my sense of what filmgoers would or should put up with: what had shocked me as fully as the films was the fact that when the lights came on after the screening, the largely student audience seemed quite responsive to what they had seen. If my memory serves, the one comment during the discussion that seemed to express a degree of my personal frustration was by Richard Leacock, who said something like, "What about boredom?"

Of course, what I felt that afternoon wasn't really boredom—though *Serene Velocity* had seemed to go on far too long, and I didn't see the point of *three* repetitions of the same continuous 3-minute shot in *Soft Rain*. I was, as most first-time viewers still are, shocked by the visceral power of Brakhage's visual exploration of the process of autopsy. And, somewhat to my own annoyance, I was captivated by *Barn Rushes*, a silent, 34-minute, 16mm film made up of, as Gottheim's description in the program notes explains,

> [a] series of eight intermittent glides past a simple upper-New York State barn. The barn, gently bobbing on the screen, reveals its changing silhouette, itself a screen. Each subsection, separated from the others by light-struck film ends into which the illusion descends (and from which it emerges), records a different day/time/light situation. A radiant serenity resolves the oppositions explored in the film: between background-movement/foreground-movement, transparent/opaque, sky/earth, figure/ground, flat/solid and others. One savors the ballet of movement, memory and anticipation, and gets to know the tragic beauty of the barn. The eye is pleased, the mind keeps transcending.

(See figs. 5a–d.)

For me and my Utica colleagues, and I would imagine for most anyone who had attended the symposium who was not connected with the SUNY-Binghamton Cinema Department, this screening offered a powerful challenge, and not simply the challenges of visceral imagery in the case of *The Act of Seeing* and what seemed the unusual duration of several of the films and of the screening itself (127 minutes, if I am correct about *Soft Rain* being the sole Jacobs film screened). The screening was a con-

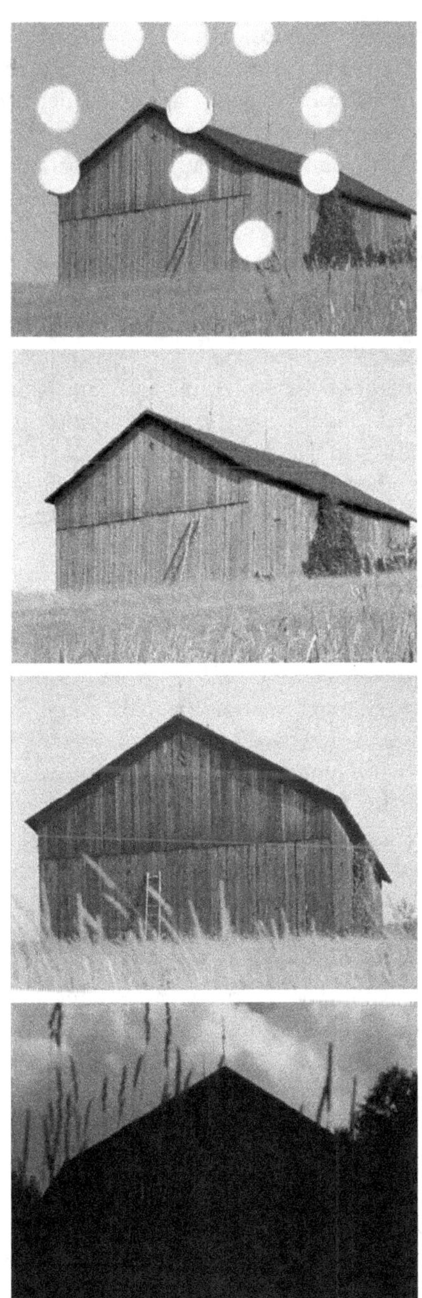

Figures 5a, b, c, d. Stills from Larry Gottheim's *Barn Rushes* (1971). Courtesy Larry Gottheim.

frontation of our conventional expectations of cinema—of the preeminence of narrative, most obviously, but more generally of the assumption that we (educated, presumably intelligent) viewers understood what cinema *is* and what it *can be*. Of course, in several urban centers (New York, San Francisco, LA) Underground Film had been expanding and invigorating the cinema scene for more than a decade, but for the most part, its various approaches and forms had not yet found a home elsewhere.

While my immediate response to the screening and the films (other than *Barn Rushes*) had been negative, I was surprised to realize, not long after returning to Utica and to my teaching week, that I could not stop thinking about what I had experienced. Very quickly, the question of whether these were good or bad films by some standard measure (by the assumptions that underlay my friend Jerome's local movie reviews or those I was reading in the *New Yorker*) vanished and was replaced by the question of whether seeing these films had something to teach about the possibilities of cinema, might in fact be valuable, even essential, for my Introduction to Film classes.

As the weeks went by, it seemed more and more obvious to me that the films I had seen at the symposium were theoretical engagements with cinema; they offered in-theater experiences that questioned what cinema is, has been, can be—what it *should be* in addition to what we already knew it was. And very quickly, some of these films (*Serene Velocity*, *Barn Rushes*, *The Act of Seeing with One's Own Eyes*) were finding their way onto my syllabi, along with other films by the same filmmakers and, soon, by the dozens of other filmmakers I was now discovering who had been and were remaking cinema history in ways that seemed independent of Hollywood and industrial film production in general.[3]

My first experience with the SUNY-Binghamton Cinema Department soon led to similar experiences elsewhere, and cumulatively, these experiences became instrumental in solving what had been a troubling dilemma for me as a young professor and a fledgling scholar.[4] At the time, I

3. I say "seemed independent," of course, because the availability of film stock, cameras, and projectors was a trickle-down from the film industry. Had Hollywood and the other national film industries worldwide not existed, the means to create alternatives to mass-produced cinema would never have been available.

4. I also attended the second SUNY-Binghamton university-wide symposium in, I believe, the spring of 1973. I remember little of the symposium itself—I do have a vague memory of a screening of a film Nicholas Ray had been working on with Binghamton students—because that weekend I was focused less on cinema than on a young woman I was hoping to have an affair with (I was married, with a small child)—though my desire did not meet with success. The level of my personal unhappiness and desperation at the time is suggested by the fact that when the young woman told me she had gonorrhea, I said, "Oh, that's okay, I'll take my chances." Fortunately, the woman was more mature than I was.

was rebelling against the assumption that publication legitimized one's academic credentials. My experience reading the work of other scholars about point of view in narrative fiction and about how point of view functioned in Hemingway's short stories, in order to write my PhD dissertation, "Narrative Perspective in the Short Stories of Ernest Hemingway" (University of Florida, 1970), had been, for the most part, frustrating. It may sound arrogant, but it seemed to me, after some months reading the even-then numerous commentaries on Hemingway's short fiction, that I had learned rather little from the experience—indeed, that I would have been better served by rereading, still once more, the stories themselves, along with additional related fiction by other writers. I had come to suspect that the primary function of the scholarly essays I had read was less an extension of pedagogy than a means to economic betterment within the industry of academe. As a young idealistic professor, I wanted my scholarly work to be more than a commitment to bettering my own status.

My personal discomfiture during and immediately after the Binghamton symposium began a process of reconsidering what I might best do as a scholar. I had come to realize that students of cinema needed to experience the kinds of films that I had seen at the symposium, but that teaching this work would quickly lead to a range of questions that I myself could not begin to answer—questions about why filmmakers might make *these* films, films that wouldn't seem like "real movies" to most of those who might experience them, and what exactly went into the production of particular demanding works. I decided to begin interviewing the filmmakers whose work most interested and challenged me, in the hope of educating myself and learning how to more effectively help to educate my students.

My first published interview was with Larry Gottheim.[5] In preparation for our conversation, I decided that the interview needed to be as

5. I had begun an interview with Hollis Frampton (several of whose films I had seen at Hampshire College in 1973, during a summer film institute sponsored by the University Film Study Association that I had attended because it seemed likely to expand on my Binghamton experience) a bit earlier than the Gottheim interview. "Larry Gottheim's 'Webs of Subtle Relationships': An Interview" was published in *Afterimage* 6, no. 4 (November 1978): 7–11. "Interview with Hollis Frampton: *Hapax Legomena*" appeared in *Film Culture* 67 (Fall 1979): 158–180; "Interview with Hollis Frampton: *Zorns Lemma*," appeared in *Quarterly Review of Film Studies* 4, no. 1 (Winter 1979): 23–37; and "Interview with Hollis Frampton: The Early Years," in *October* 12 (Spring 1980): 103–126. The Gottheim and Frampton interviews appeared together, in somewhat condensed versions, in *A Critical Cinema* (Berkeley: University of California Press, 1988).

My first conference paper was "Less *Is* More: A Discussion of Larry Gottheim's *Fog Line*," presented at the Northeast Modern Language Association Conference, University of Vermont, April 1976. And my essay, "The Expanding Vision of Larry Gottheim's Films," published in *Quarterly Review of Film Studies* 3, no. 2 (Spring 1978): 207–235, was one of my first two publications in cinema—the other, "Hollis Frampton's *Hapax Legomena*," *Afterimage* 5, no. 7 (January 1978): 8–13 (two sections of *Hapax Legomena* were filmed at Binghamton).

scholarly as possible, meaning that I should study Gottheim's films in detail, so that by the time I spoke with him, I would know these films as fully as I knew the Hemingway short stories I had written about; and, further, that our conversation should be as thorough as was manageable. In the years that followed, interviewing would become and has remained my primary scholarly activity—as is evident in the "Weave of Voices" that forms the body of this project.

The Voices

Steve Anker: Longtime Dean of the School of Film/Video at California Institute of the Arts, programmer at the REDCAT Theater in Los Angeles, Anker was director of the San Francisco Cinematheque from 1982 until 2002, served as artistic director of the Foundation for Art in Cinema, and taught for many years at the San Francisco Art Institute. He was curator of *Big As Life: An American History of 8mm Films* (MoMA) and *Austrian Avant-Garde Cinema: 1955–1993* (sixpackfilm, 1994), and is coauthor with Kathy Geritz and Steve Seid of *Radical Light: Alternative Film and Video in the San Francisco Bay Area, 1945–2000* (2010). Anker graduated in 1972, but stayed at SUNY-Binghamton an extra year.

Dan Barnett: Daniel Barnett has taught filmmaking and film theory at various institutions, including Massachusetts College of Art and Design (MassArt), where he built a film department; the School of the Art Institute of Chicago, the San Francisco Art Institute; and at SUNY-Binghamton from spring 1973 through spring 1976. For twelve years he was executive producer for Educational Projects at bePictures in San Rafael, California. A filmmaker, his work was shown widely for a time—though his films, and particularly *White Heart* (1975), completed during his tenure in Binghamton, remain underappreciated and ripe for revival. He is author of *Movement as Meaning in Experimental Film* (2008). Barnett is married to Gail Currey, a Binghamton student for a time while Barnett was teaching there; she is currently Head of Studio at PDI/Dreamworks, the northern California home of Dreamworks Animation.

Alan Berliner: Prolific installation and para-cinema artist, experimental and documentary filmmaker, Alan Berliner is a pioneer in the development of personal documentary. His *The Family Album* (1986), *Intimate Stranger* (1991), and *Nobody's Business* (1996) are canonical works in this tradition; and his *First Cousin Once Removed* (2012) won the Grand Prize at the International Documentary Film Festival. A Guggenheim fellow, Berliner has taught at the New School for Social Research and at NYU. Berliner was a Binghamton student from 1973 to 1977.

Richard Bock: Richard Bock is a picture and sound editor. He did sound editing for Mark Kitchell's *Berkeley in the Sixties* (1990) and Marlon Riggs's *Color Adjustment* (1991), and image editing for *Soweto to Berkeley* (1988, which he directed and produced), and for various television shows, including *Road Rules* (1997–1998, MTV) and *Martha Stewart Living* (2002). He edited (and was one of the lead actors in) *We Can't Go Home Again* (1978/2013), directed by Nicholas Ray. He arrived in Binghamton in the fall of 1970, graduated in 1972.

Peer Bode: Professor of Video Arts and cofounder and codirector of the Institute for Electronic Arts at Alfred University, Peer Bode has been a prolific video and media artist since the late 1970s. His work has been exhibited worldwide. He served as program coordinator at the Experimental Television Center beginning in 1976 and is currently director of the Harold Bode Archive. He graduated SUNY-Binghamton in 1974.

Tony Conrad: SUNY Distinguished Professor in the Department of Media Study at the University at Buffalo, Conrad has been a crucial figure across a range of media since the 1960s. A musician/composer and member of the Theater of Eternal Music, Conrad turned to cinema first to compose a soundtrack for Jack Smith's *Flaming Creatures* (1963), then to make *The Flicker* (1966), one of the films that instigated what came to be called "structural film." He was a visiting artist at SUNY-Binghamton in 1974, where he made *Film Feedback* (1974).

Daniel Eisenberg: Filmmaker and Professor of Film, Video and New Media at the School of the Art Institute of Chicago, Eisenberg served as chair of his department from 1994 to 1999 and from 2002 to 2008. A Guggenheim fellow, Eisenberg is a prolific filmmaker whose work has been shown worldwide and is the subject of Jeffrey Skoller, ed., *Post War: The Films of Daniel Eisenberg* (London; Black Dog, 2010). Eisenberg matriculated in the fall of 1972, graduated in 1976.

Heinz Emigholz: A prolific draftsman, photographer, filmmaker, writer, performer, and producer, Emigholz held a professorship in Experimental Filmmaking at the Universität der Künste Berlin from 1993 to 2013, and cofounded the Institute for Time-based Media there. He also teaches at the European Graduate School in Saas-Fee, Switzerland. He was made a member of the Academy of Arts in Berlin in 2013. His film series include *Photography and Beyond* and *Architecture as Autobiography*. He was a frequent visitor to the Cinema Department in the mid-1970s.

Danny Fingeroth: A leading figure in comics education, Fingeroth was longtime Group Editor for Marvel Comics' Spiderman line and wrote the entire run of the *Darkhawk* series as well as *The Deadly Foes of Spiderman*. He is author of *The Stan Lee Universe* (Raleigh: TwoMorrows, 2011) and *Superman on the Couch: What Superheroes Really Tell Us about Ourselves and Our Society* (New York: Bloomsbury Academic, 2004). Fingeroth is senior vice president of Education at New York's Museum of Comic and Cartoon Art and on the board of the Institute of Comics Studies. He has taught at the New School and NYU. Fingeroth arrived in Binghamton in 1972, graduated with honors in Cinema in 1976.

Morgan Fisher: Morgan Fisher was a visiting artist at SUNY-Binghamton in 1974, where he shot *240x* (1974). A graduate of Harvard, he studied cinema at USC and UCLA, before taking a variety of jobs in and around the commercial film industry. His precise, elegant, conceptual filmmaking often explores intersections between industrial and avant-garde filmmaking. Fisher has taught at California Institute of the Arts and UCLA, and in recent years has become widely known as a painter/sculptor/installation artist.

Hollis Frampton: Photographer, filmmaker, and theorist, Hollis Frampton's prolific career was cut short by cancer in 1984. But by the time of his death, he had produced a considerable body of films, including *Zorns Lemma*, the seven-part *Hapax Legomena* series, and the metacinematic *Magellan Cycle*, as well as a series of theoretical essays on film and photography, collected in *Circles of Confusion* (Rochester: Visual Studies Workshop, 1983). I interviewed Frampton in the late 1970s for *A Critical Cinema* (Berkeley: University of California Press, 1988) and have reworked his memories of his visits to Binghamton for this project.

Ernie Gehr: Gehr is known worldwide for his film and video work and is a canonical figure in the history of independent media. His most famous film, *Serene Velocity* (1970), was made in a SUNY-Binghamton hallway. He was visiting lecturer at SUNY-Binghamton during the summers of 1970 and 1971, and assistant professor from spring 1974 through spring 1975. Subsequently he taught film history and filmmaking at the

San Francisco Art Institute for many years, and now lives in Brooklyn, where he continues to make motion pictures and to develop installations relating to the history of moving-image media.

Mark Goldstein: Mark Goldstein matriculated at Binghamton in 1968, and graduated in 1972. During his time in the Cinema Department, he made many photographs of people and events—his is the most persistent *visual* "voice" in this project. Goldstein is currently president of the International Research Center in Tempe, Arizona (http://www.researchedge.com/), which provides "targeted and timely custom research and consulting, primarily in the communications, content and technology arenas."

Larry Gottheim: PhD in comparative literature from Yale University, Gottheim was hired as an assistant professor by the Harpur College English Department in 1964. He became involved in the Harpur College Film Society, then founded the SUNY-Binghamton Cinema Department and served as its chair for most of its early history. An accomplished filmmaker, Gottheim's early single-shot films, his first feature *Horizons* (1973) and the other three parts of his epic *Elective Affinities* series are landmarks in American independent cinema and pioneering works in what has become a modern independent cinema of Place.

Amy Halpern-Lebrun: Halpern-Lebrun has been cinematographer, gaffer, best boy, or electrician on more than fifty feature films, documentaries, commercials, music videos, and industrials, including *Cracking the Maya Code* (2008) and *Dance of the Maize God* (2014), features produced with her partner David Lebrun. She has also done theatrical lighting for music concerts and other events. She performed in Pat O'Neill's *The Decay of Fiction* (2002) and *Water and Power* (1990), and in several Chick Strand films, including *Soft Fiction* (1979). She has taught at USC and UCLA. She matriculated at SUNY-Binghamton in the fall of 1970, and dropped out after a year.

Richard Herskowitz: Director of Cornell Cinema from 1982 to 1994, of the Virginia Film Festival from 1994 to 2008, Herskowitz is currently director of Cinema Pacific in Eugene, Oregon and artistic director and curator of the Houston Cinema Arts Festival. He has taught film history at the University of Virginia and the University of Oregon and has served as programmer, trustee, and president of the Robert Flaherty Film Seminar. Herskowitz matriculated in fall, 1971, and graduated in 1974.

Jim Hoberman: Longtime film critic (under the pen name J. Hoberman) for the *Village Voice* and other periodicals, and author of *Midnight Movies* (New York: Harper and Row, 1991), *Vulgar Modernism* (Philadelphia: Temple University Press, 1991), *On Jack Smith's* Flaming Creatures (New York: Granary Books, 2001), *The Dream Life* (New York: New Press, 2003), *An Army of Phantoms* (New York: New Press, 2011), and *Film after Film* (London: Verso, 2012), Hoberman is currently Gelb Professor of Humanities at Cooper Union in New York City. He matriculated at SUNY-Binghamton in 1966, and graduated in 1971.

Ralph Hocking: A leader in the field of electronic media art, Ralph Hocking founded one of the first campus-based media access programs (at SUNY-Binghamton in 1969) and in 1970 established the Experimental Television Center in Binghamton, which for decades supported residencies for video artists and funding for the exhibition of video and film. An accomplished artist himself, Hocking collaborated with many of the pioneers of electronic media art. He taught at SUNY-Binghamton from the fall of 1968 until his retirement in 1997.

Sherry Miller Hocking: Ralph Hocking's partner at the Experimental Television Center, Sherry Miller Hocking took charge of ETC's regrant activities, supporting a wide range of production and exhibition throughout New York State for decades, until 2011 when she and Ralph Hocking retired from public life.

Lloyd Bruce Holman: Lloyd Bruce Holman taught with the Cinema Department and served as its technical guru from 1971 to 1974. He is author of *Puppet Animation in the Cinema: History and Technique* (Cranbury, NJ: A. S Barnes, 1975), *Cinema Equipment You Can Build* (Tully, NY: Walnut Press, 1975), and *Holman's Harvest from Down on the Farm* (Tully, NY: Harvest Press, 1982). He teaches photography, drawing, painting, and printmaking in the Department of Art and Art History at Cottey College for Women in Nevada, Missouri.

Flo Jacobs: Educated as a painter at Rhode Island School of Design, Florence Karpf and Ken Jacobs became a couple in 1961, "two weeks before Flo's 20th birthday," as Jacobs explains at the end of *Cyclopean 3D: Life with a Beautiful Woman* (2011). "Flo" has functioned as Ken Jacobs's partner in life and in work ever since. Their son, Azazel Jacobs's film *Momma's Man* (2008) cast Ken and Flo as the parents of fictional character Mikey; *Momma's Man* was shot in the Jacobs's Chambers Street apartment.

Ken Jacobs: A prolific and canonical filmmaker and performance artist, Ken Jacobs has taught film history and filmmaking for half a century. In the 1960s he was in the forefront of efforts to end New York State's censorship laws regarding film. Among the cinema's most accomplished autodidacts and most obsessive collectors, Jacobs has been an influence on many threads within the weave of film history (he was, for example, one of the first to recognize the significance of Oscar Michaeux). His *Tom, Tom, the Piper's Son* (1969, revised 1971) inspired many filmmakers to try their hand at rephotography, and his nearly lifelong fascination with 3-D has produced a range of shadow play, a series of "Nervous System" performances using equipment of his own devising, and in recent years new approaches to digital image-making. Jacobs began teaching at SUNY-Binghamton in 1970, and retired in 2003.

Bill T. Jones: Dancer and choreographer Bill T. Jones has choreographed and performed worldwide. He began his dance training at SUNY-Binghamton and early on, performed with his late partner, Arnie Zane, first at the American Dance Asylum in Binghamton (incorporated in 1974 as a nonprofit codirected by Jones, Zane, and Lois Welk), then beginning in 1982 with the Bill T. Jones/Arnie Zane Dance Company. He has won Tony Awards, the Dorothy and Lillian Gish Prize, and the Wexner Prize. In 1994 he received a MacArthur "Genius" award, and in 2010 was celebrated at the Kennedy Center Honors. Jones has honorary doctorates from Bard College, the Juilliard School, and Yale. Jones began taking courses at SUNY-Binghamton in 1970, transferred to SUNY-Brockport in 1973.

Daile Kaplan: Vice president and director of Photographs and Photobooks at Swann Auction Galleries in New York City, Kaplan is the photography specialist on the cable program, *Antiques Roadshow* and has appeared on HGTV, the History Channel, and the Discovery Channel. Kaplan is the author of *Pop Photographica, Photography's Objects in Everyday Life 1842–1969* (Toronto, Canada: Art Gallery of Ontario, 2003); *Lewis Hine in Europe: The "Lost" Photographs* (New York: Abbeville Press, 1988); and editor of *Photo Story: Selected Letters and Photographs of Lewis W. Hine* (Washington & London: Smithsonian Institution Press, 1992). She arrived in Binghamton in 1968, and left (without graduating) in 1971.

Peter Kubelka: Accomplished filmmaker and cook, Kubelka was one of the founders of the Austrian Film Museum. Kubelka has taught and lectured throughout his life, frequently arguing for what he has called "metric cinema," filmmaking in which the individual frame, rather than the shot, is the essential formal element. Kubelka's early metric films are landmark experiments, and his *Unsere Afrikareise* (*Our Trip to Africa*, 1966) is one of the masterworks of modern cinema. Kubelka visited SUNY-Binghamton several times and was visiting lecturer during the fall semester of 1973.

Saul Levine: Professor of filmmaking at Massachusetts College of Art and Design for more than thirty years, Saul Levine is a prolific filmmaker and champion of small-gauge filmmaking, as well as the longtime programmer of the MassArt Film Society. He received an MFA from the School of the Art Institute of Chicago, and was on the faculty at SUNY-Binghamton from fall 1973 through spring 1976.

David Marc: An associate editor for *Syracuse University Magazine*, David Marc is the author of *Demographic Vistas: Television in American Culture* (Philadelphia: University of Pennsylvania Press, 1984), *Bonfire of the Humanities: Television, Subliteracy, and Long-Term Memory Loss* (Syracuse: Syracuse University Press, 1995), *Comic Visions: Television Comedy and American Culture* (Hoboken, NY: Wiley-Blackwell, 1997), and *Television in the Antenna Age* (Malden, MA: Blackwell, 2005, cowritten with Robert J. Thompson). He matriculated at SUNY-Binghamton in 1968, graduated in 1972, and returned in 1974 for an MA.

Camille Paglia: Well-known public intellectual, author, and feminist, Camille Paglia is author of *Sexual Personae: Art and Decadence from Nefertiti to Emily Dickinson* (New Haven: Yale University Press, 1990), *Sex, Art, and American Culture: Essays* (New York: Vintage, 1992), *Vamps and Tramps: New Essays* (New York: Vintage, 1994), *Alfred Hitchcock's* The Birds (London: BFI, 1998), and *Glittering Images: A Journey through Art from Egypt to Star Wars* (New York: Pantheon, 2012) She teaches at the University of the Arts in Philadelphia. She was SUNY-Binghamton valedictorian in 1968.

Nicholas Ray: Ray, who died in 1979, is not a direct voice in what follows, but he can be "heard" in the comments of many of the voices. One of the leading Hollywood directors of the late 1940s into the 1960s, Ray's films include *They Live by Night* (1949), *Knock on Any Door* (1949), *In a Lonely Place* (1950), *Macao* (1952), *Johnny Guitar* (1954), *Rebel without a Cause* (1955), *Bitter Victory* (1957), and *Wind across the Everglades* (1958). He taught at SUNY-Binghamton from the fall of 1971 through the spring of 1973, collaborating with students on what became *We Can't Go Home Again*, released in 2013.

Susan Ray: Partner and wife of Nicholas Ray during his final years, including the years when Ray taught at SUNY-Binghamton, Susan Ray is editor of *I Was Interrupted: Nicholas Ray on Making Movies* (Berkeley: University of California Press, 1993), and in 2012–13 saw *We Can't Go Home Again* (2013), the feature Nick Ray worked on with SUNY-Binghamton students, into the public eye at the Venice and Tribeca Film Festivals. In 2012 she completed *Don't Expect Too Much* (2012), a documentary about Nick Ray and the production of *We Can't Go Home Again.*

Ken Ross: In 1972 Ken Ross collaborated with Phil Weisman and others to found the Collective for Living Cinema, for nineteen years among the most active showcases for then-current avant-garde film and related work in the world. Ross has continued to make music videos and commercials, and runs Films for Nonprofits, where he produces image pieces and films for underserved organizations. He graduated from SUNY-Binghamton in 1973.

Harvey L. Silver: Currently Executive Producer of H. L. Silver Productions, Silver sees to the management, design, production, and staging of meetings, events, and media for corporations and organizations; and he has worked as executive producer for Nathan Silver's films, including *Exit Elena* (2012), *Soft in the Head* (2013), and *Uncertain Terms* (2014). Previously, Silver was executive producer and senior vice president at Jack Morton Worldwide in Boston, producing corporate events for Gillette, Oral-B, Duracell, Reebok, as well as the Ryder Cup for the PGA and the World Cup of Hockey for the NHL. Corbis Images in Manhattan licenses Silver's photographs. He attended SUNY-Binghamton for six months during the fall of 1970.

Phil Solomon: Master of the optical printer, Phil Solomon has produced a long series of evocative and beautiful films, beginning with *Nitelite* (1975), his thesis film at Binghamton. *The Secret Garden* (1988), *The Exquisite Hour* (1989, 1994), *Remains to Be Seen* (1989, 1994), and the Twilight Psalm series are canonical works. He was awarded a Guggenheim Fellowship in 1993. Recently, Solomon has explored digital imaging, installation, and video games, most notably in *American Falls* (2010–12) and *Empire* (2008–12). In 1991 Solomon joined Stan Brakhage at the University of Colorado, where he has taught ever since. He was an undergraduate at SUNY-Binghamton from 1971 to 1975.

Philip Sykas: A research associate at Manchester School of Art at Manchester Metropolitan University in the UK, where he earned his

PhD in 2000 (he had earned a diploma in conservation from Courtauld Institute of Art in 1983). He worked as a textile conservator (1983–94), then as a museum curator (1994–98) before embarking on a full-time career as a researcher. His research encompasses the full history of textile printing in England, particularly from the perspectives of design, technology, and business. Sykas arrived at SUNY-Binghamton in 1970, and received his BA in May, 1974.

Maureen Turim: The first woman to receive tenure in the SUNY-Binghamton Cinema Department, where she taught from 1977 until 1991, Turim is author of *Abstraction in Avant-Garde Films* (Ann Arbor: UMI Research Press, 1985), *Flashbacks in Film: Memory and History* (New York: Routledge, 1989), and *The Films of Oshima Nagisa: Images of a Japanese Iconoclast* (Berkeley: University of California Press,1998), as well as dozens of articles and catalog essays. She is professor of English at the University of Florida, where she has taught film history and theory since 1991.

Phil Weisman: Cofounder, with Ken Ross (and others), of the Collective for Living Cinema, Weisman works as a freelance filmmaker and teaches in the Media Arts Department of Manhattan Community College. He arrived in Binghamton in 1969 and graduated in 1973.

Andrea Weiss: A PhD in American history from Rutgers, Weiss was the coproducer/director of *International Sweethearts of Rhythm* (1986), and has continued to be involved in writing, directing, and producing politically engaged documentaries for public television in North America and in Europe. She is author of *Vampires and Violets: Lesbians in the Cinema* (New York: Penguin, 1992), *Paris Was a Woman: Portraits from the Left Bank* (San Francisco: Harper, 1996), and *In the Shadow of the Magic Mountain: The Erika and Klaus Mann Story* (Chicago: University of Chicago Press, 2008). She teaches in the Film/Video Program, Department of Media and Communication Arts, at City College of New York. She matriculated at SUNY-Binghamton in 1974 and graduated in 1977.

Helene Kaplan Wright: After graduating Binghamton in 1972, Kaplan remained involved with independent cinema, working, for example, as Annette Michelson's projectionist during the New Forms in Film exhibition, held in Montreux, Switzerland in 1974; as sound person for Bette Gordon's *Variety* (1984), and for Susan Ray; and she continued to perform shadow play with Jacobs and several Binghamton friends. She is now an attorney.

Klaus Wyborny: A student of theoretical physics and mathematics, Klaus Wyborny began making films in the mid-1960s. J. Hoberman called Wyborny's *Unreachable Homeless* (1978) and his other 1970s films (including *Pictures of the Lost Word*, made in Binghamton) the best nonnarrative avant-garde work of the year. Wyborny's book, *Elementare Schnitt-Theorie des Spielfilms*/"Elementary Editing: Theory of Motion Pictures" (Berlin: Lit Verlag) was published in 2013. He taught at Binghamton during the spring of 1975, and later at Ohio State University, California Institute of the Arts, and the University of the Arts in Hamburg; since 2009, he has taught at Mannheim University of Applied Sciences.

The Weave

1

Emergence

Larry Gottheim: When I arrived at Harpur College in 1964, I was still working on my dissertation, which was on the ideal hero in the realistic novel, focusing on Dostoevsky (*The Idiot*), George Eliot (*Daniel Deronda*), and the German Paul Heyse (*Kinder der Welt*) [*The Ideal Hero in the Realistic Novel*, Yale University, 1965]—my adviser was the great theoretician René Wellek.

After Yale, I'd spent three years at Northwestern University, but I came to Harpur College because it was supposed to be a very special place, the *public* Swarthmore. And actually, my students at the beginning *were* fantastically literate, more like Yale graduate students than Midwestern undergraduates. Harpur was on a trimester system, which allowed for a lot of flexibility; in fact they were willing to hire me and let me have the first trimester off so I could work on my dissertation. But as soon as I finished my degree and started to face up to the rest of my life, I didn't feel so comfortable. I was being groomed in the English Department to be the new young scholar/teacher, and I could see my future laid out before me: assistant professor, associate professor, professor—something in me rebelled.

Meanwhile, Frank Newman, who, like me, was in the English Department (and much later became the chairman of the Cinema Department for a short period), had started the Harpur Film Society. I wasn't so involved at the beginning, but I felt a pull. Like everybody else in the humanities, I was interested in Fellini and Godard and the other international directors, through whom we were also discovering the earlier American cinema. So I got interested in the Film Society and because of the way things are in these organizations, as soon as you show serious interest, you're elected president of the group.

Camille Paglia: There is no way to fully express the enormous impact that the Harpur Film Society had on my intellectual development! I was in Binghamton from 1964 to 1968, seeing one major film after another. While still in high school, I began making a list of the movies I saw in theaters, so I have a complete record of films I saw at Harpur. The very first month I arrived, it was Roman Polanski's *Knife in the Water* [1962]—what a start! I'd been suffering through the perky, garish Doris Day/Debbie Reynolds era, and that oblique, minimalist film was a revelation.

There were so many pivotal moments for me—for example, the audience walking out on Antonioni's *L'Avventura* [1960], while my front row of gay guy friends and I were absolutely entranced. And the same thing happened with Andy Warhol's *Harlot* [1964]—we were riveted and stayed for a second showing. Those amazing early experimental Warhol films turned me into a "Warholite."

But Cocteau's *Orphée* [1950] captivated everyone—no disagreement there! A magical night—people were floating as they poured out onto the dark quad. And Ingmar Bergman's oeuvre always floored everyone too.

Larry Gottheim: During this same period I was also reading the *Village Voice*, and had begun to see underground films in New York—in particular some of the Warhol films. I was getting interested in this other kind of cinema that was being shown in various out-of-the-way theaters: Aldo Tambellini's theater on Second Avenue, for example—at that time the only place where you could see nudity. There were big audiences. I *was* interested in the nudity of course, but also in the other aspects of the films shown there.

I remember going with Debbie [Deborah Chess, Gottheim's first wife] to Philadelphia for a weekend, getting the newspaper to look up what was going on, and seeing a little announcement of a program curated by Jonas Mekas, whose name I knew from the *Voice*. We went to this screening and saw films by Bruce Baillie, Bruce Conner, and some others—the program helped open my mind to this new world of cinema.

Camille Paglia: My cinema experiences at Harpur remain a major touchstone for my life. For example, when the *Sunday Times Magazine* in London reprinted a piece I had written for the *Hollywood Reporter* [December 6, 2012] attacking the blandness of current women pop stars, they wanted a blurb for the contributors' page, and I instantly sent them this: "Worshiping European art films in college in the 1960s, I dreamed that the revolutionary new woman of the future would be modeled on Jeanne Moreau, Catherine Deneuve, Anouk Aimée, Monica Vitti, and Julie Christie. How wrong I was!"

I think the Film Society showed a new film virtually every week—including Hollywood classics and screwball comedies. In December 1967, I saw Kenneth Anger's *Scorpio Rising* [1963], which was followed by Jonas Mekas's *The Brig* [1964]. I remember fabulous handouts prepared for each film, with basic information and comment. In 1973, at my first teaching job at Bennington College, I organized a Women's Film Festival where I chose the films and wrote handouts modeled in both tone and format on the ones at Harpur. (See fig. 6 on pages 26 and 27.)

I've often talked about how that public film series was a model of education that should be imitated by colleges everywhere. The hushed, contemplative intensity of the Harpur audience was phenomenal—and I'm constantly nostalgic for it amid today's restless, easily distracted and disrespectful audiences.

Larry Gottheim: I was becoming more interested in *making* a film, not as the start of a career or anything like that; like a lot of people at the time, I was just interested. I knew somebody who had worked at one of the camera stores in New York and bought a used 16mm Bolex with one lens for $250. I started to learn filmmaking from the little manual that came with the Bolex, just puzzling things out. I made some little films, one of them a narrative using people I knew through the Film Society. The film was awkward—I hated some of the acting—but the experience of making it was exciting.

In 1967, I began teaching a cinema class in the English Department, the first film class at Harpur: we looked at films and did some filmmaking. There were several students who were seriously interested in film. Jim Hoberman was in this first class, and Steve Anker, who had been in a freshman English class of mine. Hoberman was already a kind of film critic. To my astonishment, he had worked out a way to get a press pass to the New York Film Festival—as an undergraduate!

Jim Hoberman: I started at what was then Harpur College in the fall of 1966, before there really was a Cinema Department. Larry Gottheim was my academic adviser, an extremely sympathetic guy. He seemed very young, and was very accessible; we were friendly from the beginning.

I was already interested in film. When I was in high school, I used to go to movies at the Bridge Theater on St. Mark's Place and at Tambellini's Gate on Second Avenue, which was in the lobby of an apartment building—Manny Farber wrote a hilarious description of it.* Jonas

*See "Experimental Films 1968," in Manny Farber, *Movies* (New York: Hillstone, 1971): 246.

State University of New York at Binghamton
HARPUR FILM SOCIETY

Film Notes
March 21, 1968

HEAD AGAINST THE WALLS (La tête contre les murs) 1958

Directed by Georges Franju

With Pierre Brasseur, Jean-Pierre Mocky, Anouk Aimée, Charles Asnavour.
Music by Maurice Jarre. Photography by Eugène Schüfftan

Short: THE BLOOD OF THE BEASTS (1949)

Directed by Georges Franju. Music by Kosma.

La Sang des Betes (The Blood of the Beasts) belongs to a small but interesting film tradition, what Susan Sontag calls "the poetic cinema of shock" (along with Freaks, Flaming Creatures, Fireworks & Scorpio Rising, & all Bunuel's films). It is a travelogue (complete with the sun sinking over a canal) of several Paris slaughterhouses, its horrible reality blunted by black & white photography, guided by an objective, thorough narrator. Dispassionately we are shown the instruments & calmly we are told exactly how each is used, & suddenly a horse's throat is slit, his blood raising steam from the ground. As we watch an axed cow's contortions (gutters are over flowed with her insides) the knowledgeable voice points out that "total decapitation" is necessary for the best veal, that butchers often develop cysts, that the headless, writing animals are dead & moving on just reflex. Now it is lunch-time in the city & a butcher hews his ax in time to the twelve chimes of a church.

But Franju is not really passing a moral judgment—most men eat meat to live & animals must be slaughtered. The moral judgment is that of the individual viewer's, Franju is showing us how, perhaps at what price, we obtain our meat (maintain our existence). The butchers have names & individual styles & histories (one was a champion boxer). The narration ends & a meatworker breaks into "Somewhere Beyond the Sea:" "…fleecy clouds like sheep…" (and we watch their bellies cut open), "…shepherd of the azure sky…" (the trained 'traitor' sheep leads the herd to the knives), "…the moist earth…" (the ground absorbs a cow's intestines).

When Andy Warhol paints a Campbell's Soup Can he asks us if we dig it, is it beautiful? Is it necessary? & if not, then why do we make or permit Campbell's Soup Cans? With the same objectivity, with the same irony (though much more graphically) Franju is examining man's more basic needs, his violent works & their rationale.

La Tête contre les murs (Head against the Walls) explores life within & without the conventional insane asylum. It is a metaphor which has recurred since films' inception, from The Cabinet of Dr. Caligari (1920) to The Titticut Follies (1967) and varying in purpose and subtledy from The Snakepit to Suddenly Last Summer to Marat/de Sade. A young, unstable motorcyclist is

1

Figure 6. Jim Hoberman's program note for the March 21, 1968 Harpur Film Society screening, as it was originally distributed. Courtesy J. Hoberman.

committed to a mental institution by his hypocritical father. He makes three attempts to escape to an outside which, excepting the possibility of love, seems (in the nightmarish shots of Paris & the grotesque gambling sequence) hardly more rational or inviting than the bizarre life of the asylum.

Franju's primary concern is with freedom. Not only the immediate freedom of escape, freedom from authority (there are two authority figures operating—the father, & Dr.Varmont who belie3ves that his job is mainly to protect the public & then to cure his patients) but also the question of how much freedom man really wants. Charles Aznavour plays an inmate who is obsessed with the idea of escape, but who also speaks wistfully of better wards & asylums by the sea. Though Aznavour seems relatively sane within the asylum, when he finally realizes his dream & does escape, he is seized by a violent fit. Gerane, the motorcyclist, exhibits the same tendency—after a successful attempt he flees compulsively from the sanctuary of his girlfriend's apartment into the arms of his captors.

Though much of the film is documentary & many of its best scenes are of actual inmates, the purpose of the film is not to illuminate the plight of the insane (in the sense that David & Lisa depicts the emotionally disturbed, or A Child is Waiting depicts the retarded). As Dr. Varmont puts it—"Insanity is a problem that publicity can't solve." Rather, Franju is concerned with the relationship between the "sane" & the "insane", between man. He is examining the nature of freedom & seems to find in it a Sartrean paradox—that the exercise of freedom is perhaps equivalent to the loss of freedom. Gerane's life before he was committed was aimless & dissolute. Only inside of the asylum was he able to fall in love with the girl who visited him, did his life have a purpose. Once he has escaped, love becomes again too great a responsibility & the burden of freedom too heavy.

--Jim Hoberman

Other films by Franju:

- Hotel des Invalides (1951)
- Le Gran Melies (1952)
- The Horror Chamber of Dr. Faustus (1959)
- Judex (1963)
- Therese Desqueyroux (1964)

Next Showing, April 4, Antonioni's RED DESERT and Brackhage's WINDOW WATER BABY MOVING.

Shirley Clarke, one of America's leading independent film-makers, will visit the campus on April 8. There will be an evening showing of her great film PORTRAIT OF JASON, after which Miss Clarke will discuss the film. In the afternoon she will show and discuss her film THE CONNECTION. Watch for further announcements.

The Film Society design contest has been won by Judith Spencer Levy. Her design will appear on the next FILM NOTES.

PLEASE, NO SMOKING IN THE THEATER

Mekas's Filmmakers' Cinematheque was moving around; for a while it was in the theater where the Blue Man Group now does their shows—I saw Warhol films there—then it moved uptown to the Wurlitzer Building, which is where I saw *Chelsea Girls* [1966] for the first time. So I was already involved in avant-garde film. And I had a Super-8mm camera and was making films of my own.

Back then, there were no film programs in any school I knew about, so I ended up in the English Department at Harpur. I was quite active in the Harpur Film Society and did the film notes for the screenings. In those days, you joined a film society because you wanted to see certain movies and you were happy to subject the rest of the campus to them. The films we showed occasionally get referenced by Camille Paglia—she was there too, as was Steve Anker. Steve started around the same time I did, or maybe a term or two later.

Camille Paglia: I can visualize Jim Hoberman at the snack bar, the college's social center—we moved in vaguely the same large circle. He was friends with my friends. It was exactly the same for Arnie Zane, a soon-to-be famous dancer/choreographer who later died of AIDS, and also Art Spiegelman: I remember them as part of my larger circle, but had no independent dealings with them.

Larry Gottheim was a revered and maybe a slightly feared name on campus. Though I often heard him mentioned in my circle, I had no direct contact with him. My big mentor was the poet Milton Kessler who had been a student of Theodore Roethke.

Jim Hoberman: Camille Paglia was a colorful personality and a cult figure for a group of gay guys I knew. She was probably two years ahead of me and widely regarded as a genius, at least by this group of guys (all of whom she's written about). I had friends in the Theater Department, which is probably how I knew her circle and heard about her. I can't remember ever having a conversation with Camille but probably we were at some of the same parties—the theater parties were great with lots of stoned charades, et cetera. I remember her as a slim, slight, elegant personage—kind of mod, with Beatle-length hair, possibly a purple or violet peacoat and matching bell-bottoms, very Carnaby Street! I was struck by the fact that she was from Upstate New York.

Camille was also a totally out lesbian and completely fearless. A legendary story is that she and a girlfriend were drinking in one of the tough working-class, mainly Slavic bars in the neighborhood called the Second Ward, where we went to live dangerously (as opposed to Binghamton's one black bar, which was regarded as friendly territory).

Some guy began either hitting on the girl or hassling them or both, and Camille took her bottle of Utica Club, smashed it on the bar, and told the guy get the fuck away from her before she rearranged his face. It could be apocryphal. I wasn't there. But she certainly seemed capable of it. (See fig. 7.)

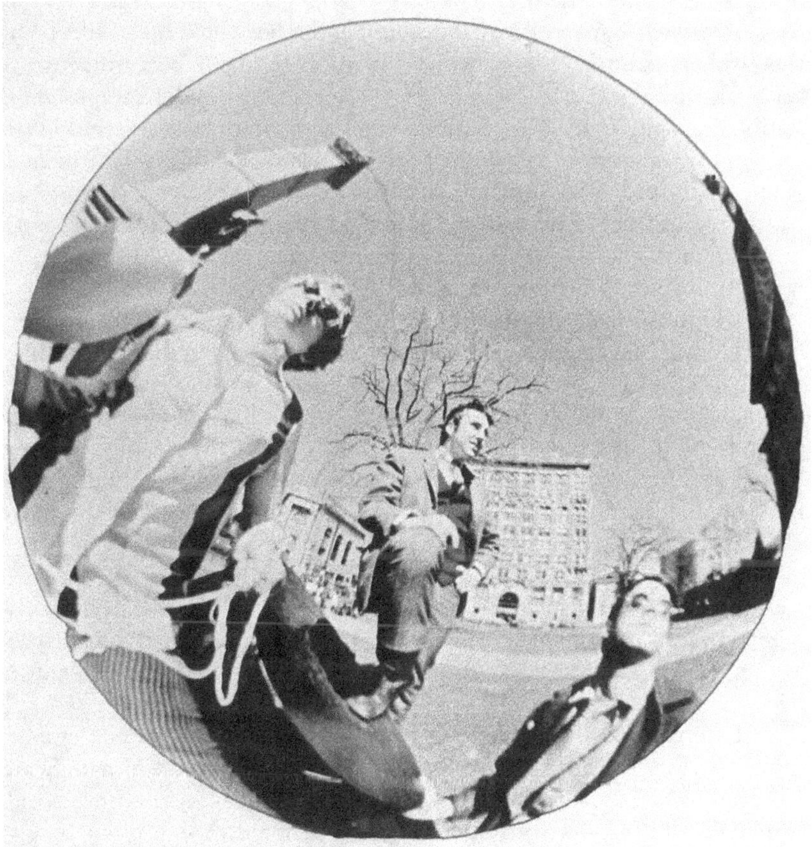

Figure 7. *Harpur Review* editors in photograph from the cover of the spring 1968 issue: in center (with foot up on a black cannon), editor-in-chief Peter Weber; on right, Hank Kune; and in foreground on left, Camille Paglia, "dressed in a trendy London mod way—unusual even at Harpur, where downtown NYC dance-leotard bohemian or studiedly unkempt California hippie style reigned"; "We're standing at the foot of the war memorial (the Soldiers and Sailors Monument) in front of the Binghamton Courthouse. There was definitely an anti-war reference there"—Paglia in e-mail to author, February 27, 2015. Photograph courtesy of Larry Lynn and Ellis Barowsky.

Steve Anker: A girl at Erasmus Hall High School in Brooklyn who I was involved with told me about Harpur; it sounded exciting. I applied and got in. As a senior in high school I'd been in theater and I played a couple of musical instruments; I was always a lover of literature and had grown up loving the movies; I'd even discovered international cinema (I'd sometimes watch the movies two or three times in a row—you could do that in theaters then).

But when I got to Binghamton in September 1967, it was like being shot from a cannon. I got involved in theater; and I became active in classical music and did a classical music program on the campus radio station. And my first week, I attended a call for people interested in the Harpur Film Society. The Film Society was run by Larry Gottheim, a young literature teacher whose lecture (on *The Brothers Karamazov*) I had heard my first day at Binghamton. I remember being knocked out by his energy and passion and his articulateness, so when I saw that he was running the Film Society I was excited.

There were seven or eight of us in the room. Larry talked about how they wanted to develop the Film Society into something substantial and that each of us would take on different assignments and run different programs. At the end of the meeting, the guy in front of me turned around and introduced himself; it was Jim Hoberman. He and I became friends and I quickly realized that Jim knew oodles more than I did about film: he and Larry and the others were talking about something called "Underground Film," which I'd never heard of.

Larry Gottheim: The Film Society started out using the Theater Department's theater, which had a projection booth fitted with large arc projectors, in both 16mm and 35mm. These were awkward to use and in need of repair.

Later on, during Nick Ray's time at Binghamton, Dennis Hopper came to visit. A 35mm print of Nick's film about the Chicago Seven emerged, and it was to be shown in that theater. A few brave souls climbed up the ladder to the booth and attempted to figure out how to work the projectors. There was a long delay, and I remember Dennis, looking like his character in *Blue Velvet* [1986], climbing up the ladder and cursing out the projectionists.

One of my earliest tasks with the Film Society was to try to develop some interest in replacing the Theater Department projectors with appropriate 16mm projectors, but nobody seemed interested, including those who later gathered around when the idea of a Cinema Department was in the air. The Cinema Department came into being just as the construction of the new Lecture Hall was completed. Our large classes were in Lecture Hall 1. At first we set up the 16mm Kalart-Victor projectors on carts amid the seats. We also used Kodak Analytic projectors. Then we had a projection booth built at the back.

Eventually we were given exclusive use of one of the smaller Lecture Halls, Lecture Hall 6, and this became the site for most of the classes and events. A projection booth was built in the back, and one of the major innovations was painting the walls and ceiling black—to some extent influenced by the original Anthology Film Archives. A black-box theater was unusual for colleges at the time.

Steve Anker: Larry was beginning to make films and was especially interested in the Underground. I remember him running rolls of film through the camera, often as single takes; he was excited by the camera's ability to create a record of real time and capture details that might otherwise go unnoticed. Dan Rowe, another literature teacher, was interested in radical art and cinema and made a feature-length experimental film. Some students who already had a serious interest in film were making their own films with the cameras that Larry had been able to get his hands on.

Early on, I also hung out a bit with Ralph Hocking—and met Nam June Paik—during the time when they were working on an early synthesizer. I was moving from one thing to another, constantly excited.

Ralph Hocking: I was brought to Harpur by Bruce Dearing, the president of the university—before he and I even figured out what I wanted to do. Whacky! Who the hell hires you to invent your job? I'd been fired from Allegheny College, where Bruce's son Jamie had been in one of my classes. At Allegheny from 1960 to 1967, I had taught pottery and sculpture, drawing and design, photography—video didn't exist yet. When tenure time came around, the president tossed me out because I didn't have "a sense of community." That year, the students dedicated the yearbook to me.

At Allegheny, we used to take students to New York, and on one of those trips I ran into Nam June Paik at the Bonino Gallery: he was running around with magnets, stuffing them into the front of TV sets. I thought, what the fuck is *this* crazy shit? But I was fascinated: Nam June was *so* passionate—as if what he was doing *had* to be done.

There was so much money available for experimentation in those days! At Binghamton, they would buy a harpsichord and then decide well maybe we need another one. I decided to try to do something with television. I discovered that Sony was making portable television units, the CV Series. I'd never seen one, but Nam June was talking about them, so I asked the university if they would buy me some. "What are you going to do with them?" "Don't know: hand them to people and say 'Here, do something.' I'm kind of curious to see what's possible for television besides what we already know."

Larry Gottheim: Ralph Hocking went through several changes in Binghamton, just as I did. In the sixties and early seventies the university allowed people to find themselves, even if that meant changing disciplines. At first, Ralph wasn't teaching any courses; he was just around. He got involved in photography, then became interested in video, in the idea of street recording, giving Portapaks to people and sending them out into the world. The Experimental Television Center grew out of that side of things. In time he connected with Nam June Paik, and he and Nam June and Shuya Abe built the first video synthesizer in the basement of the Lecture Hall building.

In 1968, through the Film Society, I heard about an independent film competition, run by Nick Manning who was teaching at St. Lawrence University. I think Manning's festival had originally been in New York, but he had moved it to St. Lawrence. A group of the students who were seriously interested in film wanted to go, so we got a college car and drove to Canton.

I think Stan Vanderbeek and Jonas Mekas were supposed to be judges, but neither could come, and Ken Jacobs came as Mekas's replacement. There was also a guy from the National Film Board of Canada.

Ken Jacobs: Jonas had asked me if I would take his place at the St. Lawrence event. When I got there, I was shocked that they had preselected films and, crazy-conscientious, asked to see *all* the films submitted. And I wrote comments on *every* film: my opinion, right or wrong. I didn't want to be this judge officiating from above, and I did find some good things that had been thrown out by the faceless prejudges.

Flo Jacobs: This was like what you had done at Millennium when it was at St. Mark's Church: you said anybody who had thirty minutes of work could show it; you weren't going to preselect.

Ken Jacobs: But you had to take your chances on what would be said afterward!

Larry, who was in the English Department at the time, brought several students to the event. They dug my unrelenting style and apparently returned to Binghamton with the idea of my coming to help start a cinema department.

Larry Gottheim: At St. Lawrence the festival judges chose winners from among the films that had been submitted (I had entered my narrative film *The Present* [1968]). You could agree to show a program of the winning films at your college, but I said I didn't want to do that. I asked if we could take *all* the films that had been entered in the festival back to Binghamton and choose our own programs. We were allowed to do this.

We filled the trunk with cans of film and when we got back to Binghamton, we looked at both the winners and the films that had been rejected. That's where I saw the first films of Ernie Gehr—*Morning* [1967] and *Wait* [1967]. And there was a Frampton film, which is how I realized that this guy I had known years before at Oberlin College had become a filmmaker! There was also a Joyce Wieland film and a Morgan Fisher film.

I began to change the direction of the Film Society—to the disgust of the regular faculty and most everybody else. Before this, there had been a tradition of the cute short film before the foreign or classic narrative feature. That's what people wanted from film societies. But we were moving the Harpur Film Society in the direction of what Jonas Mekas had called the New American Cinema.

Jim Hoberman: I remember Larry going to some sort of film festival at St. Lawrence University, which is where he met Ken, who apparently created some kind of outrageous scene. I didn't know Ken, but I was familiar with *Little Stabs at Happiness* [1963] and *Blonde Cobra* [1963]. I'd heard that Ken had gotten involved in some sort of contretemps with Stan Vanderbeek—who knows what it was about—but this struck me at the time because I'd thought all these guys were great and somehow aligned; it hadn't occurred to me that there might be warring camps among the filmmakers.

Larry brought back films from the St. Lawrence event and we did a Harpur Film Society show with some of them; that's when I first saw Ken's *Window* [1964] and *Airshaft* [1967]. Those films surprised me; they were a new direction for Ken. Nelson's *The Great Blondino* [1967] was also part of that program. Seeing those films was exciting for us, though I don't remember whether many people came to our screenings.

Larry Gottheim: Harpur had started this program where the residential units became colleges with associated faculty members teaching classes in the residence halls, rather than in the regular classrooms. The individual colleges had budgets—there was a lot of money in those days. I was a fellow at Newing College, and we began getting programs of experimental film to show at night in the lounge—a mixture of formal films and films where there was a little bit of sexuality: Bruce Conner films, Robert Nelson's *Oh Dem Watermelons* [1965] . . .

The poet Milton Kessler, who was always a supporter of the Cinema Department, became involved in these Film Society activities the following year.

Steve Anker: In the early and mid-sixties, when I was in high school in Brooklyn, the ironic/sardonic reports on television about this or that Andy Warhol film or the Factory were my awareness of Underground Film. But I remember Larry and the others saying to me, "Perhaps you could get a little Underground Film series going in your dorm complex"—when I arrived at Binghamton, I'd been assigned to live in Newing College. I proposed a little film series and the proposal was accepted. We showed several programs of films in dorm lounges and meeting rooms, and they became popular since most people had never seen anything like the films we showed. (See fig. 8.)

I learned about Underground Film by programming it. In 1967–68 I showed Anger's *Scorpio Rising* [1963], and *Chafed Elbows* [1967] by Robert

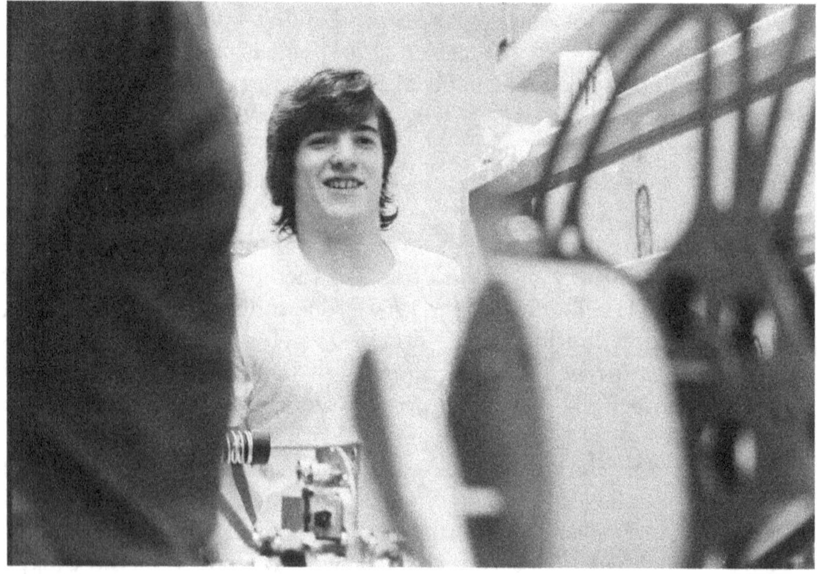

Figure 8. Steve Anker, photographed by Mark Goldstein. Courtesy Mark Goldstein.

Downey, and Taka Iimura's *Love (Ai)* [1963], which was already legendary. And Robert Nelson's *Great Blondino Preview* [1967]. I'm sure I showed *Little Stabs at Happiness* [1963] and *Window Water Baby Moving* [1959]. I'd never seen anything even close to these films and I was generally knocked out, although I was mystified by *Little Stabs* (Dan Rowe, an English professor, told me it was a masterpiece). I wasn't alone: our screenings were considered sensational and would usually pack the dorm lounge.

Early on, Larry arranged a visit by Shirley Clarke, who showed *Portrait of Jason* [1967] soon after it was finished. This was a huge, lively event that packed the four-hundred-seat theater. Fifty years later, I still remember a student attacking Shirley Clarke for being manipulative and taking advantage of Jason Holliday [aka Aaron Payne].

Larry Gottheim: I'd gotten in touch with Shirley Clarke, who had just finished *Portrait of Jason*, and through the combination of the Film Society and the money from Newing College, we brought her to Binghamton for a few days. We had a big screening of *Portrait of Jason* at the Film Society, but she also brought suitcases full of films from the Filmmakers' Cooperative that we showed at Newing College. Shirley was great, generous to the students and even to me: I showed her *The Present* and she was encouraging and supportive.

Camille Paglia: Shirley Clarke came to Harpur for two days in April 1968. The large theater was full for her evening event—standing room only. And there was an incident during that event that I've never forgotten. After the showing of *Portrait of Jason*, Clarke was onstage taking questions from the audience—the discussion was being moderated by a male faculty member (I don't remember who). Suddenly some guy in the balcony begins yelling at her—a real rant—going on and on about how exploitative she had been in the film and how unfair to Jason. I'm not sure if the guy was on drugs or not (it *was* the sixties!), but my impression at the time was that he was mentally unbalanced and that the film had simply pushed him over the edge. The audience was paralyzed—you could feel the shock.

Clarke got very quiet, very centered, listening with complete attention and respect. I remember being surprised and impressed with how she *lowered* her voice—an interesting strategy to me, because as an Italian American, I automatically *raise* my voice under attack and stress! The episode went on and on—painfully long for me and I think for most of the audience. I felt critical of the hosts of the event and thought the moderator should have intervened to protect an honored guest. But in retrospect, it seems very sixties "go-with-the-flow"—letting everything spool out without interference or assertions of authority.

Clarke was a tough cookie who knew how to handle herself when put on the spot. She made a deep impression on me and everyone, I think, as a strong and confident personality at a time when women of professional achievement were still rare in public life.

Steve Anker: Larry told us that the film festival he'd attended at St. Lawrence University had been really problematic; he didn't like most of the work and thought that the level of critical discourse among the judges was pretty low—except for Ken Jacobs, who'd challenged everybody and galvanized the proceedings. Larry asked me if I could find funding through Newing College to help bring Ken to Binghamton for a week in spring 1969, and I did.

Because the money had come from a dormitory complex and the Ken Jacobs residency was designed to last a week, we planned for the screenings to take place in one of the lounges, a relaxed setting. The space was not dark; people were stretched out on the sofas. Ken was not very happy with this, but he went through with the first program he had brought. He showed *The Man with a Movie Camera* [1929]—this is 1969 and the Vertov film was just resurfacing—and thirty minutes into the event, the lounge had almost cleared out. Jan Kaplan, my contact person with the dorm, was mortified. This was totally different and more challenging than the previous events he had helped fund.

We moved from the dorm lounge to a classroom. During the following week, Ken insisted on not doing the usual theatrical presentations and star filmmaker turns, and proceeded to lead a very intensive seminar on the aesthetics of cinema. The sessions lasted day and night. Ken showed many kinds of films (I remember him showing Baillie's *Valentin de las Sierras* [1968] several times, sometimes just the picture and sometimes just the sound), and ended up with a group of about twenty very serious, very focused, very excited young people. It was amazing how much was accomplished in terms of the depth of the discussions. It was a remarkable week.

I'm 95 percent sure that Ken was carrying Nisi on his back during the seminar. I remember marveling how different this was from the other filmmakers who had visited—and this is to take nothing away from them. It's just that their visits were more spectacle, whereas Ken was really about engaging the moment and challenging each situation, a whole different kind of experience.

Jim Hoberman: Ken Jacobs came in the spring of 1969, and basically talked nonstop for a week in one of the lecture halls. He was an amazing speaker; insight came pouring out of him. He didn't use notes; he'd just show up with movies and talk. It was fantastic. I'd been an extremely diffident student—if it hadn't been for the war and the draft, I probably would have dropped out. Ken's visit was hugely important for me; I cut all my other classes to be there. And I was able to talk with Ken for the first time.

Helene Kaplan Wright: I started in Binghamton in 1967. I was an English major and Dan Rowe, one of the English teachers, was very interested in film, as were a couple of students who were a bit ahead of me: Jim Hoberman and Michael Gersten. There was rumbling about a film department getting started.

I'd been trying to transfer away from Binghamton, and then Ken Jacobs was brought in as a visiting filmmaker, and he was revelatory. His visit was *the* most incredible event. He showed *Little Stabs at Happiness* and *Blonde Cobra*, and my memory is that—and this may be an apocryphal story—before he showed *Tom, Tom, the Piper's Son* [1969; revised 1971], which was a work-in-progress, he locked the doors to Lecture Hall 6 where it was being shown and explained that it was either leave now or stay for the next two-and-a-half hours, keep your mouth shut, and watch the screen. I don't remember anyone leaving. Ken was charismatic; he had us in the palm of his hand.

Larry Gottheim: Gradually I began to work toward a program or a department of cinema that wouldn't be part of the English Department or the Theater Department, but would be separate and equal to the other arts programs. This became my mission. The university was open to experiment at that time, and some people within the administration said, "Well, okay, let's set up a committee to examine this idea." So they set up a committee—somebody from the Art Department, somebody from the Theater Department . . . and suddenly *everybody* was interested—all of these people who had *never* supported the idea of having better projection, had *never* come to the recent Film Society programs (some of these people *hated* the changes in what the Film Society was showing). This had hardened me; I knew I didn't want these guys to be involved in the new department.

One of the people from the Theater Department had taken film courses at some university and was presenting himself as an expert in cinema, and the committee was considering a program where people from different departments would teach courses: potentially a student could major in cinema by taking courses in the English Department (Film and Literature), in the Philosophy Department (Existentialism in Cinema), and so on. There would be all these different approaches.

Some of the hidebound traditionalists who didn't see cinema as an academic discipline wanted to stop the whole thing, and other people wanted to have a little bit of it, and—this could never happen again—in some miraculous way, people in the administration actually supported my idea of a separate Cinema Department. For a couple years we had an administration that was more visionary than the faculty! After awhile, these administrators got supplanted by more academic, business-inclined types and it was all over. But at that early moment, they supported my idea, and I knew that in order to make this work, I had to find somebody who had some stature, somebody who could out-rank the people in these other departments who were claiming to have expertise.

I'd become friends with Ken, who had had experience teaching *and* making film. I proposed him as somebody who with me would be the beginning faculty of the program—it was a program before it was a department.

Ken Jacobs: I was already a teacher during my teenage years; the Police Athletic League had after-school programs in poor neighborhoods. I still remember some of my students. This was a poor Irish area of Brooklyn, and I had three kids, a sister and two brothers named Jacobs—Irish but "Jacobs"—who were unbelievably talented. The littlest one would draw a picture and when it was done, he'd put swastikas all over it. I'd ask, "How come you do this?" And he would answer, "They're very exciting!"

I was a teacher whenever somebody would allow me to talk—I was so wound up. Even as a middle teenager, I was beset by ideas and if somebody gave me a signal to be forthcoming, I would roar. At some point after I got out of the Coast Guard (pressure of the draft: my aim was to be useless—Korea had clearly been a con—but I was okay about guarding the coast), a friend of mine who was teaching painting in Bronxville gave me her job teaching adults there—women mostly, very rich and very nice. I'd also taught some amazing old people at the Home and Hospital of the Daughters of Israel. There was a woman named Rose who'd come here from Russia with her husband to proselytize for the Revolution; she was very talented. I've kept some of the things she gave me all these years.

I also taught filmmaking at the Dalton School, and at a summer program at Fieldston [Ethical Culture Fieldston School]. I didn't have a license so I couldn't teach in public schools.

Flo Jacobs: Don't forget Millennium.

Ken Jacobs: And at Millennium, starting in 1966–67. I made Millennium into a kind of "university of the streets." I taught filmmaking—practical, historical, and theoretical; and we had the use of the St. Mark's Church in the Bowery to show films. Peter Kubelka's first screening in the USA was there. We began the practice of conversation after the films—not to everyone's liking. If people got the conversation going themselves, I wouldn't say anything; but if they didn't, I would speak and candidly. Bob Downey needed no help; he was deadly charming.

The first Millennium was destroyed by monsters of personal ambition, but we kept it going outside of church control with the help of other people, including Ernie Gehr.

I also taught at St. John's University in Queens, a Catholic school. The Art Department contacted me after the Millennium fracas, which had made the papers. Whether the kids were rich or poor, whatever color they were, whatever religion they were trying to rescue themselves from, I saw them as individuals and I did my best for them.

One memorable thing from St. John's: at some point I screened this Marxist South American film, *The Given Word* [1962, directed by Anselmo Duarte], that showed the failure of the Church to care for people. A semiretired priest—bad heart—who attended my classes and who had spent a lot of time in South America said to me afterward, "It's worse than that." The film was devastating but he said, "It's *worse* than that"! You never know what to expect from any individual.

The Art Department at St. John's wanted me to start a media center, then they suffered a big drop in funding. Binghamton made a surprising offer to us, and there were two other offers: one came from Stan Vanderbeek in Tampa, and Manny Farber recommended me for a position in California.

Flo Jacobs: I didn't want to leave our loft in New York. At Binghamton, Ken would get a three-year contract and we could keep our place. Stan Vanderbeek had offered Kenneth $18,000, but it would have meant leaving here, as the California position would have.

Ken Jacobs: Say how much money we were living on.

Flo Jacobs: We were living on $3,500 a year.

Ken Jacobs: Even back then, that wasn't much.

Flo Jacobs: I wasn't convinced about the move to Binghamton; I thought it might be like living in Albany, where I'd spent my first six years—I hated it there.

Ken Jacobs: You'd had a very bad experience with small-town anti-Semitism.

Flo Jacobs: But if we went to Binghamton, we could sublet our loft. I'd already put Nisi on the waiting list for Hunter Elementary School; I wanted her to go to school in Manhattan, not in small-town America.

Ken Jacobs: We'd met some of the Binghamton students, including Jim Hoberman, and they were great.

Flo Jacobs: Yes, they *were* great. So I thought, well, maybe after three years Kenneth will be able to get a job at a university in Manhattan and things will be fine.

Jim Hoberman: Larry was working to create a film department and already trying to figure a way to get Ken to teach in Binghamton—which, looking back, seems pretty extraordinary; I don't know if Ken had even gone to college.*

Larry was successful and the summer before Ken came to teach, he had a job teaching at the Aspen School of the Arts in Colorado. I basically invited myself to go along as Ken's assistant, and believe it or not, I got them to comp my tuition and maybe even my board—so that I could be Ken's projectionist and gofer. It was the sixties: I hitchhiked to Aspen. (See fig. 9.)

Michael Gersten, a buddy of mine from Binghamton, was in Aspen with us; he was another film buff, probably involved in the Film Society too, and wanted to be a filmmaker—so we spent that summer, or part of it, with Ken. I wasn't totally reliable: at a certain point a bunch of people I knew passed through and I took off with them to California, and then came back.

In Aspen I had to learn how to work with the Kalart-Victor analytic projector; Ken had a number of them. He was working on *Tom, Tom, the Piper's Son* at this time. You can't understand the Cinema Department

*Jacobs: "I took two courses, an intro to the movie camera (faces this way) and an intro to 16mm editing. That was my college education and not sure if it was graded, more likely another Certificate if that much. Hans Richter interviewed each potential student, said nothing, and was never seen again, as his assistant on his later cine-junk, Arnold Eagle, taught the class. Richter out-takes were given out to do the editing assignments and Bob Fleischner did his impressively, and so we met. . . . It was pathetic and most students, on the G.I. Bill like me, dropped the course before it was over." E-mail to the author, June 13, 2014.

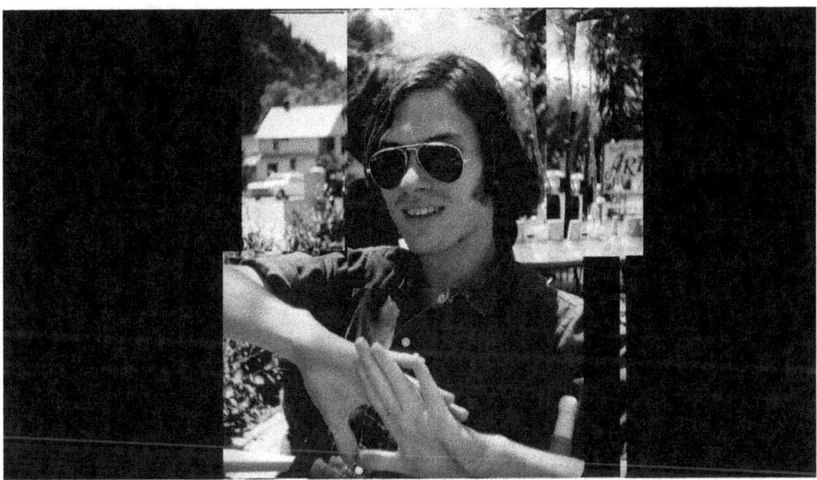

Figure 9. Jim Hoberman in an early Ken Jacobs stereopticon photograph (c. 1970). Courtesy Ken Jacobs.

apart from the Kalart-Victor projector. The first thing Ken did when he was hired at Binghamton was order two. Essentially they were variable speed projectors: you could show films one frame at a time, and you could stop on a single frame. But they were extremely sensitive. The threading was extra complicated; there were all these little safety triggers; it was nerve-wracking to use them. They had been developed during World War II, and now were very cheap—Ken probably paid twenty-five bucks for them on Canal Street. He was a devotee of the Kalart-Victor. Later, at Binghamton, I was Ken's projectionist—it was my work-study job.

Daile Kaplan: I arrived in Binghamton in 1968, a naive girl from Brooklyn, and immediately developed culture shock. Campus life was much freer than life at home and required some adjustment. I had planned to major in Russian (like Larry Gottheim!), and was interested in becoming a diplomat. I was making photographs and interested in photography, but only as an avocation, a personal form of artistic expression.

I attended a film screening that Larry organized and was transfixed. I transferred to the Cinema Department in my sophomore year, soon after Ken Jacobs had conducted a visiting artist program that dazzled many of us—and subsequently was invited to join the brand new department.

Ken was/is an amazing presence, a charismatic lecturer who linked cinema, painting, performance, and other art forms in visceral and dynamic ways. I suppose he could be construed as a guru, given how we revered him. I should also say that Flo, Ken's wife, was his partner and equal. Given the feminist revolution that was underway, this made a strong impression on me.

Larry, the academically trained professor-turned-artist, had been teaching at Harper College and living in Johnson City for several years; he was the yang to Ken's yin—a quiet, kind, and smart guy who, like his students, seemed to be groping for a new identity.

To a great extent my decision to move toward the arts was due to my being away from my parents, whose worldview was quite protective and limited (true of many of my friends' parents at the time). We students were caught up in the remarkable cross currents of what was then known as the "counterculture." After my parents met Ken, they recognized his positive influence on me.

Steve Anker: Larry managed to find a way to get Ken hired and in September of 1969, my junior year, the Cinema Department came into being. Larry was the architect of the program, and even then it was clear that he was a visionary who, in the right place at the right time, was bold enough to move from literature into the new academic area of cinema; and he was smart enough to be able to take advantage of the university's resources during a time of growth. Most importantly, he was drawn to the most radical possibilities of how this new area of study could be brought to the campus, and he was unwavering in wanting the most creative and challenging people to be involved. Hence, Ken Jacobs and, soon, a remarkable course of study for both film production and film appreciation.

Larry Gottheim: It's amazing how much can happen in a short time. The first actual cinema program courses were offered during the summer of 1970, after I had received an NEH grant and took a year off. By this time, I had transformed from an English professor who was interested in cinema into a filmmaker, and I had invited Ernie Gehr to teach with me that summer.

I'd been fascinated by Ernie's *Morning* and *Wait*, and at one of our projections one of his films got damaged. I went to see him to arrange to replace the print, or do whatever we could do, and we became friends. That was the summer when Ernie made *Serene Velocity* [1970].

Ernie Gehr: In the spring of 1970—around the time of the Kent State shootings—I was invited to show films in Binghamton. I showed the four films that I had completed up to then—*Morning*, *Wait*, *Transparency* [1969], *Reverberation* [1969], and possibly a section of *History* [1970]. Afterward, there was a long discussion, partially about the work and partially about why someone would make such works in a time of turmoil.

Later on that evening, there was a reception at someone's home, and Larry asked me if I would be interested in teaching a course at Binghamton that summer. I told him that I'd never taught before, had never even thought about teaching, and didn't feel I could do it. Larry said, "Oh, you handle yourself quite well." We left it at that.

Back in New York, I purchased a copy of Ed Pincus's *Guide to Filmmaking* [New York: New American Library, 1969]. I read a bit of it, called Larry back and said, "Larry, I don't work with film the way Pincus writes about film, and if his book is the standard textbook, I'm not the person to teach filmmaking. I don't want to spend my time talking about equipment." Larry's response was, "But we're not asking you to teach a standard filmmaking course. We're asking you to teach filmmaking *according to Ernie Gehr*." I told Larry, "Well, okay, it may be a disaster, but if that's really what you want, I'll try it."

So in the summer of 1970, I went to Binghamton to teach an introductory filmmaking course. I don't remember what on earth I did, but apparently I did it well enough so that most of the students liked the two courses—introduction to filmmaking and film history and analysis, mostly analysis—and I was asked to teach again the following summer. (See fig. 10.)

During those years, the energy of the film department was great: inquisitive, and quite hopeful for the possibilities of film as an art form.

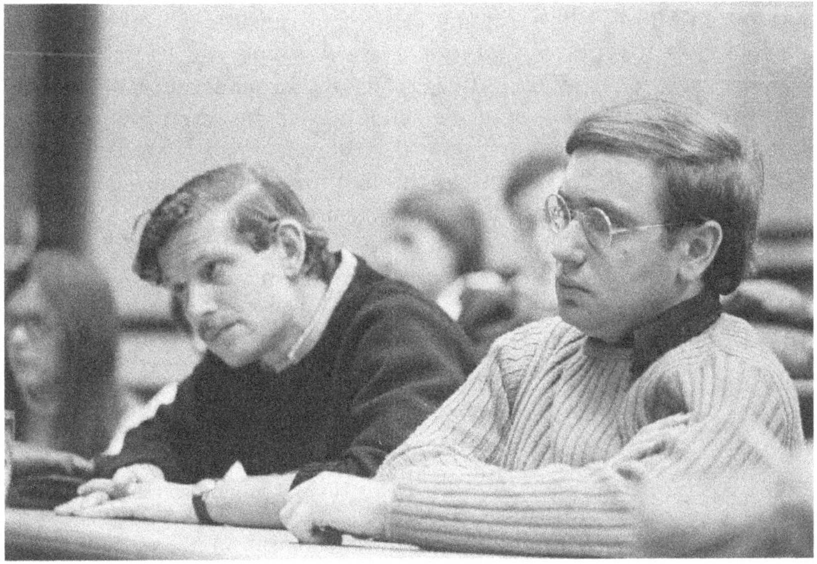

Figure 10. Larry Gottheim (left) and Ernie Gehr. Courtesy Mark Goldstein.

We were looking at all kinds of movies, and the kind of dialogue that was taking place during this time and the positive atmosphere that prevailed was largely due to the efforts of Ken and Larry.

Among other individuals I befriended at Binghamton were Jim Hoberman, Helene Kaplan [Wright], Ann Kruger—and Art Spiegelman, who was not a student, but was living in Binghamton and coming to screenings as well as to some of Ken's presentations. We became good friends and are still close.*

In the summer of 1970, I recorded footage for several films: *Serene Velocity* [1970], *Field* [1970], and *Three* [1970]. *Three* was just a 100-foot roll; it was shown once or twice, but after *Field* and *Serene Velocity*, I didn't think much of it and eventually withdrew the film from distribution. The following summer I did the final edit for *Still* [1971] in Binghamton, because they had the equipment I needed to synchronize sound and image.

Larry Gottheim: Ernie was involved in the beginning of what became *Horizons* [1973]. I don't know whether he or I wanted to film some sheep; he was at loose ends in Binghamton, and we would spend time driving around and talking. There was this hillside where I remembered seeing some sheep, and that's where I conceived the idea of *Horizons*.

Ernie Gehr: I recorded some other material in Binghamton in 1970, or maybe 1971, that didn't result in a work, for something I was calling "Animated Shorts." It was going to be approximately 60-minutes long, composed of a series of 100-foot takes. At some point I shelved that project, but I remember Larry driving me around the winding back roads near Binghamton, with me shooting out the rear window, telling him, "Drive a little bit faster, now a bit slower, now a bit faster"—those 100-foot rolls took forever to go through the camera! I never used any of the footage I shot in Binghamton for that project.

I think it was during the summer of 1971, though it could have been 1970, that Nam June Paik came up to Binghamton to do some work with Ralph Hocking at the Experimental Television Center. Nam June, who I had known from New York, invited me to the ETC studio. For several days that summer I played with the equipment. The technology

---

*At the beginning of part one ("My Father Bleeds History") of his Pulitzer Prize–winning *MAUS: A Survivor's Tale* (New York: Pantheon, 1986), Art Spiegelman thanks Ken and Flo Jacobs and Ernie Gehr. The importance for Spiegelman of Ken Jacobs's lectures is made clear in his cartoon, "Ken Jacobs" (see Appendix 2).

was intriguing, but at that point in time, I didn't care to work seriously with video.

Larry Gottheim: I owe a lot to Ken for his ideas and insights, and a lot of valuable creative tension came out of my struggles with him over the years. When we were on the same side, as early on we often were, for example, on cinema aesthetics or defending the department against enemies within and outside the university, we were a powerful duo, each supporting and influencing the other.

But right from the beginning there were some hurtful problems that had to do with personality. Ken was well known in the "Underground" community, for whom Jonas was a public voice. So when Ken came to Binghamton, Jonas trumpeted his arrival with little knowledge and thus little recognition of the years of work I'd put into nurturing the birth of the Cinema Department.*

The original purchase of some filmmaking equipment and the assignment of a room for editing resulted from my agreeing to make a publicity film—*Our Harpur Film* [1969]—with my students; that and some of the early Film Society programs (the guest appearance of Shirley Clarke and even Ken's original visit in connection with the Film Society and the film class that I was teaching in the English Department) indicated the direction the department would be heading, even had Ken not joined it.

The basic sequence of courses was put together with the help of Robert Pawlikowski, a poet who was the assistant dean; he emerged as our guy within the administration. He helped to hammer our ideas into a shape that would accord with a regular undergraduate program.

---

*Mekas: "Harpur . . . must be the most exciting place for any serious film student to be these days: At Harpur Ken Jacobs is setting up the most exciting (and the most advanced) visual arts workshop in the world today." See "On Ken Jacobs, or Images and Sound in Space," a June 4, 1970, *Village Voice* column, reprinted in Mekas, *Movie Journal: The Rise of the New American Cinema, 1959–1971* (New York: Collier, 1972): 384–385

2

First Flush

Ken Jacobs: I was hired at Binghamton to start in the fall of 1970. Larry and I were given our freedom. The school was adventurous in those days and we had lots of resources. That was the only time in American history that someone like me, without even a high-school diploma, could have been considered for such a position. Dean Peter Vukasin told me they'd decided I was "a natural." (See fig. 11.)

Flo Jacobs: Dean Vukasin and President Bruce Dearing were both very supportive.

Ken Jacobs: Amazingly so. Dearing's son was an artist, and I've always assumed he figured into my selection.

Part of the sixties for me was attempting to remain myself in all situations, not to go into special modes of behavior because of this or that social situation, so our movement from how we lived at home to how we lived in the classroom was seamless. I was a father and my parenthood was part of my teaching. I'd be holding forth and Flo would be nursing Azazel in the back.

Flo Jacobs: And Nisi would be drawing on the blackboard or coloring on the steps. She asked once why her friend Diana had her own mommy and daddy and why *her* daddy was everyone's daddy.

Ken Jacobs: My approach to students had always to do with recognition of the individual; I never saw students as a mass. For me they were individuals as much as I was.

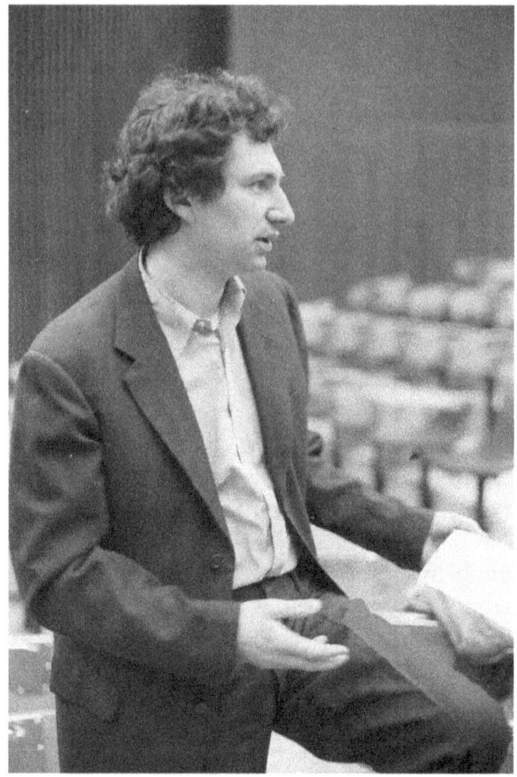

Figure 11. Ken Jacobs lecturing. Courtesy Mark Goldstein.

What I brought into the classroom was a kind of theater, teaching-theater, didactic theater. Many of the class-sessions were artworks, juxtapositions of this against that, making a thought-unit at the end. The classes were countless works of art—at least *I* considered them that, though I never *said* that.

Flo Jacobs: Yes you did.

Ken Jacobs: To *you*, not to students.

Flo Jacobs: That's true.

Ken Jacobs: I was never a big one for syllabi. In fact, I would rarely know what I would be doing in class until I stepped into the room. I was just *consumed* with stuff; I would carry shopping bags of materials to class. Sometimes I would end up talking the whole session or going into one little section of a film and never use the contents of the shopping bags, but I brought them every class, so I was always loaded and ready to go. Spontaneity was important to me. Each session had to have a charge, usually supplied by that morning's news.

Flo Jacobs: Classes were often structured the way *Tom, Tom, the Piper's Son* is: he would screen a film, then do a detailed analysis of it, then screen the film again—that could take nine hours, for one class.

Ken Jacobs: No one ever told me how long a class was supposed to last.

Flo Jacobs: At that time, 1970–71, there was no problem about this, or at least I don't remember any. A class could meet pretty much at any time for as long as you wanted. Later on, classes had to fit into time slots, but at the beginning there was nothing like that. You could do everything on a Tuesday; you could come in at 10:00 and go to 12:00, take lunch, then come back again from 1:00 to 3:00, then come back again in the evening, and people were fine about it: they had lunch and dinner together and came back.

Steve Anker: This was the sixties, a critical period of growth for film studies, and Larry got a budget to buy equipment, including an Arriflex BL, for its time a very fancy camera, and a Nagra—nice basic equipment to expand the filmmaking possibilities. I wasn't involved in filmmaking at that point although I went out with Larry a couple of times on shoots for what became *Horizons*, and I think I was involved with one of Larry's early single-shot films.

Looking back, I realize that Larry had a profound impact on me during my first years at Binghamton. He caused us to think about perception, to take note of smallest details during a moment in a landscape, of things we'd otherwise barely be aware of. One large three-hour lecture class was conducted totally in the dark, and over time Larry pointed out objects in the room and qualities of light that few of us had ever noticed or thought about. That was also how he approached cinema, that it was both totally simple, yet wonderfully complex, a miracle medium that we could discover for ourselves.

I decided to become a cinema major, and I often wonder why ultimately I was drawn to Ken—during my last two years I didn't have a lot to do with Larry, and I regret that. I guess it has to do with my looking for a certain kind of father figure. Ken was fiery and confrontational, always shaking things up with unexpected responses to the startling and strange material that he brought to his classes. Larry was gentler, but also deeply thoughtful and questioning. He had a different way of exploring new ways of thinking and perceiving that allowed more room for each person's responses to emerge. Both were remarkably articulate.

Ken could be incredibly supportive and passionate and was nearly always compellingly articulate and poetically analytical: Ken's penchant for words is very strong. But he could be very severe and uncompromising (even brutal), and often unpredictable and seemingly inconsistent in terms of what he was looking for from a student. Many people rose to the occasion and were able to produce, but his criticisms were often sharp and humiliating. I wasn't very productive—maybe I just didn't have filmmaker in me. How many people do? But I saw Ken take some students apart in a way that was quite shocking, even scary. He expected us to put ourselves on the line every day.

Soon after Ken arrived, I got involved in the shadow play he was doing, among his earliest forays into 3-D performance. He used a translucent screen with a couple of bulbs lighting the screen from one side with polarized filters in front of them, and you would watch from the other side with polarized glasses.

Jim Hoberman: I'd thought *Larry* was an open-minded teacher: one year I came up to Binghamton with my girlfriend and didn't have an apartment yet, and Larry let us stay in his house! But with Ken there were no boundaries at all; in Aspen, Michael and I had practically lived with Ken and Flo and their daughter Nisi; at SUNY-Binghamton Flo and Nisi were present in every class.

Ken is much mellower now. When I met him, he was not an easy guy. He arrived in Binghamton with a lifetime of resentment and would air grievances in class. He would talk about his childhood; his lectures were almost like stand-up routines: he would free-associate, although he was so good at it that he never lost the point. He was always drawing on his personal experience, which he made very mythic. Jack Smith was a mythic character to us and what happened at the Millennium was a set of mythic events. For Ken, to remember something is to relive it. There were a lot of things that had happened recently in New York that he was still working through, and it was just amazing to have this charismatic artist talking about his life.

Ken was going to make a movie with the title "Binghamton, My India." For him—and this was true in a sense for everybody who grew up in New York City and landed in Binghamton—it was the most exotic place he had been, but not in a good way, at least for Ken. Ken and

Flo lived in the Stair development, a set of prefab garden apartments up the hill from a shopping plaza. I was naively shocked that he would live there. I think he and Flo were living out of boxes the whole time they were in that apartment.

Helene Kaplan Wright: Once Larry Gottheim had brought the Cinema Department into being and Ken had been hired to teach, I was a work-study student, the assistant to Mrs. Aigen, the Cinema Department secretary. Mrs. Aiken was very maternal and unflappable and knew everything; she made sure that all the *t*'s got crossed and the *i*'s got dotted. Barbara DiBenedetto was also an assistant, the equipment hand-out person, so she and I were always around the building where the cinema classes were held in Lecture Halls 1 and 6. I was also a projectionist, and for a time I ran the Film Society. Larry and I used to brainstorm about what films we wanted to show.

For me personally, the beginning of the Cinema Department was the end of dropping acid every other day; I don't know if it was the same for other people. My original peers were Ken Ross and Phil Weisman. Steve Anker, Linda Karpel, Hali Breindel, and Renée Shafransky came a bit later. Jim Hoberman was older by at least a year and didn't seem at all interested in being a critic in those days. I was actually in one of his early films, a background odalisque, lying on a couch, not reacting while all sorts of odd behavior takes place in the foreground.*

I have to say that I would have followed Ken to the ends of the earth. He was the most extraordinary, riveting teacher. To listen to him talk about narrative film, to have him stopping and talking as he showed us a Bresson film or one of the Italian Neorealist films or some of the early French avant-garde films, to see him deconstruct film on the narrative, political, and visual levels in a way that was so passionate—all this was entirely different from every other teacher that I've ever had. He was just *on* for three hours at a time and never ran out of things to say.

Ken's film*making* classes could be terrifying; Ken was no-holds-barred in his criticism, though he also was supportive in recognizing authenticity. As I think back on it now, some of what he was doing was paralyzing rather than liberating, at least for me. But in class there was a lot of enthusiasm and it seemed as if we were all becoming filmmakers. If you look at who came out of the program during that early era, it was Steve Anker, who went on to become a curator and more recently the

*Wright is referring to *Customs & Immigration* (1971), which was shot partly on the SUNY-Binghamton campus and partly in an apartment in Johnson City (a town next to Binghamton).

dean of the Film School at CalArts—*not* a filmmaker. And Jim Hoberman came out *not* as a filmmaker (though I think of Jim as *Larry's* student). I gave up filmmaking for a variety of personal reasons.

David Marc: I arrived at Binghamton in 1968, and met Larry Gottheim when I was a freshman; he was a Yale-educated English professor lecturing on *The Odyssey* to a class of four hundred students who met with graduate students once a week for discussion. Larry put that behind him to develop the Cinema Department.

The Cinema Department classes were like none other. All you really had to do was attend, though as we quickly found out, attending meant more than physically being in the lecture hall; you had to *attend* to what was going on. You were either involved or you were put out of the room!

Larry and Ken didn't want to be bothered with reading papers, grading standard assignments; you handed in your notebooks at the end of the semester and the grades came from that.

Ken Jacobs, who had never gone to college—he'd studied informally with the painter Hans Hofmann—was the professor and he put a value on knowledge that was much more rigorous than anything else I experienced at Binghamton—and Binghamton had a good faculty! Ken was attuned so directly to learning how cinema worked and taking the text, as the French would say, anyplace it led—that being in his classes was very exciting. I majored in English, but for me the Cinema Department was the intellectual center of my education.

You were expected to be so dedicated that, in addition to the scheduled three-hour classes, you would be available when there were visiting filmmakers: Stan Brakhage would show up and you had to be involved for the whole weekend. I didn't know anybody else in the class who was familiar with the kind of nonnarrative, abstract cinema Brakhage made, and I found a lot of it deadly, beyond my comprehension. I wasn't alone. We had a "fraternity of suffering." *The Weir-Falcon Saga* by Stan Brakhage—if you just sat through it, you deserved a medal.

The British poet Basil Bunting was at Binghamton for a semester. Brakhage was very interested in him, so I arranged for the two of them to meet at Larry's house. At Binghamton social occasions were just as important as the classes.

Larry and Ken wanted *real* education or nothing, but of course what *they* thought of as real education the "real educators" on campus thought *was* nothing! Larry and Ken seemed rather isolated from the rest of the campus, though there were others on the Binghamton faculty they'd made links with: Milton Kessler, the poet, was certainly one, and

I studied with him. Robert Crouch, the Canadian novelist who won the Canadian Book Award for a novel called *The Stud Horse Man*, was my adviser in the English Department. Kessler and Crouch gave a lot of time and effort in the traditional way, but there was a sense in the late sixties that something new was going on in education, and the Cinema Department was definitely where the new was happening.

Amy Halpern-Lebrun: I arrived in Binghamton a shy sixteen-year-old in the fall of 1970. There was so much newness around that, looking back, it feels as if I was born with the department. By the time I arrived, I'd already decided that my life would be making film, and I'd seen enough film when I was younger to know that what I was interested in had little to do with Hollywood. I was lucky enough to have a film-maniac father, Ben Halpern, who did publicity for United Artists—hey, when I was four, Cary Grant proposed marriage to me! (He and my dad were working together.)

I was at the Museum of Modern Art watching films with my father all the time. He would say, "This is great! That is great!"—without any genre snobbery. So I'd already seen and enjoyed a huge amount of experimental film.

When I arrived and saw the Binghamton campus, made entirely of salmon-colored brick in a place where it's always overcast, I walked around literally reeling with horror, thinking how could *anybody* with eyes *do* this? But when I saw the films that were being made there, I thought, "Aha!"

The first films I remember seeing were *Barn Rushes* [1971] and *Blues* [1969]—Larry's stuff. It went right into me, as did Hollis Frampton's *Lemon* [1969]. Film suddenly seemed more open than literature or painting or sculpture; there was so much still to be done.

Harvey L. Silver: I was only at Harpur for six months—fall of 1970. I'd transferred up there from Queens College in New York City (a personal relationship soon brought me back to Queens). Until I arrived in Binghamton, I didn't realize how incredibly noncommercial the program was; Larry and Ken taught us an appreciation for Pure Cinema. We used to watch entire films with sound, then again without sound; and the department preached, "If you're bored, that's *your* problem. In this program you'll need to learn to rise above boredom."

We were basically taught to shun Hollywood films. The only contemporary Hollywood film I remember being recommended to us was *Joe* [1970] by John Avildsen. We did see a lot of Ingmar Bergman. As a result of Harpur, I got into Ken Russell, Sam Peckinpah, and Robert

Downey Sr. (*Putney Swope* [1969] is one of the great films: what happens in that film when a black man takes over an ad agency has parallels to what happened when Obama became president).

I got a lot out of the months I was there: Larry and Ken were great teachers and fascinating individuals. Jacobs was well-known, already described in books as the Father of Underground Film, so it was a big deal to actually know him. And to this day, I remember watching Larry's film *Blues*.

Jim Hoberman: I think that Ken was very threatening to other professors, particularly in the arts, because they saw that he wasn't an academic. His ideas seemed very advanced, and he was very straightforward at putting them out. Ken was, and remains, extremely opinionated. All this made for great excitement.

His was an authoritarian classroom; there wasn't much give and take. Ken was very sensitive and took everything very personally. He would be holding forth and anything could throw him.

The classes were devoted to analyzing movies. There were certain movies that Ken loved; I know them by heart because I showed them over and over. In effect he would create a new *Tom, Tom* out of whatever the day's film was. His favorites included *They Live by Night* [1948]—ironic, given what would happen later—and *The Bicycle Thief* [1949]. I remember that we also looked at a lot of Griffith.

Ken was open to things that Michael Gersten and I would suggest: *Detour* [1946, Edgar J. Ulmer], for example, and *Touch of Evil* [1958, Orson Welles]—a movie that, except for the opening dolly shot, he was not that impressed with. *Breathless* [1959] he liked, but he *hated* everything else that Godard did. I was shocked by this, never really could get over it. He also hated *Blow-Up* [1967]; I had mixed feelings about *Blow-Up*, but to *hate* it seemed extravagant to me. Hitchcock—forget it! He found Hitchcock not just manipulative, but evil—to this day you can't talk about Hitchcock with Ken.

Ken *taped* his classes on a Wollensak recorder—I mean *everything he said* was taped. I'd love to hear these lectures again because, a few specific remarks aside, I don't really remember them very clearly. I do know that Ken's teaching style came back to me when I started to teach—I'm certainly no Ken Jacobs, but I did assimilate certain things and had also learned *not* to do other things.

In all these college towns there are students who never leave or who come back, so there's a rich off-campus existence. Since Ken was the most interesting thing happening on campus, there were lots of people who would show up to sit in on his classes. Art Spiegelman is an example; he had been at Binghamton, dropped out and did other things, then suddenly came back and was showing up in Ken's classes. Bob Schneider, who I was very friendly with, did the same thing. (See fig. 12.)

Ken overshadowed Larry in a way that I feel bad about to this day. Larry was a supernice guy, very bright, and I liked *his* films too. But Ken was a genius, and when he started offering courses, those were the courses I took. Michael and I had to have been the first people to graduate with a BA in film, and in my case, it must have been film/English—probably Larry helped me cobble together some kind of joint major. I stayed around for a bit longer than four years.

Helene Kaplan Wright: And there was Flo, this incredibly soft-spoken woman making Ken's life possible. Linda Karpel, Barbara DiBenedetto, and I used to look back at Flo, who would always be sitting in the rear of the lecture halls, and wonder, "Where do women fit in here?" Because Carolee Schneemann was the only avant-garde woman filmmaker—besides Maya Deren, who was dead—who was ever shown or spoken about; it seemed like there were no women filmmakers, just women who slept with filmmakers. We were kind of dumbfounded at the relationship that Flo had with Ken, especially because she's so soft-spoken.

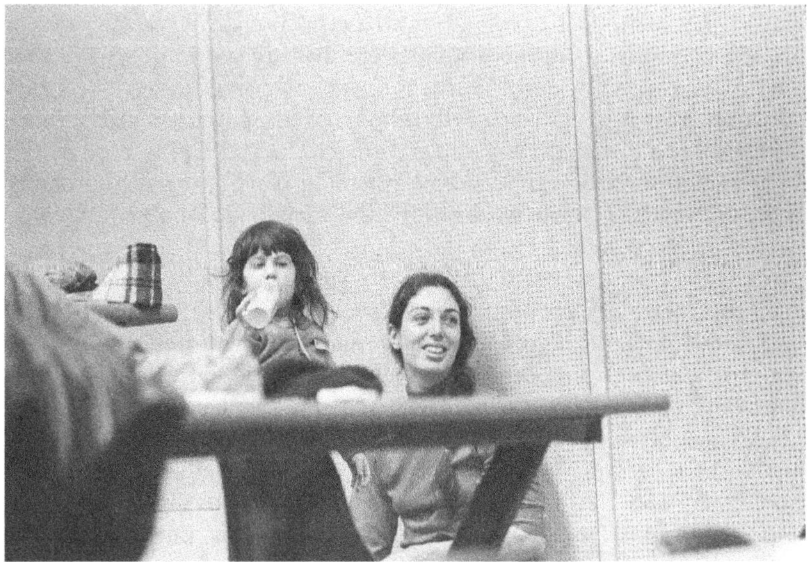

Figure 12. Flo Jacobs and Nisi in back of classroom. Courtesy Mark Goldstein.

In retrospect, and because I've now been friends with Ken and Flo for thirty-five years, I see Flo in a completely different light—someone who was a painter, studied at RISD, and married Ken as a fellow artist—and out of choice, at least to some degree, gave up painting, or showing her painting. She was always a stronger voice than we assumed back then; she was his collaborator and best critic—we didn't recognize this because she seemed so retiring, so in the background, and so dedicated to Ken. He was always looking to her and saying, "Do you remember that, Flo?" or "Will you get that, Flo?" or "What happened there, Flo?" We made terrible jokes about this. As women we were trying to figure out how we could function in this world, and we sometimes felt like Ken was grooming us to *marry* filmmakers, not *be* filmmakers.

Ken was never overtly sexist; I think he just assumed there was no issue. It was a given that there were women in *Little Stabs* and in *Star Spangled to Death* [shot 1957–59, completed 2004], and in all of the early footage that Ken showed of his works-in-progress, but there were very few of them and often they were just somebody's girlfriend.

David Marc: The students were always treated as people by the faculty, which at the time included a lot of things that are no longer allowed in a university. The kind of socializing that went on is now associated with sexual exploitation, but I didn't see much in terms of manipulation or bad behavior (much worse went on in the English Department). I don't know what affairs occurred and didn't occur, but there was no onus on it. A door was being opened; adults were inviting you to be part of their real lives, and sex was not considered some separate thing. Back then, we took great pride in being fully who we were, not just fledgling intellectuals, but full-functioning adults. *Animal House* [1978] is a movie that continues to reverberate; Donald Sutherland plays an English professor who is having an affair with one of the female students, and it's very accurately portrayed.

I was trying to make a life as a young openly gay man. At Binghamton, there was no particular encouragement to be gay, and so far as I know, none of the professors were gay, but there was absolutely no onus on homosexuality. In speaking about sex, you felt you were on the moral high ground, because the faculty certainly spoke about many sexual things that were not in the mainstream. I could speak about being gay in the first person with no fear, which was very important to me and something that I refused to give up later, at times when I might have feared being honest. I'll always appreciate that about Binghamton.

Ken Jacobs: Now we have DVDs and computers. But in those days we had analytic projectors, which was like a dream; it was wonderful that the school was able to respond to my request to buy them. The machines themselves led to a lot of my performance-work.

The Kodak analytic projector wouldn't stop on a frame, but the Kalart-Victor could, and because I had one of those, I could make *Tom, Tom*.

Flo Jacobs: You taught with the Kalart-Victor because you could go through a shot, frame by frame by frame.

Ken Jacobs: And really see how the cuts worked.

Flo Jacobs: Then you'd run the soundtrack without the imagery; then you'd do the sound and the image together. The students called the classroom "the house of pain"!—from *The Island of Lost Souls* [1933, directed by Erle C. Kenton].

Ken Jacobs: That's a film I spent a lot of time on. It's quite a movie, with Charles Laughton and Bela Lugosi.

I was very critical of the films I showed *and* very impressed by the things that were there. In other words, I could be impressed even by things in films I hated. I wasn't doctrinaire, so I could look at things that I was politically *for*, critically. I could look at something that worked as art and not be in a fit of blind love about it. I once estranged Brakhage over *23rd Psalm Branch* [1966]. I was teaching during the summer in Boulder and Stan came over. By that time, Stan and I were very candid with each other. I'd worked that day with *23rd Psalm Branch* and told him he'd aestheticized World War II: explosions were flowers. He'd made the war a symphony. He didn't take it well, said I was betraying what it was to be an artist, and it was years . . .

Flo Jacobs: Three years . . .

Ken Jacobs: Three years, before we spoke again. He called on my birthday and sang "Happy Birthday" to me, and we just went on from there—never discussed what had happened and continued as if only a day had passed.

Bill T. Jones: Arnie Zane was a biology and art history major who had developed an interest in photography while he was living in Amsterdam, and when he moved back to Binghamton and he and I had begun our relationship, our shared interest in modern art and photography was fed by the Cinema Department. I especially remember auditing Larry Gottheim's and Ken Jacobs's intriguing classes, and we got to know the cinema students too: Kenny Ross, Hali Breindel, Renée Shafransky. We became fixtures in the department.

We were watching *Gold Diggers of 1935*—and Ken was demystifying the experience. There's this shot of a woman standing on a piano, dressed in an amazing white gossamer outfit and turning in a weird way, and then suddenly from every direction thousands of white pianos come in to make one huge piano. Ken yells, "Don't be seduced! Don't be seduced by cinema! This is just still pictures that are manipulated, and how do you think that she made that weird turning movement? Very simple: it was shown in reverse." Did I resent Ken taking away the magic of Hollywood? As a beginning artist, I appreciated someone pulling back the curtain and showing that in some ways it *was* all technique.

At the time, I also wondered if Ken's approach came out of his jealousy of the position that Hollywood held in the national aesthetic conversation. Did Ken and Larry and these other young Turks think they were going to take Hollywood down by showing its secrets—or were they in fact just revealing their deep love of it?

Ken's use of the analytic projector turned out to be very important for me. The way in which Ken manipulated the images, moving them forward and back, and sometimes stopping them, made us very aware of the power of still pictures becoming movement and vice versa. Arnie and I were movement people and we became *very* interested in performing arrested movements, in creating moving figures that would stop or that would build into movement from a series of "stills." (See fig. 13.)

Steve Anker: I graduated in May of 1972—I stayed a fifth year and for my last three years, I worked pretty closely with Ken, although I also remained deeply involved with the radio station. Ours was often a difficult relationship. Many weekend nights, three or four of us, sometimes one or two, would go down to the basement room that Ken had set up and practice shadow play. A number of the shadow plays were pivotal for me personally, and I think they were significant moments in Ken's work. I would perform, although rarely on screen, as well as be an assistant. Ken became the closest teacher for me at that point; when he did events in New York City, I'd assist him. I was still friendly with Larry and we would spend time together occasionally.

In my first year of working with Ken, a group of us did a show at Anthology Film Archives, when it was on Wooster Street. On our way down we stopped at Robert Breer's house in New Jersey, where Breer was having a huge party for his New York artist friends. That might have been when I met Ernie Gehr. It was very exciting being there with all these people—I'm still a kid at this point—and there were colorful

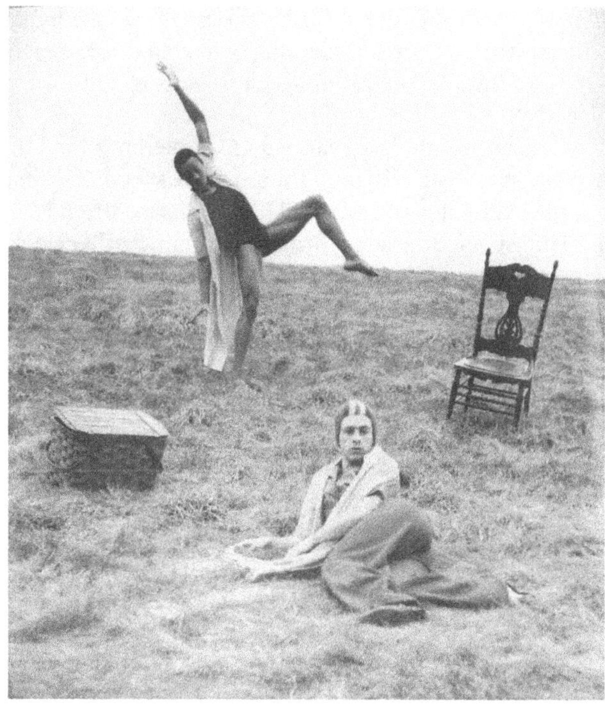

Figure 13. Bill T. Jones (in background) and Arnie Zane, in Arnie Zane photograph, *On the Hill in Johnson City* (1972). See *The Photographs of Arnie Zane* (Cambridge: MIT Press; Riverside, CA: University of California Press, 1999) for other images in the series. Courtesy Bill T. Jones.

people coming and going. Then we did a performance that Jonas Mekas wrote about, in a Wooster Street loft that I believe was owned by Richard Foreman; it included shadow play, abstract sound pieces, and different kinds of projection.* That trip remains one of my fondest memories.

One summer, Ken took over the Bleecker Street Cinema for a night and did a twelve-hour performance piece. He showed films in multiple projections, sometimes projecting on the ceiling, sometimes superimposing films—all kinds of films, from obscure features by Oscar Micheaux (who was almost totally unknown at that point) to his own films and to

*See "On Ken Jacobs, or Images and Sound in Space," a June 4, 1970 *Village Voice* column, in Mekas, *Movie Journal: The Rise of the New American Cinema, 1959–1971* (New York: Collier, 1972): 384–385, for a review of this show.

cartoons, strange features, and documentaries, the whole panoply of the kinds of cinema that he was discovering. He called that performance *A GOOD NIGHT FOR THE MOVIES*. Helene Kaplan and I were assistants on that piece.

And then, during my last year, we did something for John Lennon and Yoko Ono. Ken had run into John and Yoko on the Staten Island Ferry or somewhere downtown, and they became friends for awhile. Yoko had a fantasy about a large Broadway avant-garde celebration, and she was going to include Ken's shadow play. We set up several pieces in Ken and Flo's loft down on Chambers Street, and eight or ten of us performed for John and Yoko. They enjoyed it, but that larger celebration never materialized.

David Marc: During the shadow play performance for John and Yoko, we tried not to be nervous, not only because we wanted to be cool but because at the time we felt we were actually living on a higher plane than popular art. So we couldn't betray envy.

I guess to demonstrate how little he cared to be part of "the poisonous culture of the USA," Ken often told the story about how, after *Little Stabs at Happiness* had been shown somewhere, *Time Magazine* called him for an interview, and Ken said he wasn't interested. They called several times and actually sent a reporter to knock on the door at 94 Chambers Street, but Ken wouldn't let the reporter in.

Larry Gottheim: After Ken had come on board, we began to develop the visiting filmmaker series, which would remain an important part of the program. I knew some people—Hollis Frampton, for example—and Ken knew others, including Brakhage. I think I'd met Hollis again at a program at the Paula Cooper Gallery that Michael Snow and Hollis had arranged. During the next couple years Hollis came to Binghamton several times and made several films that became part of *Hapax Legomena* [1971–72].

Jim Hoberman: Certain visitors to Binghamton were important for me. Ken brought Seymour Stern, who had done a special Griffith issue of *Film Culture* [No. 36 (Spring–Summer, 1965)]. Seymour was a pistol, so nutty and great, a real man of the thirties. And I remember Ernie Gehr, who was very shy; I got to know him during the summer of 1970, when Ken got me a job as a film cleaner at the Filmmakers' Cooperative in New York (I replaced Andrew Noren who had all these funny quasi-pornographic R. Crumb drawings pasted up in his space). Ernie worked as the Coop bookkeeper, and we became friendly. (See fig. 14.)

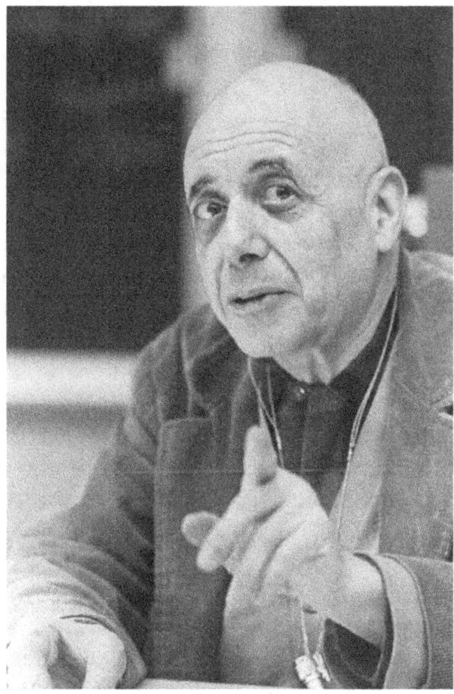

Figure 14. Film historian/scholar Seymour Stern at Binghamton. Courtesy Mark Goldstein.

Ernie shot *Still* [1971] during that summer. Larry assisted him with the sound. I'm *in Still.* Shelley [Hoberman] and I are the pair that cross the street to go into the diner. I was in a bad mood that day because we'd planned to drive out to the beach, and Ernie took a lot of time to make the shot.

I also remember Frampton visiting Binghamton, and Kubelka; but the most important visitor was Brakhage—I remember a weeklong visit in the fall of 1970. Steve Anker was very big on the campus radio station, and he managed to put Ken and Brakhage on the radio; it was a "Special Live" conversation—as if more than a tiny group gave a damn about this! I was involved somehow—maybe it was a panel and I was the student representative. We got into a conversation about *Joe* [1970, directed by John Avildsen] that became competitive: like who could voice the most hysterical view of what was happening in America.

Ken clearly loved Brakhage; he figured prominently in Ken's discourse and Ken always showed a lot of Brakhage films. We watched the entire four-hour *Art of Vision* [1961–65] in preparation for the visit.* Ken gave a wonderful introduction to the film, and I still remember asking (I was a kid), "Oh, Ken, should I drop acid for this?" He gave me a look but just said, "No. The film will be enough." And he was right.

So Brakhage came for a week and, like Ken, Brakhage could *talk*. For four days it was Brakhage's show; he would screen whatever he wanted and hold forth. Ken just sat there in the front row. But on the fifth day, Ken engaged Brakhage, and this was something epic: King Kong versus Godzilla. It wasn't hostile, but it certainly *was* competitive. Their points of view were very different, because while Ken was very involved with current events, Brakhage had moved to Colorado and had retreated from politics. Ken was this New York wise guy who had an opinion on everything, talked very fast, enjoyed all sorts of films, and cared about things that struck Brakhage as horrible junk. Although Brakhage did go to the movies, he couldn't draw on them in the same way Ken could.

They were going to bring out a book of the conversation; Ken wanted to call it "Holidaze Inn"—because Brakhage was staying at the Holiday Inn on Route 17, just across from the campus. The cover photograph was going to be an image of the sign out front, "Holiday Inn Welcomes Filmmaker Stan Brakhage." What I heard—I cannot confirm this—was that Jane [Stan Brakhage's first wife], who was also there, didn't want this debate to be published. (See fig. 15.)

Peer Bode: I was a freshman at Binghamton in the fall of 1970. I went there to study film. I'd been living with my folks in North Tonawanda and had been planning to go to nearby SUNY-Buffalo [now the University at Buffalo]; exciting things went on there. As high school students we used to go to UB to see Ferlinghetti and Ginsburg do presentations. But my folks encouraged me not to live near home. I was aware of SUNY-Binghamton, and delighted to find out about the Cinema Department. I decided to go for a semester to see if it was the right place for me. I remember showing Larry Gottheim some of the 8mm films I'd made, and him saying, "You should come into the department!"

I took a number of classes with Larry, and though I had some interaction with Ken, didn't take him for production—five years ago when he visited us at Alfred University, he gave me a hard time about that!

*"In *The Art of Vision*, Brakhage presents all the layers of film which went into the making of *Dog Star Man* [1961–64], individually and in superimposed combinations"—P. Adams Sitney, *Visionary Film: The American Avant-Garde, 1943–2000* (New York: Oxford University Press, 2002): 203. See Sitney's chapter 7 for his analysis of *Dog Star Man* and *The Art of Vision*.

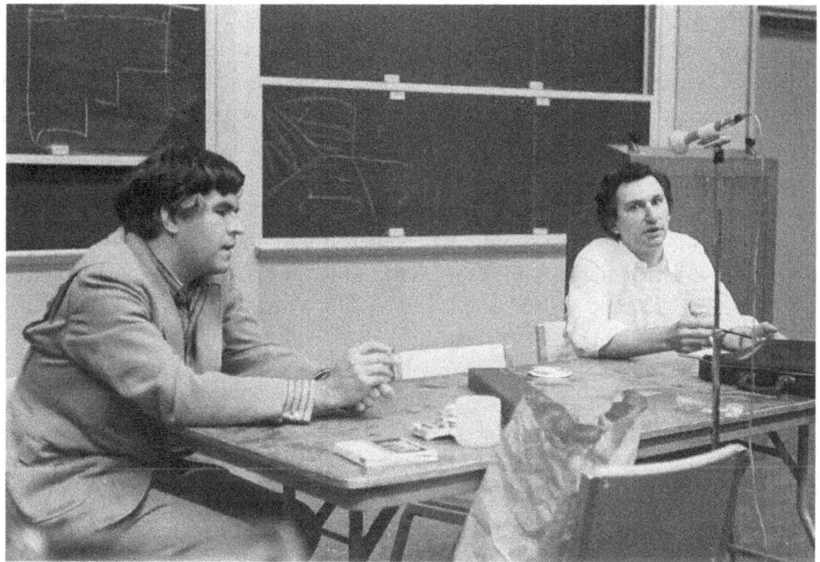

Figure 15. Stan Brakhage (left) and Ken Jacobs. Courtesy Mark Goldstein.

We had these large analysis classes in Lecture Hall 1 that Ken led. I remember being really impressed by those, and by the visiting artists program. Ken and Larry made those artist visits extensive and intensive.

Brakhage came a number of times, and there were all kinds of heated exchanges where he was challenged and he challenged Ken and Larry back. When Hollis Frampton and Paul Sharits and Tony Conrad and P. Adams Sitney visited, the same thing happened, and I remember thinking, "God, we're really lucky to be able to hear this stuff!" These weren't just school exercises; the visiting artists program was more like a public forum where real issues that people were passionate about got addressed.

All kinds of people came through. Peter Kubelka was with us for a semester and Hermann Nitsch came with his *Orgien Mysterien Theater* ["Theater of Orgies and Mysteries," many performances since 1962]. Ernie Gehr and Taka Iimura did some teaching; the Warhol group came to show *Lonesome Cowboys* [1967–68]. And Jack Smith, Alfons Schilling, Dennis Hopper, and Jane Fonda.

And I remember the first time I visited the Experimental Television Center in Binghamton. Ralph had set up his own sculptural video installation, a sort of automated marching-band piece that included video feedback and a siren and a light that was spinning and balloons or prophylactics that blew up, then went limp, then blew up again. I thought, "Whoa! Fantastic!" But despite my excitement about the piece, I have to admit that at the time I was a film snob, as many people in those days were—it was kind of a theme at Binghamton.

Bill T. Jones: I remember Hollis Frampton's *Works & Days* [1969]. I think he had found old footage and had re-mastered and organized it into a very glorious formalist film, and Arnie and I were very much into that.

Stan Brakhage visited the Cinema Department several times, and I remember Paul Sharits, who was a legend. I saw Michael Snow's *Wavelength* [1967] at Binghamton. And I remember Peter Kubelka: the first flicker film I ever saw was Peter Kubelka's [*Arnulf Rainer*, 1960]. Jonas Mekas was the patron saint of the department—I remember him showing *Reminiscences of a Journey to Lithuania* [1972]. Ken and Larry made these events so appealing, so *urgent*, and every one of them was branded onto my consciousness—they were all so fresh and so powerful.

Peter Kubelka: For me the environment of Binghamton itself was a great experience. I'd come from Vienna, so it was quite something to be for the first time in small-town America. The neighboring city to Binghamton is called Johnson City, and there was a huge sign at the entrance to Johnson City: Home of the Square Deal. I was amazed that a *town* could put a slogan like this on its doors! And there was a *wonderful* diner that everybody at SUNY-Binghamton seemed to loathe. I loved it, because they did home cooking—they would broil liver for you. And in Binghamton I discovered the language of American short-order cooking: "Two fried, over easy!" These were for me key sensations.

And here, in the middle of small-town America, and inside the normal structure of a university (we were not really respected by the other faculty; they looked down on us), was this jewel of a film department.

At Binghamton, apart from Larry and Ken, the secretaries were the most important people. There was Marilyn Aigen and the students who helped her run the office; they always had a central position in what went on in the department. Marilyn was completely nonbureaucratic and nonacademic; and she continually did things to keep the whole adventure moving.

At that time, film departments had not been academicized the way they are now, and at Binghamton there was a very interesting community of students who were always together. I remember Helene Kaplan [Wright], who was a projectionist and a key figure for the other students.

Philip Sykas: I began my undergraduate career at SUNY-Binghamton in the summer of 1970 and finished in summer 1973, formally receiving my BA in May 1974. As a young student, I'd been discouraged in the pursuit of art, but with the start of university I was finally free to follow my instincts, though my choices were constricted by practical matters. I'd obtained a New York State Regents scholarship, which paid my tuition, and it was this that sealed my choice of Binghamton. My father provided me with a sum each month equivalent to his income-tax deduction for claiming me as a dependent, and I also received a small social security payment arising from the death of my mother.

In those days, registration for courses was arranged on a competitive basis, with students allotted earlier opportunities to register according to grade point average and with freshmen at the bottom of the heap. As a result, the studio art classes I desired were filled before I had a chance to sign up, and the money from my father would not cover more than a modest expenditure on required textbooks, so an art history course was out of the question. The Cinema Department required no set texts, and, seeing this as my best chance of including an art subject in my schedule, I took Cinema 101: Introduction to Cinema in my freshman year. Cinema was to become my minor, alongside my major in printmaking and drawing.

Cinema lectures took place in a large lecture theater packed with students, and were gently but ably led by Larry Gottheim, whose mellow voice and rambling impromptu thoughts opened a new world to me and many others. Larry, with his slightly unruly side-parted quiff of hair, button-down collars, and tweed jackets, looked the part of the university professor, yet he preserved an attractive, youthful, and unpredictable quality. His vibrant eyes and halting vocal delivery embodied his deep thoughtfulness. Without us knowing or even having to know, he was able to convey the complexities of Heidegger in an everyday vocabulary and a totally unassuming manner.

Ralph Hocking: Ken and Larry were both very supportive of my working with video. They thought video itself was just terrible, crappy—no resolution; you couldn't hold it up to the light and look at it. They *hated* the fucking stuff! For Brakhage, of course, video was a death ray and if you got anywhere near it, you would fry! But Larry and Ken also felt, it's here and we've got to do something with it; we'll let Ralph do his thing. They were willing to support my passions. Our ability to work together was all based on a kind of thoughtful, passionate belief in each other.

I began to understand a little bit about the world of grants and, realizing that I had to organize things, I was able to get the university's lawyer to help shepherd me into what Sherry and I called the Experimental Television Center. We moved off campus, to Court Street, and the idea of handing out cameras to students expanded into the community.

Sherry Miller Hocking: In 1971 Ralph hired one of his Allegheny students (my boyfriend), and I came along with him to Binghamton.

Ralph Hocking: And broke up my marriage!

Sherry Miller Hocking: I was the Other Woman for a long time, but we've been married longer than Ralph was married to his first wife, so I'm claiming the position now.

I had a lot of informal interaction with the Binghamton students; the video classes Ralph was teaching were held at ETC and the kids used the equipment. I'd look at what they were doing and we'd talk about their work.

Ralph Hocking: The university didn't have a problem about organizing the Center off-campus; in fact, they were *for* it, but they couldn't figure out a way to create a formal financial connection. In the end, the university bought some equipment and the students used it through the ETC.

Video artists showed up at ETC. Nam June came up quite often; he would stay with Sherry and me. Woody and Steina Vasulka would come up from New York, and Walter Wright was sort of an artist in residence for a long time. Beryl Korot was a visiting artist at the university; she installed some work, but we had nothing in video exhibition comparable to the density of the film people coming through.

Ken Jacobs: I liked what Ralph brought to Binghamton. The Vasulkas worked with Ralph and did great, great work. We didn't see much of them before they went to Buffalo, and then they moved to Santa Fe. They were among the few people working with analog video who were doing things that impressed me. Also, Ralph's *Slow Scan* [1980] is *great*.

It was impressive that Ralph moved the Experimental Television Center to the middle of Binghamton, to an area that seemed like a stretch of the Bowery. I admired that. I wanted the Cinema Department to get a building *in* Binghamton and do the same kind of thing. I wanted a building with a turret top that would move with the sun, like the original Black Maria. For a while the administration spoke about this, but then the will to do it evaporated.

Bill T. Jones: When I went to Binghamton to begin my freshman year, I treasured the image of myself as a nomad. The university was simply a way station. As freshman year drew to a close, I decided that I didn't want to return in the fall, that I wanted to go back to San Francisco. Arnie suggested that we go somewhere I'd never been—Amsterdam. He'd been there just before I'd met him and had friends there. All we needed was the money.

By luck and happenstance, Ralph Hocking had just gotten a grant to open an experimental video center in Binghamton, and he hired Arnie and me to move the bulky videotape recorders, tapes, and files to the new location. When we decided we were moving to Amsterdam for the summer, Ralph was angry. Through a government program, he had been able to hire us as laborers, and even paid us upfront. Suddenly, after our having shown up irregularly or hardly at all, here we were, coming to ask for a final payment and leaving him in the lurch.

During the time we worked for Ralph at the brand new Experimental Television Center, we were sometimes allowed to borrow the clunky though state-of-the-art "portable" (the power source had to be pulled in a children's wagon!) equipment, and we made videos of each other. I remember two of them in particular. In *The Devil's Gonna Get You*, I wore a vintage polka-dot dress and straw hat—both of which suggested Bette Davis's rejected wardrobe in *Now Voyager* [1942]! I lounged about against the Binghamton skyline to Bessie Smith's admonishment, "Devil's gonna get ya, chile, just as sure as you born!"

Women in Art featured Arnie. His hair shoulder length, full and black with a streak dyed platinum-blond, he wore pink 1950s pedal pushers and executed a dance that was a cross between a religious ceremony and a low sexy shimmy. Placing a kiss on the Madonna's lips, he let the sculpted image slide suggestively down his body as he undulated to Gil Scott Heron's insistent wailing, "Who'll pay reparations on my soul," in the benign morning sunlight of our third-floor walkup.

Richard Bock: Ken Jacobs taught a class on film history at St. John's University, which I took in 1968. It was just a coincidence; I'd never considered art as a pursuit, though I loved movies and found the films coming out at the time thought provoking. Ken was a visiting professor, a tough-talking New York Jewish guy lecturing about film art.

I still remember Ken's analysis of D. W. Griffith's *Birth of a Nation* [1915]. I remember the screening—a 16mm print—with black students jeering at the stereotypes. I didn't realize at the time why they were angry, but their reaction made me see the power of film, how it can hurt. It was a challenge for Ken to talk about the film, but he had an intricate, nimble, and deep understanding of any film he would present. He went below the surface. His lecture rambles entranced me. I'd never had a teacher like this.

Later, through a friend, I found out Ken was teaching at SUNY-Binghamton; Ken wrote a letter of recommendation for me, and so in the fall of 1970 I moved to Binghamton.

Most of my requirements had been satisfied at St. John's, but I stayed in Binghamton for three years, spending most of my time in the Cinema Department, watching hundreds of films and starting to make films. I lived and breathed the experience of learning about all kinds of film: underground films, silent films, Hollywood films.

Philip Sykas: Ken Jacobs shared his work with us, including *Tom, Tom, the Piper's Son*, made with the analytic projector. However, my strongest impression of Ken's work was a 3-D shadow play performance. Since birth, I've had no sight in my right eye, so I could not experience the intended 3-D effects, but the impressive outcomes achievable by simple means through the shadow medium remain strongly with me. Jacobs's interest in early cinema also ensured that we saw the work of the Lumière brothers and George Méliès, both of whom had formative roles in my aesthetic development.

Jacobs had worked with Jack Smith, and the "classic" status accorded to Smith's *Flaming Creatures* not only presented students with another direction in film, but helped to deemphasize the heterosexual bias that might otherwise have been felt in the department.

Jim Hoberman: Ken could be very difficult. There were plenty of ways to fuck up with those Kalart-Victors. Go forward! Go back! Freeze! I was getting these directions from him during class, and it was stressful. Ken was not a generous boss; he was much too tense for that, and this complicated my feelings for him. I resented the way he treated me, especially since I figured I had known him before he was a faculty member and was a totally devoted fan.

At one point Ken envisioned a kind of tripod that would move freely in space, and he wanted Michael Gersten and me to build it for him. Michael, whose parents were Holocaust survivors and who was himself a very tense guy with his own issues, was handy. He understood carpentry. So, Ken drew some plans on a napkin for us, and Michael and I went to the lumber yard and a hardware store, got some stuff and tried to build this thing. I wasn't much help, but Michael really tried to do what Ken wanted. In the end, of course, we couldn't make what Ken envisioned, and he was furious with us. That was it for Michael. He'd had enough. A year or so later, we saw *La Région Centrale* [1971]: who knows whether Ken got the idea from Snow, or Snow from Ken, but that doesn't really matter; basically Ken wanted us to build a $50,000, computer-driven tripod out of wood, working from plans on a napkin! And threw a tantrum when we couldn't!

Richard Bock: At Binghamton, the idea was that one had to learn to make films by doing. Not by sitting in a class listening to lectures. Working with Ken Jacobs on the Apparition Theater of New York and 3-D shadow play, showing films to each other—we were *doing*.

We learned much about the vital necessity of art and its power to give audiences a heightened sense of being. We learned to take account of the visual and auditory parade of the world—the poetry. Use your eyes! Think for yourself! Interact with the reality! Work to make the world better by creating beauty or finding beauty or making someone think!

Film artists and film historians were visiting continually. Then Nicholas Ray came along. Our cup ranneth over with personalities and events and egotistical geniuses!

Ken Jacobs: In 1971, we made the calamitous error of hiring Nick Ray; Nick was awful and got the department punished. In the end, this decision—and our later hiring of Saul Levine, an extreme leftist who was into student demonstrations and pretty much led the taking over of the SUNY-Binghamton Library—caused us problems.

3

Maelstrom

Larry Gottheim: The question had come up, if a department can't be just two people, who's going to be the third? Some of the people we considered, like Ernie Gehr who had already taught at Binghamton, didn't have academic credentials; later on, Ernie did come as a full-time faculty member, but at this earlier point he didn't seem a possibility. We went through the whole list of the people we knew or knew of, but no one seemed right to Ken.

During this time, I remember getting an issue of *Film Culture* that had to do with the Hollywood 10 [*Film Culture* 50–51 (1970)]. I happened to be looking through it, and in a footnote there was something about Nick Ray—I don't remember the details.* Ken and I shared a love for early American cinema and for odd corners of cinema; and one film we both liked was *They Live by Night* [1948], Nick Ray's first feature. Maybe because the article said that Nick Ray, who had been an important Hollywood director, was making a film about the Chicago Seven, we said, "What about Nick Ray?" I called Tom Luddy, or whoever had written the article, and he gave me Nick's number and we invited him to come for several days, which turned out to be a major event.

Susan Ray: I met Nick in the fall of 1969, when he was already, career-wise, on something of a downward slide. He had been living primarily in

*In "Two Film Books on Joseph Losey" an anonymous reviewer mentions "James Leahy, who now teaches film at Northwestern University in Illinois and is assisting Nicholas Ray in organizing a film on the Chicago Seven trial." This is the only reference to Ray I could find in *Film Culture*, no. 50–51.

Europe for ten years, trying to get films done there, and already had a wild and woolly reputation. It would be simplistic to attribute this to drink and drugs—and I certainly wouldn't underestimate their influence—but I couldn't say it was exclusively that. There was a certain self-destructive thing in him, but also, he was so bloody ahead of his time that usually people just didn't get him. All that said, in the winter of 1970–71, Nick bumped into Dennis Hopper, which led to a night of carousing, and in the spring of 1971 he went out to Taos to Dennis's ranch—I met him there a few weeks later, and we stayed with Dennis for a while.

Sometime during that stay, Nick was invited to speak at SUNY-Binghamton. I didn't go with him, but apparently it was an extraordinary visit: he inspired these people very quickly and out of that appearance came an offer of a job. Nick was a gifted teacher and gave teaching a great deal of thought.

Dennis claimed some credit—I'm not sure it's due—for Nick's getting the Binghamton job; I don't know whether it was for writing a letter of recommendation or whether he made the initial contact for the speaking engagement. But Dennis should have credit for other things: he was a very generous host to us, perhaps more generous than he intended to be. (See fig. 16.)

Larry Gottheim: Of course, lots of people came to see Nick when he visited campus that first time. He got all of the equipment we had around and

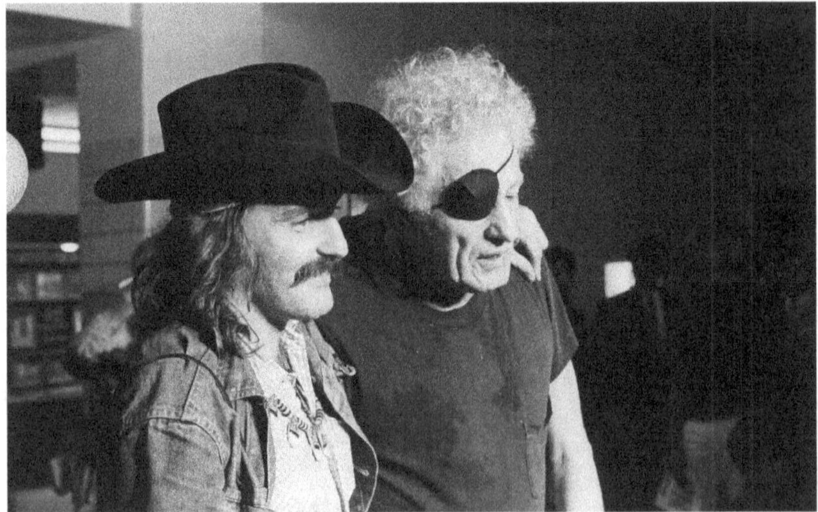

Figure 16. Dennis Hopper and Nick Ray in Binghamton. Courtesy Mark Goldstein.

created a big, outrageous, but really fascinating event—and we decided that he would be our next colleague. We envisioned that Nick would have the kind of freedom with us that he wouldn't have anywhere else; he wouldn't have the constraints of Hollywood and money, and we imagined that he would become an experimental filmmaker. Nick seemed attracted to the idea of the department, and, this being that moment when the administration was being adventurous, we were able to hire him for three years.

Nick's being around was very heady for me. He stayed at my place during the summer before he started teaching, and that was a delirious time. I remember coming into the City and filming something with Ernie and Nick. It was exciting to be working with somebody from the movies, somebody whose work we respected.

Nick loved *Harmonica* [1971], and he drove the car for one of the shots in *Barn Rushes* [1972]. And he was filling my head with ideas. Nick was an incredibly successful manipulator because he seemed to believe so much in what he was doing. He could make everybody working with him crazy in some strange good way, and infuse actors with the force of his own personality, driving them into a state where they would outdo themselves. It could be dangerous, but it was also amazing.

At the end of the summer, before classes began, Nick (and Sue when she came up from New York) moved into the guest apartment in the Infirmary, and once classes began, Nick attracted a large group of students—he had conceived of a complicated narrative where the secretary of the department played a nurse and there was an ambulance—all very elaborately choreographed like in a Hollywood movie. I was the assistant director; it was my job to say, "Roll!" Like most people, I had a lingering dream of getting involved with Hollywood, and during this moment the possibility seemed *so* close. But I was also saying to myself, "I'm outa here; this is definitely *not* what I'm into"—being manipulative with people wasn't me.

That sudden feeling of resistance was very influential in the transformation of my own work. *Horizons* [1973] could have been just another short, pure film like *Barn Rushes*, but it grew to be feature length, and the beginning of a kind of epic—though I didn't yet know how *Elective Affinities* was going to evolve.* Having Nick around helped me develop the idea of something large-scale *and* embrace a way of working that was an alternative to what Nick was doing.

Ken Ross: I arrived in the fall of 1969; I went to Binghamton because it was a school in the SUNY system known for liberal arts and it was a place

*In the end Gottheim's *Elective Affinities* series included four films: *Horizons* (1973), part 1; *Mouches Volantes* (1976), part 2; *Four Shadows* (1978), part 3; and *Tree of Knowledge* (1980), part 4.

I could afford. I began by studying theater, don't quite know why—and Russian. I would also nose around to see what was happening. I knew there were films on campus, and one day I was in the Lecture Hall building and happened to see a sign that a filmmaker was having a screening. I popped in and what I saw was completely bewildering: the theater was silent and the screen was full of little dots of light, and an audience was watching in rapt attention. I felt I was in a church, and I was completely enthralled.

When the lights came on, I found out it was a film by Ernie Gehr, called *History* [1970]. It was my first experience seeing an avant-garde film, and it related very much to my early childhood love of going to the movies, where I was as much involved with looking at the light beam and the projector as I was with what was happening on the screen. I decided I wanted to find out more about this, and so I enrolled in Cinema 101, with Larry Gottheim.

From then on, I was a full-time cinema student, and for the next three and a half years my other coursework tended to fade into the background—I don't remember much of anything except making films and going to screenings. Then, of course, when Nick Ray arrived on the scene, I was part of that experience as well. Working with him on *We Can't Go Home Again* was pretty incredible. It felt like Binghamton was the epicenter of cinema.

In his production class, Ken Jacobs treated students as great-film-makers-to-be. He would respond to some of our first films with, "This should be shown at Anthology," so we had an elevated sense of our work, tremendous excitement, and very high expectations.

But being at Binghamton wasn't just studying with Ken and Larry and Nick; it was studying with the entire independent film world; it seemed like there wasn't a weekend when somebody wasn't visiting. Thinking back, I don't know how they got the funding, but it was Paul Sharits; Hollis Frampton for a week; it was Brakhage and Kubelka and Hermann Nitsch and on and on and on. To see films is one thing, but to see the films of these filmmakers and then actually be in their presence and hear what they had to say—an unbelievable environment for a young student, for *anybody*. It reminded some of us of what it must have been like to be in France in the 1920s: the pulse of art was throbbing around us and we were living it; we were eating, sleeping (and not sleeping) art—working with Nick we could be up for weeks on end. (See figs. 17 a and b.)

Philip Sykas: The cinema sphere was one mainstay of my undergraduate world, but this was overlapped by other important spheres. One of these was Off Campus College [OCC]. I moved six times during my stay at university, always living off campus. I didn't wish to live in campus dor-

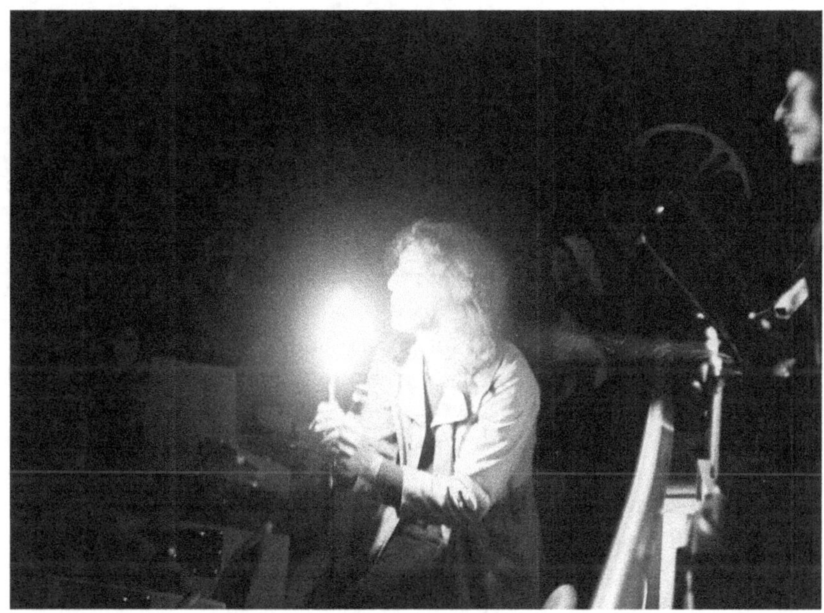

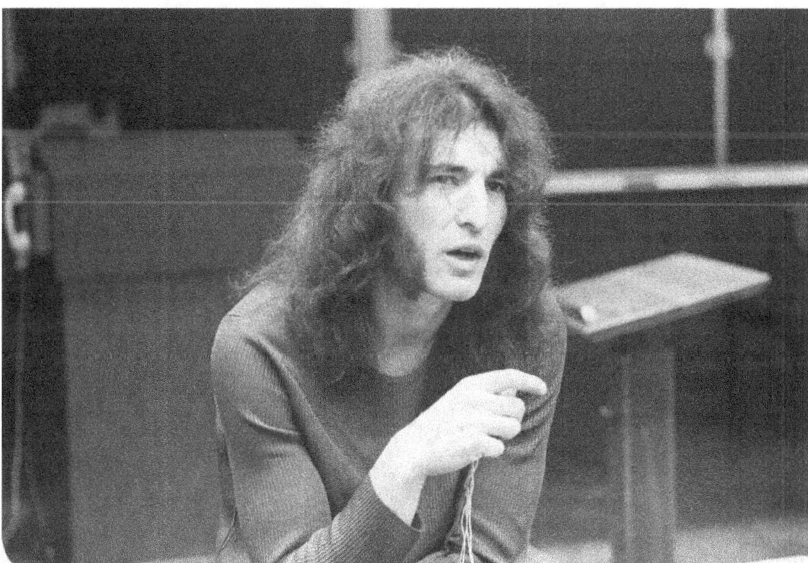

Figures 17a, b. Paul Sharits performing at Binghamton, and lecturing. Courtesy Mark Goldstein.

mitories and couldn't have afforded them anyway. So in August 1970, my brother and I rented a flat at 1282 Vestal Avenue in Binghamton. Upstairs lived three female students: Karen Voight, whose boyfriend at the time was Jan Hacha of the Starry Night Puppet Theatre; Julie Coutts; and a third, whose name my memory refuses to unlock. They were a friendly and welcoming group and introduced me to a wider circle of people and to the seeming sophistication of New York City Jewish culture—I was a provincial boy, brought up in rural Vestal, New York, with little exposure to cultural activity beyond what was available on television and in paperback editions of the classics.

Another social circle was formed around students in drawing and printmaking classes, and especially those in contact with the dedicated and dynamic printmaking teacher, Linda Robinson Sokolowski, who was the first female to teach in the Art Department. Sharp as a burin, hair pulled back exposing large eyes out of proportion to her tiny figure, with unquenchable enthusiasm, she was quick to smile and had a warm, earthy laughter. I took my first drawing course in summer 1971, and began printmaking with Linda in fall 1972. It was within these classes that my closest friendships arose. I especially admired the work of Karen Dauler (who later went on to work in the field of architecture), and David Harvey and Cecily Dunham (who later married, with David eventually pursuing a career in museum design and Cecily in book illustration). My memories of Binghamton are strongly infused with the smell of burned linseed oil, asphaltum, stop-out varnish and nitric acid from the print studio.

There was also the Gay Liberation Front (GLF). This title now seems aggressively confrontational, but it must be remembered that at the time homosexual activity was still a felony in New York State. With trepidation, I attended an inaugural meeting of the group, spearheaded by the tall, curly-haired, boyishly handsome, flamboyant Martin Levine, whose other passion was the black music scene. It was Marty who arranged for the Gaduntz to play at the first GLF dance. He had many friends in the black community at SUNY-Binghamton, bringing together two unlikely minorities that might otherwise have shunned each other.

It might have been at a GLF meeting that I first saw Arnie Zane and Bill Jones, but we were to meet again somewhat later through a mutual friend, the musician Charles Seltzer. All my social circles were to coincide in my friendship with Arnie and Bill: both of them modeled for drawing sessions, sat in on Cinema Department classes, and participated in OCC activities. When I first encountered them, they were still bathed in the aura of Amsterdam where Arnie had fledged his career in photography. Their flat had a European sense of style, with bare floorboards and beautiful decorative objects acquired from charity shops. Arnie and Bill were both strong personalities, but there was not yet a sense of steel rubbing flint, just great warmth.

Daile Kaplan: Visiting filmmakers Hollis Frampton (a most erudite man); Andrew Noren (who featured Stephanie Sarokin and me in the film originally called *Kodak Ghost Poems* [1968; now called *Huge Pupils*, part 1 of *The Adventures of the Exquisite Corpse*]); Stan Brakhage (so emotionally complex!); Ernie Gehr (a delicate sensibility and a giant of filmmaking); and Paul Sharits (very artsy) embodied the quintessential early seventies liberal arts education—daring, and interdisciplinary in thought. It was an incredible time, and these guys demonstrated a new (visual) way of thinking.

Larry Gottheim: Though different universities within the New York State system were developing different kinds of cinema departments, in those days there was a program within the system to bring people together from across the state so there would be cross-fertilization among the campuses. We hosted two of those statewide events, the first in the spring of 1972.

Ricky Leacock was at the first of these. The new possibilities of portable sync-sound recording were his big thing, of course, so he came as a celebrity for his use of sound—and here we were showing all these silent films! He was furious. (See fig. 18.)

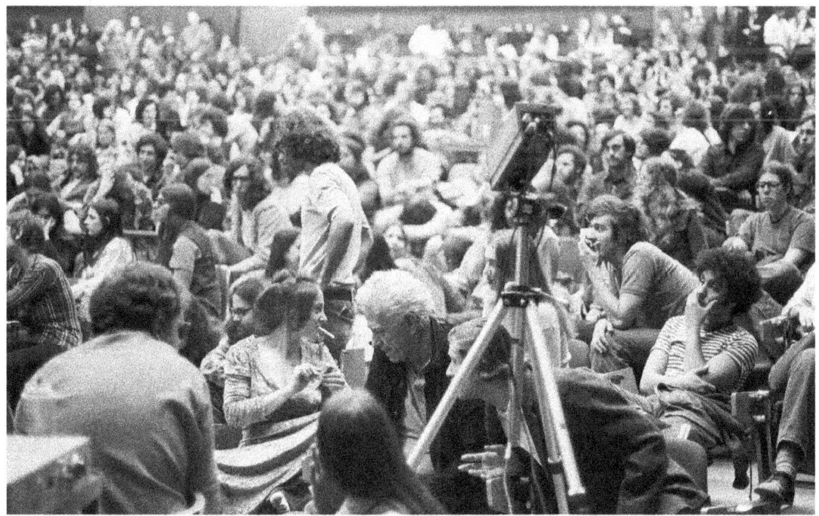

Figure 18. Audience possibly on second night university-wide Film Symposium; in foreground is Susan Ray (lighting a cigarette), Nick Ray, and (behind tripod) Larry Gottheim. Courtesy Mark Goldstein.

The second event was a year or so later, when Nick had assembled a version of the film he'd been shooting in Binghamton (it came to be called *We Can't Go Home Again*), using different media: he had bought a surplus 35mm camera, so there were some things in 35 mm, some things in 8mm.

One of the amazing things about the Cinema Department was that even though there was total turbulence from the first minute to the last, whenever we had visitors from the outside—another department, the administration, people from another university—we bonded together. In some way we all knew that we had something special, and even if we were always fighting over what it should be, we all *loved* it and our lives were completely entrenched in it.

My house in the country outside of Binghamton was becoming a center for visiting artists and for department events. Students were always hanging out there. On the day of the second university-wide film symposium that we hosted, Nick and Ken came out to my place (I remember giving the remains of my marijuana crop to Nick), and I recorded a moment from that afternoon and used it in *Horizons*.

Peter Kubelka: In 1970 I brought Hermann Nitsch to America—to Cincinnati, to New York, and to Binghamton. In Cincinnati Barry Zelikovsky was the director of programming at the university, and he lost his job as a consequence of the Nitsch appearance. The event in New York, which Jonas Mekas had vouched for, also caused a scandal.

Harvey L. Silver: Because I was already a photographer (I grew up with photography: my father managed a photography store in Manhattan and Garry Winogrand, W. Eugene Smith, Duane Michals, and many other well-known photographers were his customers), I recorded a lot of what was going on in Binghamton, including the blood-orgy performance by Hermann Nitsch.

For that performance the college cafeteria was covered in sheets of plastic, and the organs of various animals were arranged on tables. The focus of the performance was the crucifixion of a dead lamb. Nitsch, a little guy who looked like Beethoven, worked himself into a frenzy and sliced open the lamb and pulled the insides out. During this, there was a student lying *underneath* the crucifixion; and other people had jugs of blood that they poured down on the poor guy. Still other students formed a noise band providing a soundtrack for the event (in my photographs, the kids in the noise band, covered in blood, all look stunned). Later the lamb was cooked and served.

It was an antiwar, anti-Vietnam performance—one of the more interesting happenings of that period. I was there the whole time, photographing in both color and black-and-white—sometimes the camera is a good excuse for being in a place you don't really want to be! I think the event was designed to take you to the point where you're immersed in so much blood that you reach an epiphany and are cleansed.

That event became controversial, not so much because it was performance art gone bad or because Nitsch used animal body parts and blood: what was controversial was what the performance *meant* politically. There were very right-wing, pro–Vietnam War legislators in Albany.

I handed over my Nitsch-event photographs to Ken before I left Binghamton—he needed them because the department was being investigated by the state legislature. In the end, I lost touch, and with a couple exceptions never got the negatives back—some of the few negatives I've ever lost!

Philip Sykas: When Hermann Nitsch brought his *Orgien Mysterien Theater* to campus in October 1970, cinema students were invited to participate. I went along to a rehearsal and was selected for the part of the ritual sacrifice, possibly because I was of slight build and easy to carry. It was not a demanding role, requiring mainly passivity. At the time, we took Nitsch's art lightheartedly, delighting in his Austrian accent and quirky pronunciation of the word "scaffolding." The dry rehearsals were fairly straightforward, marking out the basic movements. On the day of the performance, Larry Gottheim and Nitsch collected a lamb carcass and large quantities of animal blood and organs from a local abattoir that were to be used in the theatrical event in a ritualistic way.

Amy Halpern-Lebrun: We were rehearsing in the gymnasium and I'd never screamed in my life, literally—yelled but never screamed—and during this rehearsal I let out a classic, female, blood-curdling scream on cue and scared the fuck out of myself. That scream was part of what made that very shocking, weird, amazing piece so powerful.

At one point, there were two people under the sacrificial lamb, a boy and a girl—I was the girl. I was covered with blood, and looked like Kent State or something, which of course was part of the larger context of that performance. (See figs. 19 a, b, c on pages 78 and 79.)

Phil Sykas: During the performance I was dressed in white, blindfolded, and at one point quantities of animal blood and organs were heaped over me before I was dragged away screaming. Nitsch thought deeply

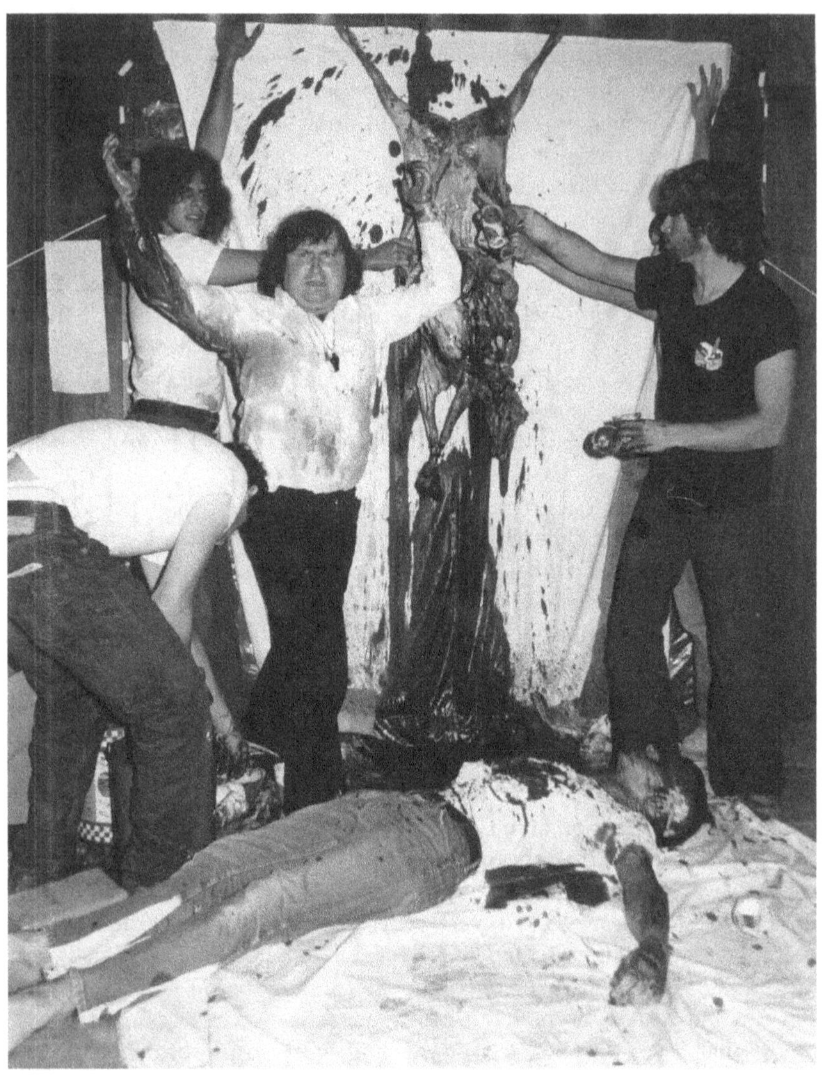

Figure 19a. Hermann Nitsch performing his *Orgien Mysterien Theater* at Binghamton; Philip Sykas is the person lying on the floor. Photograph by Harvey L. Silver. Image available at Corbis Images, New York, NY.

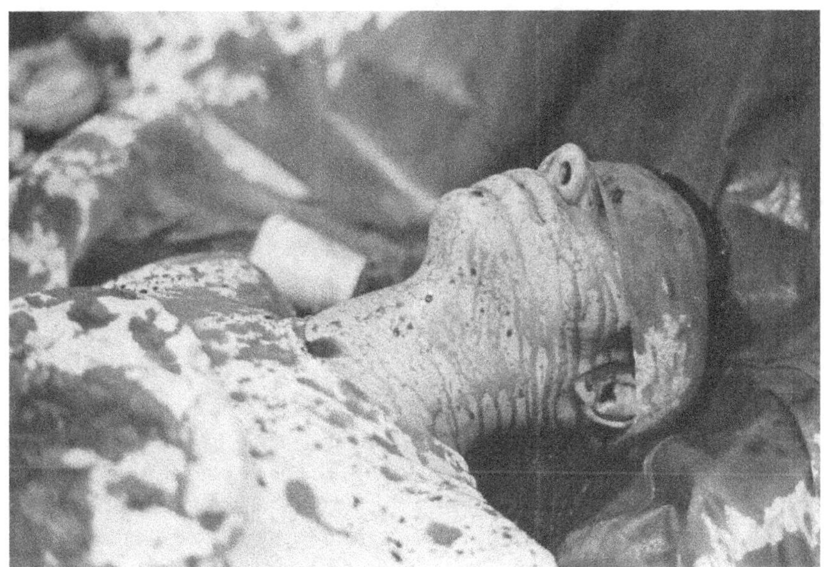

Figure 19b. Philip Sykas during Herman Nitsch performance. Courtesy Mark Goldstein.

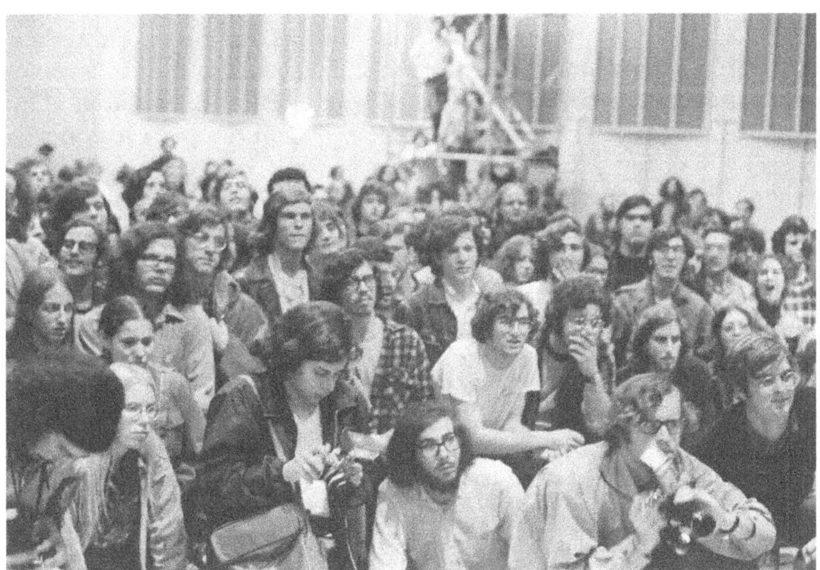

Figure 19c. The audience at the Herman Nitsch performance. Courtesy Mark Goldstein.

not only about the meaning of his theater, but about practicalities. The blood was warmed so that the experience was sensual and pleasant rather than cold and clammy. The smells and sensations were primal and evoked thoughts of ancient rites. Having been brought up in the Greek Orthodox Church, I was accustomed to ritual, and none of this seemed unduly extraordinary to me. But it did upset quite a few others, perhaps most of all the university janitorial staff.

Some time later, Larry Gottheim showed me a copy of one of Nitsch's books, which gathered together rare archival images of criminal acts linked to the realm of sacrifice, and this helped me realize the depth of study that went into Nitsch's work.

Steve Anker: The most notorious event during my years at Binghamton was when Peter Kubelka brought Hermann Nitsch to campus to do an Actionist performance. I wasn't involved in the early preparations. I know that Nitsch spent the day gathering the various parts of the animals, the blood and the entrails, that were going to be part of this event. It was a ritualistic experience, a kind of abandoning yourself to your senses: the people involved in the performance were almost hypnotically engaged in very repetitive physical gestures interacting with the different parts of the animals.

The Student Center, a sprawling new building with many wings, was the site of the Action. I remember on the afternoon of the show, opening the door into the part of the building where the radio station was and walking into what felt like a bank of odor; the smell of blood had permeated the entire building. The people in the radio station were gagging, and the station's general manager said to me, "Anker, if you had *anything* to do with this, I'm never going to speak to you again!"

I had helped set up the sound system, and that evening, I spent most of the performance holding the wire to one of the speakers because somebody had ripped it out as they moved about in a frenzy. But I was blown away by the whole experience, and I didn't begin to make sense of it for days. The event led to repercussions, beginning with an outraged article in the local press, and later, a state Senate subcommittee investigation and a big article in the *New York Times* (see facing page). My parents and relatives, who read the story, were horrified. I heard that Ken and Larry were warned that if anything like that happened again, the department would be shut down.

Larry Gottheim: Nitsch involved many students whose lives were transformed by working with him. The event involved a lot of mess and much attention to the details of cleaning up after the event, but it became a scandal that had national reach: I was interviewed by Pacifica Radio.

HARPUR 'EXHIBIT' STIRS CRITICISM

Dismemberment of a Lamb on Stage Is Protested

Special to *The New York Times*.

BINGHAMTON, N.Y., Nov. 28 [1970]—A controversy has started here and in surrounding Broome County over an "orgies mystery theater" performance during which a slaughtered lamb was opened and disemboweled in the student union at Harpur College here last month.

The local city council and the Broome County Legislature have begun considering resolutions to curb such practices and open a complete study of the administrative policies of the college, a unit of the State University of New York at Binghamton.

The exhibition in question took place October 14 and was conducted by Hermann Nitsch, a young German [Nitsch is Austrian], who says the dismemberment is art. The "exhibition," as it was also dubbed, was observed at first by about 300 students, but after the actual work on the carcass began, the number dwindled to barely half that figure.

During the show, several students became ill. Some of the girls in the crowd were sobbing.

"It was a corruption," a youth said softly outside the room.

Indignation Mounts

Rumors spread through the community the next day that a live lamb had been sacrificed during the show. And although newspaper accounts of the presentation emphasized that a conventionally slaughtered lamb had been used, indignation quickly mounted.

As letters and telephone calls denouncing the event and its sponsors poured into the college and local newspaper offices, the city council and county Legislature quickly became involved.

The Legislature named a committee to meet with university officials in an effort to develop a "mutual understanding." The city council adopted a resolution calling for a study of the university's administrative policies.

Dr. S. Steward Gordon, acting president of the State University of New York at Binghamton, told the city council in a letter: "In my view it was distasteful, and if I did not believe the university should make it possible for students to experience all forms of art and to hear all shades of political opinion, I would be inclined to condemn those who permitted this presentation to be made."

Basically faculty members, who were not there and who I guess hated the Cinema Department anyway, complained that we were killing animals.

Even the local government got involved. When Brakhage was visiting, Ken, Stan, and I appeared before the Broome County Legislature to defend the event. Finally, the Legislature asked the Binghamton Council of Churches to investigate, and they became if not supportive, at least convinced that this was a serious artistic work.*

The Nitsch performance was a great event, and afterward, we went to my place in the country where we cooked the lamb and had a feast together that lasted all night.

Jim Hoberman: The Hermann Nitsch event took place in the new Student Center. The space, which was used for dances and performances (Ginsburg chanted there), totally reeked of blood. I can smell it now! There was noise, music, and hysteria—at least inside. Outside, life went on with amazing indifference. You could walk back and forth from an antiseptic study lounge full of dozing students into this truly crazy bacchanal. It was a fabulous disconnect.

The feast that Kubelka prepared at Larry's afterward was great. Amy Halpern [Lebrun], one of the maenads under the cross, was pissed at me because, snot that I was, I teased that she had finally found her "nitsch." The rumors afterward were fantastic. You'd hitch a ride to campus and the driver would say, "I hear they crucified a giraffe up there at the college."

Helene Kaplan Wright: The teaching environment in those days was amazing, and seems even more amazing now as I look back. Here's an example: Ken brought Peter Kubelka, who spent a week not only showing his films and talking about them, but cooking these incredible feasts and lecturing about cooking. We'd all go to Larry's house, and Peter would bring a giant roast out of the oven, with Bach playing on the stereo. We were all so sensitized to aesthetics. In retrospect you could make *New Yorker* cartoons out of all this, but back then we all took it incredibly seriously and were moved and excited by the idea of having art be part of our everyday lives.

I had had art history teachers who showed slide after slide of incredible works, providing the *dullest* explanations of what you were looking at. With Ken and the visiting filmmakers, we were seeing, *really seeing*, with new eyes, *experiencing* art, and it was a whole new world.

*Anthology Film Archives has made available a portion of the discussion between Gottheim, Jacobs, and Brakhage (some students seem also to have been in attendance) and members of the Binghamton Council of Churches: www.ubu.com/sound/afa.html.

Phil Weisman: I got to Binghamton in 1969, as a transfer from Syracuse University. I'd known Steve Anker since we were children—we went to the same sleep-away camp! When I told him I wanted to get out of Syracuse, Steve said, "Come to Binghamton and be in the Theater Department." By the time I got there, Steve was already working with Ken Jacobs. I spent one semester in the Theater Department, where I met Ken Ross: we were both in a graduate production of Arthur Miller's *The Crucible*. Then we both took Cinema 101 with Larry Gottheim and transferred into the Cinema Department.

Larry's an excellent teacher and he was introducing us to great films: European and world cinema, as well as the avant-garde. I didn't really know Ken Jacobs at first, but I knew Larry and Ken were bringing major artists to campus—Brakhage and Ernie Gehr, whoever had something to premiere. The euphoria in the Cinema Department was that we recognized that we were getting things *from the source*, all the time.

Looking back, I think the big sixties thing was starting to pass, and a lot of the filmmakers who came to Binghamton—Hollis Frampton, Paul Sharits, Brakhage, Ken himself—were finding their way into colleges as a way of trying to keep a community together.

Helene Kaplan Wright: I met Hollis Frampton at the Flaherty Seminar in 1970, which turned out to be a very frustrating experience for me—not because of Hollis, but because Jonas Mekas was there and wrote a column about one of Ken's students filming in the middle of the night and how that was what the Flaherty Film Seminar was really about.* *I* was

*Mekas: "There we were, at the Flaherty Film Seminar, trying to learn something about cinema, talking until 1 A.M. It was after 1 when we were walking to the dormitories. It was pitch dark. One could see stars, but all around us was an impenetrable blackness. As we were walking so, and looking at the sky and the barely visible silhouette of the lake, suddenly there was a dark figure sitting by the roadside, in almost complete darkness, I almost stepped on it.

I leaned over, and I recognized the figure of a girl, from Harpur College, one of Ken Jacobs' students. She was sitting on the ground in the dark, and she had a Bolex in her hands, and she was sitting there motionless and silent and an inseparable part of night and occasionally she clicked her camera: She was filming. I looked into the distance—there was some kind of light there. There was nothing else. I had no real idea what she was filming, nor how. But there she was, completely involved in her work, at 1 A.M., and it was clear, as I leaned and looked into her, that she knew completely what she was after, although to us it was a total mystery—so we stood for a moment, and continued walking. Soon her dark silhouette disappeared in the darkness, she merged with the night: a filmmaker at work, in the deep darkness of the Connecticut night. That's where the cinema is born, talk or no talk, books or no books: the creative process is continuing in its own night of privacy"—Mekas, *Movie Journal: The Rise of a New American Cinema, 1959–1971* (New York: Collier, 1972): 399.

that person, but was never identified; it was the first of many instances where we were stereotyped as "Ken's students" and didn't have our own identities. Of course, this wasn't Ken's fault.

Phil Weisman: The experience at Binghamton changed our lives. Both Larry and Ken were/are extremely articulate, really good teachers—and in their own ways, deeply introspective. From a student's point of view, they seemed to have things down—though, looking back, it's obvious that they were experiencing these new films with us, and struggling, often in class, to grapple with the issues around them—rather than presenting the kinds of prepared lectures you might get in a normal college setting.

At Binghamton, education was freewheeling. I don't remember ever getting a syllabus. I don't remember tests—there must have been projects or something, but I have no memory of them.

Now, another aspect of this is that the teachers were very exacting, and at times, not great to be around. I don't fault them for this; they were into their own work, like good artists are—plus they were on a steep learning curve in terms of teaching. People skills, in our current sense, were not a priority. Both Ken and Nick Ray were extremely strong-willed individuals, with tempers. If you could bear up against that or if you could push back—I pushed back many times—you could learn a lot. (See fig. 20.)

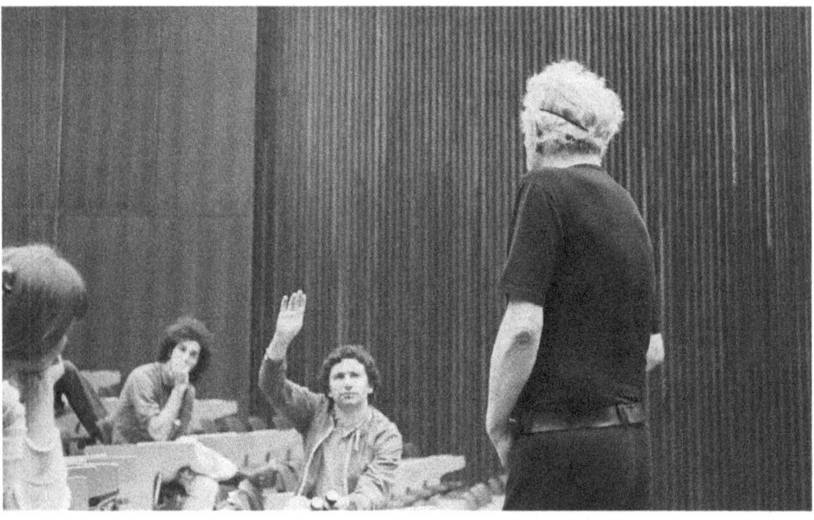

Figure 20: Ken Jacobs raising his hand during a talk by Nick Ray. Courtesy Mark Goldstein. (p. 81)

I was *totally* involved in Nick Ray's project, and I was *totally* involved in Ken's Apparition Theater of New York, and I went regularly to Larry's classes. We were inundated and didn't mind it. We didn't think there had to be a limitation on class time; we would stay for hours; we'd stay into the night—happily.

If we hadn't been twenty, I don't know if we'd have gone through all we went through, and not everybody lasted. As tempers flared, some people dropped out. You had to be extremely committed to Cinema as a higher calling in order to stay with either Ken or Nick.

Richard Herskowitz: When I decided to go to Binghamton, I had no idea I was going to a school where the emphasis was going to be experimental film. I got to Binghamton in 1971 and when I enrolled in Cinema 101, I was assigned to Ken Jacobs (he and Larry Gottheim alternated years). You could take a two-year sequence. I had Cinema 101 and 102, then Cinema 201 and 202, four semesters in a row with Ken. If you came in the year before me or the year after me, you were assigned to Larry and would have your two-year sequence with him. And who you got assigned to became a major influence. By the spring of 1972, I was a convert and wanted to make experimental films.

Jacobs's personality was *so* strong that my first reaction was extreme aversion. He was just oppressively intimidating. I *hated* him for the first semester. When I think back, I wonder if he was more intimidating during the first semester as a way of trying to slim down the class. So many students would register for Cinema 101; they figured it was going to be a gut. The second semester, Ken was still intimidating, but he was less obnoxiously authoritarian than he'd been the first semester.

Ken was a dictator in the classroom; you had to sign in both before and after the break, so that he could make sure you didn't escape—these were three-hour sessions, three days a week: Wednesday through Friday, 4:00 to 7:00 p.m. *And*, during that time, *only* Ken spoke. He was not the kind of professor who engaged students in dialogue. I may have said a total of four sentences in the course of the four semesters that I was his student.

After intimidation and anger, the next phase was to be in complete thrall. Ken was fascinating to listen to on almost any topic, and I was learning so much. He was one of a number of experimental filmmakers—Stan Brakhage was another—who were *great* talkers. It was a different kind of education than I had gotten from anybody else. By the end of the second semester, I'd realized that this was an extraordinary experience.

An unforgettable moment was the day Ken walked into the classroom carrying a pile of books. He stopped midway down the stairs and turned to us: "You idiots! I had a forty-seven average in high school and am still trying to catch up on all the education I missed. You're in college and just messing around!" I swear my attitude changed at that moment and I started taking research and scholarship seriously.

I began keeping a kind of diary by writing to my parents about what was going on with me in this class, and I've just recently discovered they kept those letters. [See pages 87–88 for an early letter from Herskowitz to his parents, probably written in 1972.]

During the two years when I was taking that four-semester sequence, Ken brought in a lot of guests, a lot of his friends. There was an intimacy to these presentations because Ken treated the classroom like it was his living room. It was a big lecture hall, but at the back sat Flo nursing Azazel; and four-year-old Nisi would be running up and down the stairs playing. Occasionally Ken would turn and say, "Nisi, cut it out."

I remember a moment when Ken was talking to Jonas Mekas. He turned the lights down low and got really personal; he said something like, "Jonas, you never got over the woman you left in Lithuania." Jonas's eyes widened, and it was like, "Ken, this is something you and I talk about, not something for a class!" But Ken looked at him, "No, no, don't worry—they're fine." *Anything* could be talked about, and part of what made me embrace experimental film was how much the films were an extension of these people's lives and experiences.

I found that knowing the difficulties these filmmakers had experienced, whether it was the poverty of 1950s New York or escaping from Nazi Lithuania, was valuable for understanding what was going on in these films.

Peer Bode: By the time I got to Binghamton, I'd been a fairly stable, if alienated person for a long time and didn't need to be part of a crowd. I tried to develop my own relationships with the faculty. Things didn't always go as I planned. Ken threw me out of his apartment one time! I'd brought over some stuff to show him and then made some comments about his class: I told him I didn't understand why he felt he needed to make people cry. He became angry, packed me up (I had my two speakers and amplifier in hand and whatever on top of that—I could barely see: Flo looked very concerned) and backed me out the door, which was, as if to finish a scene, slammed in my face.

Helene Kaplan Wright: I've heard recently that P. Adams Sitney has said that when visiting filmmakers would come to Binghamton, women students were expected to sleep with them. P. Adams's take on things is exaggerated. I don't think there was an *expectation*, but I do think that's

Dear Mom and Dad,

Very strange weather we're having. Yesterday it was 62°, people were going to classes in shirtsleeves, the snow was melted completely. This morning I woke up to 18°, the campus covered with 5 inches of snow, and all morning classes cancelled. Last night it was beautiful here. When I got out of Cinema it was just about to pour. It was the meanest looking sky you ever saw, and it was throwing shadows over the campus. There was a wind starting that added to the effect, which was something like Kansas before the tornado in "The Wizard of Oz." It was getting darker and darker as I walked to the dorm, so by the time I got back I couldn't take pictures.

It's crazy how fast the weeks go. I'm amazed when it's Sunday and I feel like I called you yesterday, it's why I don't write letters, I really have no conception of time. My weekend really runs through Tuesday, you know my schedule, and I usually leave my work for Monday & Tuesday while I keep Saturday & Sunday for myself. Because I never seem to finish all I wanted to, Tuesday night comes really fast. Wednesday thru Friday I'm packed with classes, but more than half of that is seeing movies and a lot of it is gym, so that part of the week is over before I know it.

That Cinema class is becoming more & more the greatest thing happening to me here. They have just added another three hours to the nine I go a week. On Wednesday the class runs from 4–10 p.m. with a break to eat. On that day, all three cinema teachers conduct a forum, usually on a Nicholas Ray film we'd see in the beginning of the class. I see in the Times that Ray's films are on at least two or three late shows a week. The movie we're studying now, his first *They Live by Night* is remarkable. One scene, which was exquisitely shot and cut, drove Jacobs to scream "This is Beethoven!" The change in Jacobs is astounding, almost as astounding as the change in me in relation to Jacobs. I'm learning more from him than I can handle, but I really try. The fact is he knows so much, has done so much, him with his 47 high school average can compete with Cantor [distinguished history professor Norman Cantor with whom Herskowitz was taking a course] in scholarship. His mind digests everything then he spits it out at us, sarcastically, first, defensively, but we get all this information. It's taking too many words to explain that his class is the only time I have to work my mind to its capacity, and I find out that capacity isn't enough. Jacobs has control of the class' emotions. I have come out of that class shivering, I've seen a girl crying after he yelled once, he makes everyone see how lacking we are in perception. This class is not training us to understand movies, it is training us to put up a mind-block against the bombardment of media outside. We don't just study films now, we study commercials, men's and women's magazines, newspapers, all information media. Understand he's not claiming to be doing any of this, it's taken me a long time to understand the class' direction. Jacobs chose Cinema because he sees it as the most volatile media, people don't realize the subliminal power of Cinema, the media which throws information at you which you have no time to reflect on, you can't turn back the page and re-read, you have to accept it all as it's coming at

continued on next page

you. It's taking all my effort to keep my distance from Jacobs. He's a sad person, he has very little hope for anything. He is not the type of person you want to idolize, but it's taking effort. I still do not want to make his kind of movies. He has tried hard to convince us that personal cinema of the underground variety is what's important now. It's funny that in his Cinema class what I buy the least are his opinions on Cinema.

What I want is to "learn" Jacobs' kind of perception. Right now I'm sarcastic and critical without any direction. I told you that I get depressed because I've got too much to think about. Watching Jacobs, I'm learning how to think in his way, which is about the only way possible to stay sane.

Finally, I'm writing again. I've had to do a movie review and a composition "The Movies, Sex, and Me" so far. They're both the kind of smart alecky clever writing I used to do. I just haven't done it in so long, I'd thought I lost it. Because I don't practice, the writing, I feel, is not much more mature than what it was in high school. The only time I write is when I'm forced to, when I'm given a title and forced to be creative. Jacobs is the only one doing that now. I'm not going to take creative writing. Ask me to explain why sometime. I'm going to try to write, though, especially this summer.

I've got to end the letter because I've got a class, Cinema. This is going to be a good weekend—five movies and a concert. Whatever else I have to say I said yesterday when I called. Dad, you can write too.

Love, Richie

what happened. Ken and Larry brought a constant flow of filmmakers, and my memory is that there was a lot of interaction.

In those days if you were an unattached young woman and there were unattached filmmakers around, people kind of wound up in bed together. I certainly was very guilty of sleeping around; I slept with Hollis Frampton at the Flaherty Seminar (*not* when he came to Binghamton), but with lots of other people too, not just filmmakers. William Kunstler, the guy who defended the Chicago Seven, had a partner who came to speak in Binghamton, and my roommate told me she slept with him. When I was a freshman in Binghamton, there was no Cinema Department; I was in the English Department, and when visiting poets came, *they* slept with students too. And when Nick Ray brought Dennis Hopper to Binghamton, Dennis wanted to sleep with everyone!

We were starry-eyed nuts about the work these talented guys were making, so for us girls it made perfect sense to sleep with them—I say "girls" because we really didn't think of ourselves as *women*; it was early for making those distinctions.

But basically, all this had nothing to do with the Cinema Department, but with the fact that sex was very casual then (as was marijuana). And I don't think it meant all that much; these were just one-night or two-night or four-night stands. Nobody was *expected* to sleep with anyone; they just did. I think Ken knew this was happening, but nobody said anything; it was all done very discretely and privately.

Jim Hoberman: I finished my class work in the spring of 1970, which was when everything shut down because of Kent State, and I stayed another semester, working on my film. I was gone by May 1971. Ken and I parted on bad terms. I wanted to do some refilming as part of my movie, and a student monitor checked out the Kalart-Victor for me (I wasn't a gangster: I went through the department procedures). I took it home and did my thing. Apparently Ken had wanted to use the Kalart-Victor and I guess he thought all the projectors were *his*, even though this one was the department's. Or maybe he didn't like the idea of my doing refilming. Of course, after sitting in his class for two years watching films on the Kalart-Victor, it wouldn't have been *so* strange if I'd had some ideas along this line.

Anyway, Ken got furious at me, accused me of *stealing* the projector. It's a little hard to remember clearly because it was so disturbing. I was outraged and lost my temper. The student who checked out the projector was intimidated by Ken and said I'd not followed procedures, and nobody, not even Larry, stood up for me. I was the first student in the Cinema Department to make a movie as a senior project, and suddenly I was eighty-sixed, wasn't allowed to use any of the department equipment.

Ralph Hocking, who'd created his own little fiefdom in the basement with two-inch video technology, those early clunky Portapaks, was someone I still got along with, and I switched to video to finish this movie [*Customs & Immigration*, 1971]. I felt *horribly* mistreated by Ken and the others; they were shits. Even thinking about it now, I'm being like Ken—*reliving* it. I managed to finish the movie, editing in my parents' apartment in New York, and graduated, then went off to Mexico.

I thought then and still think that Ken was horribly competitive with his students. And why? As a teacher, it's madness to compete with your students. I mean if a student of yours does well, it's partly *you*!

Marsha Bronstein was also at Binghamton, and she took it on herself to get me back to show my film. Ken still has never commented on it, but I guess in the end I accepted that, and we became friendly again. After I graduated, Bob Schneider and I got involved with something that *wasn't* filmmaking—we called it the Theater of Gibberish: performances with slide shows and drama—and maybe because this *wasn't* film, Ken could love it. I revisited the school a number of times in the early seventies as a guest artist with the Theater of Gibberish, so in that sense Ken was very generous.

Lloyd Bruce Holman: I had just returned from making documentary films in India for the New York Department of Education. Before departing for India, I'd resigned my position as director of Graphic and Photographic Production at the Sperry Learning Resources Center at SUNY-Cortland, so upon my return I needed to find employment. At that time I was writing and illustrating articles for *Filmmakers Newsletter*, and stopped at the office in New York to drop off that month's piece. I mentioned to Suni Mallow, the editor, that I was looking for a job, and Suni said an advertisement had just come in from SUNY-Binghamton: they were seeking a tech person for the Cinema Department.

I called and talked with Larry Gottheim, who was a little surprised at getting such a quick response, and on my way back home, I stopped at Binghamton. Larry explained that the Cinema Department was focused on developing appreciation for film as an art form. He also pointed out that I appeared overqualified for the position; the job could actually be filled by a nuts-and-bolts guy who could repair equipment. Larry mused over this, then said he would look into having the position upgraded so it could also fill a teaching line they hadn't been able to get approved.

A couple of days later Larry drove up to my place in Labrador Valley. He was pleased to tell me that he'd been able to get a better salary for the position and student workers to help with the equipment. But best of all, he asked if I would be interested in teaching classes in animation and advanced film production. I said yes, and served in the Cinema Department for the next three years.

Richard Herskowitz: My generation of students were aware of the fact that the generation who had come through Binghamton before us were already stars in the making. Hoberman came back with Bob Schneider; together they had formed the Theater of Gibberish—this is before Jim became a critic. And Ken Ross and Phil Weisman soon went on to form the Collective for Living Cinema.

Amazingly, I later fell into programming by getting the job as director of Cornell Cinema in 1982, the perfect role for me. At Cornell Cinema I could do a collage of all kinds of film exhibition: commercial films as well as avant-garde films, along with art films—a temperament I had developed during the four semesters of Ken's film appreciation classes, which included Frank Capra films, *The Wizard of Oz* [1939], *The Big Sleep* [1946], *and* experimental films *and* home movies *and* industrial films. *Everything* was thrown into the blender. I came to call it the "School of Experimental Film Viewing" because what I learned at Binghamton was less about making experimental films than about teaching people to watch films experimentally. I think the importance of Ken's teaching and found-footage filmmaking was that it taught me how to look at mainstream commercial products experimentally, how to open up their closed systems.

Ken would stop *The Big Sleep* and shout, "You're falling into the film!" I remember him once tilting the projector up and showing a film on the ceiling because we were getting too absorbed. It wasn't like he was trying to deny pleasure; he was trying to get us to think critically, think politically, think formally, to *think*.

I remember an amazing session when he brought Nick Ray into the class. This was going to be a series of classes during which the two of them would go through Nick's films. During that first three-hour session Ken was talking about *Knock on Any Door* [1949] or maybe it was *In a Lonely Place* [1950], about the rectangular shape of the newspaper bundles that were thrown onto the screen and how rectangular shapes played out in many of Nick's films (Nick, by the way, was incredulous).

Anyway, Ken was fundamentally an education in watching all kinds of films experimentally, and I took that as my mission as a programmer for the rest of my life. A lot of Binghamton graduates became programmers; more seem to have become programmers than filmmakers, and I'm surprised that most of them—Mark McElhatten, Steve Anker—have tended to program experimental film more exclusively than I do.

Larry Gottheim: In time I think Ken and I took it for granted that Hollis Frampton would be the next tenure-track person we would hire (the program at Buffalo didn't exist yet). Hollis had taught at Hunter College with Bob Huot, who got him that job and, later on, got him interested in living in Central New York State. (See fig. 21.)

In the Cinema Department it was always true, at least to some extent, that we were more like friends working together than like typical faculty and students; we were our own little world. For example, to make *Harmonica* [1971], the first sound film in the series of single-shot films I'd been working on, I needed a car. Barbara DiBenedetto had a car and loaned it to me. Frank Albetta was the guy with the sound recorder, recording Shelley Berde playing the harmonica.

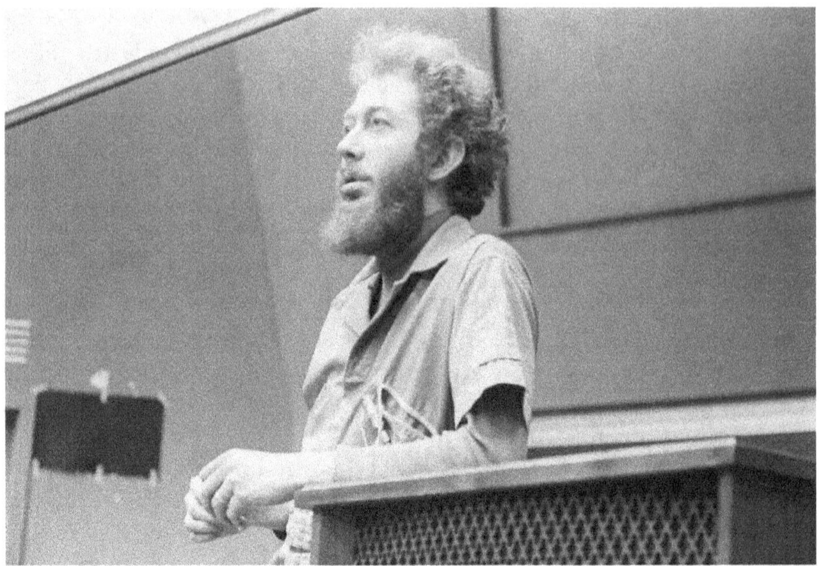

Figure 21. Hollis Frampton in class at Binghamton in February 1971. Courtesy Mark Goldstein.

On one of his visits Hollis said that he had an idea for a film, and it seemed as if he was working in more or less the same way I was: let's see what will happen if I do *this*. He wanted to get some people together, and I suggested Barbara and Frank. We all went into this room with the tape recorder and the camera, and Hollis made the shots he needed. (See fig. 22.)

Hollis Frampton: I spent several days in Binghamton at screenings and workshops. At that time Binghamton consisted of thirty typical state university specimens of immaculate penal modern rising from a sea of mud. I had an idea of what I wanted to do and asked around the Cinema Department, which was well populated by volatile personalities, for the names of the two people, the man and the woman, most likely to fly off the handle. There was virtual unanimity that Barbara DiBenedetto and Frank Albetta were my two best bets. I asked them if they would be willing to perform and gave them a set of conditions—namely, that they had been living together for about six months, that he had disappeared for a weekend and refused to offer any explanation. I let them stew in that juice over night. We shot the following evening. It was one take, the

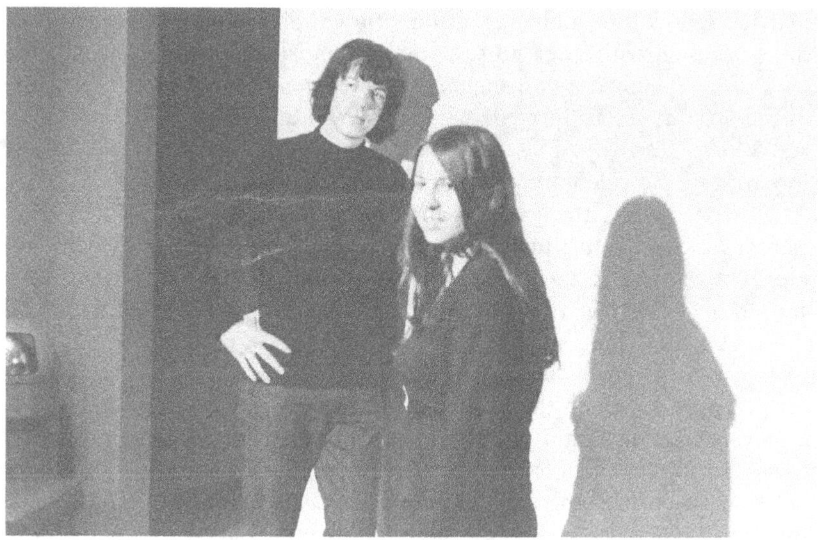

Figure 22. Frank Albetta and Barbara DiBenedetto at the shoot of what became Hollis Frampton's *Critical Mass* (1971). Damaged photograph. Courtesy Mark Goldstein.

first time and the only instance in a film I had made to that point where I used lip sync.* Larry Gottheim crewed on the job as sound recordist: at the time I didn't know a Nagra from my elbow.

By the end of the shooting—it was 10 minutes at the most—everyone in the room was absolutely limp. We filmed in March 1971, but it was October before I had anything like a clear notion of how I would edit what I'd shot. I didn't spend much time looking at the footage, which is fairly blank, but I spent a great deal of time listening to the tape, which became a source of references to the way the film itself behaves: lines like "This is getting us absolutely no place" came forward in high relief.

Larry Gottheim: Hollis came back to show the film, *Critical Mass* [1971], on March 11, 1972, his birthday. He and Marion Faller were staying with Debbie and me. Hollis was also going to show *(nostalgia)* [1971].

*In his notes on *Critical Mass* for the Criterion DVD of Frampton's work ("A Hollis Frampton Odyssey") Ken Eisenstein explains that actually, Frampton shot "two hundred-foot rolls (less than three minutes each) of the improvised argument."

We decided to have a birthday celebration at an Italian restaurant before the screening, with Nick and Susan Ray, and Ken and Flo.

We'd planned to meet at six for dinner, assuming the program would start at seven thirty or so, and we're waiting and waiting for Ken and Flo to show up. Everybody is starving, and at long last, Ken and Flo arrive—the celebratory mood now dampened.

At that time, the students in the Cinema Department—and there were a *lot* of students: hundreds were taking our classes—were into the idea that there were no strict rules about time. Finally we get to campus and, even though we're an hour late, the lecture hall is filled.

The first thing on the program was a new version of *(nostalgia)*. In this version Hollis used Michael Snow's voice (I think there was an early version in which the text was spoken by Hollis). "Do you see what I see?" is the final line of the narration, which is followed by Hollis's then-new logo; and as soon as the screening is over and the lights come on, Ken says something really inflammatory, something like, "You ruined the film! Why did you do *that*?" and Hollis immediately gets like, "Who are *you* to tell *me* what to do!?"

Ken Jacobs: We'd invited Hollis to show films, and it happened to be his birthday. The films were *very* good, but each one would end, and—Ow!—there'd be this HF. And the damned thing resembled a swastika; the *H* and the *F* were joined in a way that evoked a swastika.

Flo Jacobs: Less a signature, more like a brand name.

Ken Jacobs: He wanted to brand your fucking mind with this *HF*! At that time, I did not defer to persons or situations, and felt it was my obligation to speak up, especially with a lot of my students there. So I said how much I appreciated the work but that I deplored that the films were setting people up to have this *HF* thing imprinted on their brains. Hollis took umbrage and didn't speak to me for a year.

Flo Jacobs: More than a year.

Ken Jacobs: More than a year.

Hollis was like Stan in the sense that he had a private and a public persona; his private persona was very endearing, and humorous. But in public he would be the most pompous, bloated, nineteenth-century ass. I couldn't stand that. I don't think he was that way in classrooms, but you know, he was developing that pompous persona more and more—and at the same time his work was deteriorating. I think that, as with Jack Smith, public acclaim did not do Hollis a lot of good.

Larry Gottheim: Hollis's challenge back to Ken was extremely rare, even unique. Ken often dominated the presentations by our frequent visiting artists. He would immediately raise issues that would tend to deflect the discussion toward issues that the visiting artist hadn't expected to talk about. Generally the visitor would have to endure the direction of the discussion, or accept it as flattery.

Then Hollis shows *Critical Mass*. Barbara DiBenedetto is standing in the back of the lecture hall, seeing herself for the first time in the way she comes across in that film—because in fact something really strange and completely unexpected had happened during the filming: this little improvisation of a conflict between Barbara and Frank had transformed, in some amazing way, into a real thing between them. It was no longer *acting*; it became some kind of totally unexpected *reality*. And Barbara was now seeing this improvisation, heightened by Hollis's great disjunctive editing. She completely freaked out and started shouting, "You *can't* show this; if you dare to show this, I'm gonna sue you!"—another horrible moment on top of everything else that had happened that evening.

Steve Anker: I was good friends with Barbara DiBenedetto at that point and the roommate of Frank Albetta, and if I remember correctly, they had just finished an affair. When Barbara saw the film, she hit the roof in a way that I still remember vividly; I thought she was going to have apoplexy. I don't agree with her reaction, but I think she was sensitive about seeing herself on screen in that histrionic way, with that voice, and so cut up in the editing and in the middle of an altercation with somebody who, on top of everything else, she probably had real feelings about. Of course, Hollis was looking for true chemistry and he got it.

I remember Nick Ray saying that it was the funniest film since Lubitsch.

Hollis Frampton: Barbara was a volcano of energy, a young woman with astounding powers of projection. When she saw the film, she was, to my regret, deeply troubled by it. I don't know why. Had I delivered myself of an interlude of that magnitude, under conditions of such sanity and control, I would consider it one of the grand achievements of my life. Barbara's was a Mediterranean rage. My own bad tempers are essentially Celtic, which means that they go off like Roman candles and are immediately spent.

Ken Jacobs: Afterward, Hollis said that he wouldn't work in Binghamton: I had insulted him on his birthday *in public*—what I had said was the kind of thing you say to someone in private.

Flo Jacobs: Everybody had expected him to be teaching at Binghamton until this thing with the HF occurred.

Ken Jacobs: Larry must not have been happy with me over the loss of Hollis.

Larry Gottheim: In the end, Hollis's visit created a rupture that made it impossible for him to be our fourth faculty person. Somewhere, I still have a letter from Brakhage where he tries to patch up the rift, but it had become impossible: Ken wouldn't have supported Hollis coming, and Hollis wouldn't have wanted to come—and at that exact moment the whole thing at Buffalo opened up and Hollis ended up there. It was a big loss for us, but we had to move on. (See fig. 23.)

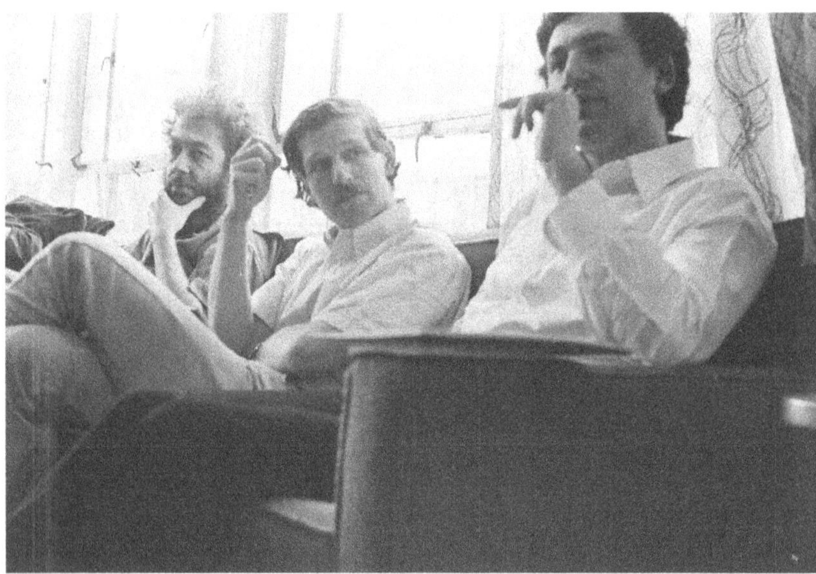

Figure 23. Hollis Frampton, Larry Gottheim, and Ken Jacobs. Courtesy Mark Goldstein.

4

Collision

Larry Gottheim: Even before Nick Ray arrived, it was clear that to be a student in the Cinema Department was a twenty-four-hour-a-day involvement, virtually a life commitment. I'm not sure it was that way in other departments. In fact, now it seems a little embarrassing.

Once Nick had arrived, the department changed character, partly because of Nick's own emotional issues (there was a lot of drug involvement that was driving him more and more fully off the edge). Of course, ours was an explosive mixture of people who all had their own psychological issues and dynamisms. Instead of us all wanting to be part of this relatively harmonious thing, everybody began to have their own particular vision; and especially with Nick and Ken, it had to do with a need for control and for loyalty.

Of course, it was always true that the cinema students tended to be separated from all the other students, in their own world; and within the department we each had our own group of students. From the beginning to the end, there was rivalry about who would receive students' primary allegiance. I think many of them would now say that part of what they're grateful for is having had to wend their way through these different aesthetic and personal allegiances.

In time it became clear that Nick wanted to take over *all* of the equipment, *all* the facilities, *all* the students. This was a really tough thing for me as the chair—a job I always *hated*, at least after the beginning flush of getting the thing moving. I didn't enjoy having to hold all of this explosive stuff together. The students whose aesthetic and personal allegiance was to Nick's group were so committed to what Nick was doing that they could no longer be part of the personal filmmaking thing that Ken and I were involved with. This was damaging to the program and to some of the students, I'm sure. For others, working with Nick was the best thing.

Tom Farrell became deeply involved with Nick's work and he's still involved with Nick. Just a couple years ago I was in touch with him, and it was interesting to get his perspective: he had seen me as the Bad Guy, the chair who was trying to put the reins on Nick—because I was trying to keep some equipment available for the other teachers and students.

Phil Weisman: Nick was mesmerizing for some students because the promise of Hollywood loomed large for them, but Nick was an alcoholic and struggling. He taught me a lot, including how directors can manipulate you to draw out emotions, and I learned to control gestures and emotions for the screen rather than for the theater—and used that knowledge when I was working with Ken in the Apparition Theater of New York.

From the outside we might have seemed like some sort of cult, but we were just young, impressionable, vulnerable young adults. After a while we were so in sync as participants in Ken's, Larry's, and Nick's projects that it felt like a perfect education. The experience was *alive*, and it was all first-person.

Bill T. Jones: There were battles in the department. Nicholas Ray had been invited to be artist in residence. A living legend, he certainly had an aura about him: he was tall, craggy, patch over one eye—an exile from Hollywood. Enmity grew between him and Ken Jacobs, who became quite moralistic about Nick's involvement with drugs and his involving the young students who were working with him in cocaine or whatever it was. Little did we know that in a few short years many of us would leave the confines of the university and move into the larger cocaine art world—Binghamton was a foretaste of what was to come. But it was exciting.

Peer Bode: I'm reflecting on my own experience of teaching and how little I know about my faculty colleagues' activities. Larry showed a number of his films—*Barn Rushes*, and *Harmonica, Blues* [1969]—and I can't remember Nick Ray specifically saying that he wasn't interested in them, but I do remember having a sense that he wasn't. Did he go to the Brakhage films? Nick was sixty or so, far along in his artistic development; and multi-image films were something he'd wanted to do for a long time. So how much attention he paid to whatever else was going on in Binghamton, I don't know.

Lloyd Bruce Holman: Early in our conversations Larry Gottheim mentioned that Nicholas Ray was resident filmmaker in the Cinema Department. Oh, I thought, Nick Ray was once the highest-paid director in Hollywood: *Rebel without a Cause* [1955], *Johnny Guitar* [1954], *55 Days at Peking* [1963], *They Live by Night*, *Flying Leathernecks* [1951]—I used to be able to rattle off his whole filmography. But Nick himself had dropped out of sight.

Larry told me that he'd invited Nick to come to Binghamton so the students could benefit from his experience. That had been a year ago, and Nick had become the Man Who Came to Dinner. Nick had instigated a film project and had attracted a cadre of student followers, which had created a film department inside of the Cinema Department. This had become a problem, since the department had a limited supply of movie cameras and production equipment.

For Nick it must have been frustrating to find himself in a college film department with children who had no industrial experience and who hardly knew his name. And his income must have been below what he had once been accustomed to. When Nick had first come to the Cinema Department, Larry ushered him through the university's business office; they asked how many dependents he wished to declare. Nick told them he didn't pay income tax; he was so far in arrears that the IRS just dropped around from time to time to ask if he could spare something, and Nick simply told them no.

Flo Jacobs: Nick Ray was involved with cocaine and alcohol.

Ken Jacobs: Yuk.

Flo Jacobs: He got the students into cocaine.

Ken Jacobs: Yes.

Flo Jacobs: And he had this Almaden wine bottle with a little hook on it that he'd carry over his shoulder . . .

Ken Jacobs: The students learned to take swigs with the bottle perched on their shoulders, just like Nick.

Flo Jacobs: And they would put out cigarette butts on the Arriflex, and the Arri lens-caps would be used for ashtrays.

Ken Jacobs: Nick had a contempt for technology, for our equipment.

Flo Jacobs: Kenneth would just go *crazy*, and they'd have meetings continuously because Nick's crew never brought back the equipment for others to use. Barbara DiBenedetto would get so angry, you can't *imagine.*

Ken Jacobs: Nick demanded that the students who worked with him be loyal only to him and the work he was doing. He called Larry and me "masturbators," said what we did was "masturbation."

Lloyd Bruce Holman: Nick may have been the premier director in Hollywood, but he had little technical knowledge about filmmaking or film exhibition. For example, he had a revelation that movie screens could be made brighter if the screen's surface was covered with tiny pieces of glass. Toward this end Ray and his student followers emptied hundreds of beer bottles and stockpiled them in a corner of the classroom that Nick had commandeered as a studio. When I arrived, Nick's students approached me, asking if I knew of an easy way to crush the beer bottles and to adhere the particles onto the studio wall to form a screen. I tried to be gentle when I informed them that Nick had just reinvented the glass-beaded movie screen, which had been standard for the past thirty years.

Nick and his student crew were hard at work producing a film. Nick's personal direction was critical since there was no written script; the plot depended on Nick's inclination. He would show up in the late afternoon to empty more beer bottles and begin shooting. The shooting sessions often ran late into the night which took a toll on the students, and probably on Nick as well. It was rumored that he was receiving vitamin injections which sustained him, but sometimes the late hours caught up with the students. I remember a student coming to me with a Sennheiser microphone that had been dipped in the college swimming pool when the student, the sound-boom man that night, had fallen asleep.

On another occasion two of Nick's crew brought in the department's only Nagra tape recorder and announced sadly that it had stopped working the previous evening—could I take a look? I checked the Swiss-made tape recorder, smaller than a loaf of bread but more expensive than some automobiles, and noticed that the battery compartment hatch was ajar. "Oh, that's the trouble," I said, "The batteries probably aren't making contact." I opened the hatch and a double-handful of shredded green leaves fell out onto my desk.

After the students had gone, I found a large brown envelope, swept the "oregano" into it, sealed it, and sent it to the director of campus security, Mr. Faraldo. I carried the envelope to the next building and put it in their campus mail drop. Despite the fact that I had not included a return address, I got a phone call from Mr. Faraldo the next day, asking if

I knew anything about a brown envelope. "Uh . . . Oh, *that* envelope—I found it in the road, somebody must have dropped it; I sent it to you because you're in charge of Lost and Found." I could hear Mr. Faraldo chuckling—he was known to have a sense of humor. "Did that road run anywhere near Nick Ray's studio?" "Golly," I said, "That would be awfully hard to say . . ." Pause: "Yes, I suppose it would." Mr. Faraldo wished me a good day and we both went back to our work.

Danny Fingeroth: I always felt I had a creative flair. I'd drawn a lot as a kid, inspired by comic books, and I was always writing. I was on the editorial board of my high school literary magazine at Bronx High School of Science. I thought I would grow up to be Saul Bellow; I used to go to bookstores to see where my novels would fit on the shelves—between Faulkner and Fitzgerald! After high school I went briefly to Boston University where I was an English major, but I wanted to "experience life," so I dropped out, lived in Cambridge with a high school friend, hitchhiked cross-country and traveled to Israel and Italy.

In high school and at BU I'd made a couple of films with a friend, and had found the experience very satisfying. We "invented" sync sound with a Super-8mm projector and a Wollensak tape recorder. I liked manipulating images. Boston University has a well-known film school, but I didn't take film there—although I did take a filmmaking course at the Orson Welles Cinema in Cambridge, taught by a guy named Austin De Besche, who would show up in Binghamton a couple of years later as the cinematographer for *I'm a Stranger Here Myself: A Portrait of Nicholas Ray* [1975, by David Helpern Jr. and James C. Gutman], a documentary about Nick Ray that people affiliated with the Orson Welles Film School were making.

After my travels, I went back to college in the fall of 1972. I said to myself, "I want to study film, but I shouldn't waste my mother's money on tuition when I'm not even sure that this is what I really want to do with my life." Since I was a New York State resident, the SUNY schools were very low cost, and at the time Binghamton was the only university in the state system that I knew offered a film major. I applied and was accepted at Binghamton.

My first inkling of what the Cinema Department was about was a letter from Larry Gottheim, which they sent to prospective cinema majors. It said something like, "We just want to make sure you understand that this is not a traditional filmmaking program; we can guarantee that our program is *not* going to prepare you for a mainstream *Hollywooden* career." Larry wrote "Hollywooden," the implication being that Hollywood movies were generally stiff and formulaic, lacking in life. So

I can't say I wasn't warned, though I don't think I really got what the letter meant. And when Larry mentioned that Ken Jacobs was part of the department, I probably confused him with Lewis Jacobs, the film historian/theorist.

Steve Anker: During my last two years at Binghamton I was the arts director of the radio station, WHRW-FM. I had Ken do an hour-long radio program every Tuesday night—an exciting, totally unpredictable, sometimes harrowing experience. Ken might show up very close to showtime and give me a variety of not-simple directives that I might succeed in carrying out. The radio programs were sometimes musical anthology evenings, sometimes interviews or readings, and once there was a dramatization.

Ken might play music he was interested in, ranging from Messiaen and Janáček to early blues to stage and screen music from the twenties and thirties. At the end of one show, Ken and David Cohen, the person he was working with that day, had extra time and read random scraps of paper lying around the studio—a Dadaist moment. I remember the station manager, Joe Molloy, storming into the booth where I was engineering and screaming that he had never been so embarrassed in his life, then storming out. Moments later, Ken came in, thrilled with what he had done, and when I told him that the manager had just stormed out, Ken erupted into fury, stating that this was one of his best shows. Then *he* stormed out. Of course, Ken was always into confrontation and was very good at confronting and embarrassing *me*.

I had to defend the shows; sometimes people were livid because the music Ken was playing was not pop fare—but it was all exciting; every week was different and inventive. The program was called "Mister Radio Man," I think after a thirties song of the same name. It was Ken's theme song, an old recording with which he began each show. Once he forgot the recording and asked me to sing it (I hummed it).

Soon after the Hermann Nitsch event, Ken produced a powerful segment of the *Mr. Radio Man* show that he and I hosted; the segment was a collage of writings that discussed conformity, openness to unknown experience, and the complexities of dark and hidden emotions within contemporary American society. It was a passionate intellectual exposé—though Ken's anger was controlled throughout.

I was primarily working with Ken until Nick Ray came along during my last year. Nick was hired for the fall of 1972, but I'd met him when he came to do a seminar for a few days in the spring of 1971—similar to the way Ken had come for a week in 1969. During that seminar Nick had the students pull out the cameras and run around directing scenes with each other.

Nick had a background in early radio—I found that very interesting. He had been involved with Alan Lomax in the thirties, for the first time bringing people like Leadbelly and Sonny Terry to a large public audience, on the radio program *Back Where I Came From*. Nick was like an Orson Welles figure in the sense that as a young man, he'd cut a swath through different media. By the time he made *They Live by Night*, he'd already had quite a career, so he really blew everybody away when he came to Binghamton. Nick was deep-voiced and very charismatic and filled with endless stories about famous people. He loved to let you know what James Dean would have said in this circumstance or that.

I'd gotten to know Nick and his wife Susan in New York the summer before he began teaching and ended up getting together with him a number of times. One night he had me take a 16mm camera and go out shooting with him in Times Square around midnight. This was when Times Square was very seedy and after dark, dangerous, and he asked me to film a group of hookers; I was threatened by a pimp who demanded I put my camera away or else he'd smash it. Later I finished shooting the roll from the fire escape of Nick's office. When Nick moved to Binghamton, Larry helped him make the transition, and Helene Kaplan [Wright] and I hung out with him until school started.

Nick thrived on setting up situations that had an air of danger, anything from actual physical danger to just the imminent threat of confrontation. I think that's palpable in his films; one of the things that makes them so strong is the unspoken tension between the actors and how that affects the entire landscape. Nick would set up situations between members of the crew, as well as between the actors, that would establish real contention, which he would then manipulate. I don't mean this necessarily in a negative way; it was clearly a creative tool for him. He said that the first day on any set, he would figure out who the alpha person was on the crew, and he would set up a confrontation with that person during which he would force the person to back off.

So Nick came to Binghamton and set up a situation where, not unlike Ken, he demanded complete dedication, to the point where it ended up becoming a communal situation: the people involved with him had relatively little going on in their lives outside of working with him on the production, and the film became more and more entwined with their lives: although the film was fiction, fantasy, it was also very clearly tied to the individuals involved in making it.

Amy Halpern-Lebrun: I was walking with Larry in the hallway when I ran into Nick Ray for the first time; he said, "How would you like to be script clerk?" I'd been typing for a living since I was sixteen and had already decided I'd be damned if anybody in the film world would ever see me with a typewriter, because I knew what people's brains do when they have a picture of a young woman at a typewriter—so I declined. I was stunned that the next time I saw Nick, he remembered my name, which I've come to recognize as standard power equipment in Hollywood. I liked Nick immensely, was knocked out by him like anybody would be. But I also knew right away that he was a vampire.

Steve Anker: Nick's film was never fully finished, at least not at Binghamton. Nick had a story in mind when he first got there, called "The Gun under My Pillow," but he scuttled it almost immediately. What I noticed is that he would come up with an idea and then routinely undermine it or change his mind. He worked in fits and starts, trying things, then undoing them or basically sabotaging them. It could be very frustrating. He might begin assembling people to make a shot or two in the afternoon; but before the planning was fully worked out, it would be evening; and before the actual rehearsing would begin, it could be well into the night. The shooting itself might not happen until 3:00 or 5:00 a.m. I became his first assistant director when school began, but that relationship didn't last very long; I was still too interested in other things to devote myself 100 percent to Nick.

He always wanted to have a camera and crew around, and I remember that on one of the first days of class he suddenly asked me to direct a scene with the entire class, though nothing had been discussed. So I had the camera make a long tracking shot through a corridor with students popping out of the doorways as the camera passed and joining the growing throng. Another time, after I had mostly dropped out of the group, he asked me to do camera for what became a steamy scene between Richie Bock and Leslie Levenson. No one on the crew had any idea of what the two would be doing, and the filming didn't begin until the middle of the night, even though the setup had begun in the early afternoon. During the filming, Nick asked me to make many camera moves and zooms, even though we hadn't rehearsed and I had never been the DP before. The action became more and more startling as Richie removed Leslie's blouse, the camera moving in for a close-up.

When we saw the footage, I was proud of how the filming had gone, since the camera was in tune with them in the way Nick had wanted. But he was furious because in fact there was no "head room"—not much space over their heads (I had misread the inner-frame symbol within the eyepiece of the camera). For me the scene was still powerful and the tight composition fit the scene, but Nick said that it needed to be reshot. I told him that maybe he'd need to have someone else film it, but he insisted that I do it again, and I did. And this time the scene, still strong and erotic, came out the way he wanted.

Susan Ray: Nick felt that the only way to teach filmmaking was by *making* a film, and I can't imagine *any* context in which Nick would not in some manner be trying to make a film. Making films was as essential to him as his liver and kidneys; it was another excretory function for him, another means of expression.

For me, being in Binghamton was very complex. I was not there full-time; I had a job in the City at Viking Press for part of the time (before that I'd run a real estate office, then was an assistant to the publisher at Arbor House). I would fly up on Allegheny Airlines for four days a week.

I was the same age as the students, but in a very different role—and part of that role was privilege and part of it was anything but. The way the students related to me was complicated, and not always easy. Some of them became friends and are still friends, but it was always a bit loaded to be the Great Man's Wife. I've talked to a number of other Great Men's Wives, some of whom are great women in their own right, but the same dynamic almost always applies: the women are treated as obstacles, or as some kind of foolishness on the part of the Great Man that people need to indulge. (See fig. 24.)

There were many instances when I felt this in Binghamton, but I remember one very clearly. Nick had picked me up at the airport and brought me to where the students were gathered at his place. I'd been

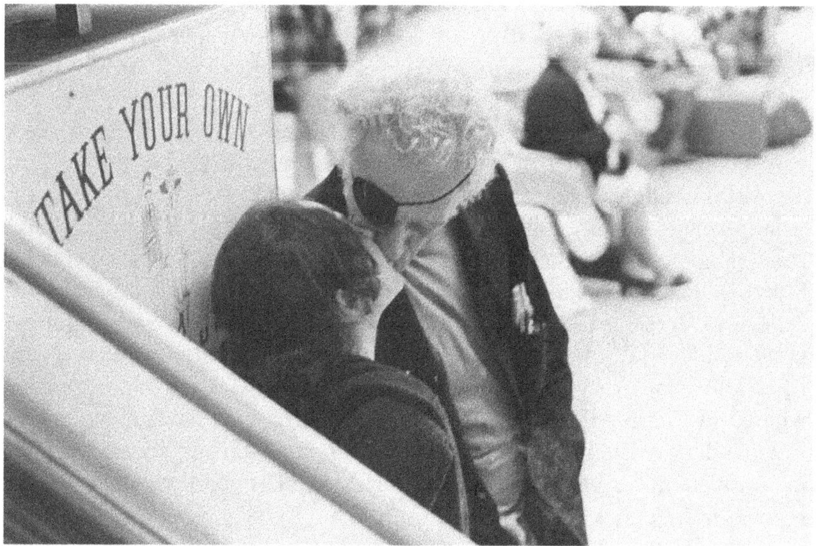

Figure 24. Susan and Nick Ray. Courtesy Mark Goldstein.

working all day, had been traveling, and was hungry and tired—and suddenly it became quite clear that everybody was waiting for me to cook dinner!

During those two years, there were lots of struggles: struggles over equipment, over money, and over who would be center stage. Ken was a fairly hip presence, at least to begin with, and a charismatic figure at Binghamton—not from *my* point of view, but certainly for a lot of the students. I think he thought of himself that way, and he certainly had a following. Then Nick came along, and Nick never took second place to anybody.

Let's face it (this is highly subjective, but it's my point of view), Nick was just a bigger guy than Ken—in terms of accomplishments, but also just as a man. He was more expanded, an extraordinary guy—whatever you've heard, he was *more* so. In my book [*I Was Interrupted: Nicholas Ray on Making Movies*], you can see what kind of teacher he was and what kind of a person he was. Nick was blustery and full of bravado, but he was also extraordinarily emotionally honest with himself. He could be selfish, but in other ways, particularly with his students, he was incredibly giving.

Danny Fingeroth: I grew up in New York during what people now think of as the bad old days, the high crime era of the fifties-sixties-seventies, when you'd find your parents' car broken into and they'd say, "Oh, it must have been a junkie!"—when eight-year-olds knew what junkies were and nobody thought that was weird. In those days, City kids took the subways and buses and walked all over the place in a way that kids aren't allowed to do now—though these days New York is statistically much safer. And when you went away to college, your parents kept a certain distance. Maybe, given the era, they were glad you weren't in a crash pad in the East Village or a battle-zone in Vietnam.

If a student today called home to say, "Hi, Mom and Dad, I'm having this great time, learning a lot. Oh, and there's this sixty-year-old teacher named Nick Ray, and he and a bunch of us students are making a movie called *We Can't Go Home Again*; we're all sort of living with Nick and sleeping together and smoking dope; it's this great communal, creative lifestyle experiment . . ."—your parents would already be in the car coming to save you! In that era—although I'm sure there were cases where this wasn't the case—it seemed important to develop your own independent existence apart from your parents. Maybe parents who had lived through the Depression and World War II figured their kids could survive film school shenanigans.

Nick was a fascinating character who seemed to have been everywhere. He knew everybody from Woody Guthrie to Frank Lloyd Wright to Elia Kazan. I was not directly a part of *We Can't Go Home Again*, but what I understand from talking to people back then and seeing Susan Ray's recent documentary [*Don't Expect Too Much*, 2012] about the making of the film is that essentially Nick collapsed his classes into one large film crew and went about making this movie about a burned-out Hollywood director who comes to an Upstate New York college to teach cinema. Everybody took turns acting and doing all the different technical roles. It was a very fluid situation, and I'm sure it was very educational. I think for a lot of people involved, it was one of the peak experiences of their lives. Of course, most of those students also studied with Ken, Larry, and the rest of the department faculty, too.

Jim Hoberman: I missed the whole Nick Ray moment, though during my visits friends gave me a sense of what was going on. Apparently the department split into factions: some people were devoted to Ken (sometimes so totally devoted that it was creepy); others were devoted to Nick, who had a degree of glamour that Ken didn't—it must have been horrible for Ken to have his acolytes changing sides. One guy who changed teams from Ken to Nick was Richie Bock.

From what I understand, Nick was totally irresponsible; I mean Ken was pretty irresponsible in *his* dealing with students, but nothing on the scale of Nick. In fact, I think that Ken may have learned from Nick what you could get away with! When I would visit during the early seventies, there seemed to be a whole new level of emotional confusion and turmoil.

Richard Bock: I loved my teachers, all three: Ken, Larry, and Nick. All were *very* devoted to their students! They *cared* about us! Each one in his own way.

I liked painting B-32 and making it into an incredible film room. The surplus World War II equipment lying around was staggering. Beautiful 35mm Mitchells and old Moviolas, tripods—the works. Nick put it all to use. It was quite something for us to learn about the collaborative nature of moviemaking in the face of Ken's and Larry's solo-artist emphasis. For Nick, film was the cathedral of the arts, incorporating sculpture, dance, painting, music. It took the efforts of many talents to create it. We learned to do the jobs on and off the set necessary to produce his kind of film. We learned about acting and directing actors. We learned that film was an adventure and that this adventure has only just begun.

The possibilities were endless. But even when I was working with Nick, I still attended all of Ken's classes.

Maybe I should call them Ken's Happenings—whatever you call them, they were terrific, something to behold. The ideas that Ken brought to our appreciation of film! We must've spent two weeks studying Todd Browning's *Freaks* [1932]. And three weeks looking at Nick Ray's *They Live by Night*—frame by frame. Ken's deep love and appreciation of directors and actors and writers and photographers was a way to begin *understanding* film. Ken taught us how to see. His lectures were a verbal music—like a brilliant Beat riff. He loved film and we caught on. He was a stern teacher and stood for little fooling around. Quiet and concentration on what he was saying and the imagery and sound he was showing us were the real requirements of the class.

Steve Anker: There was increasing tension that became animosity soon after I left, between Nick's assumptions about narrative conventions and his background, which he felt made him an authority, and Ken's and Larry's understanding of what film was—even though Ken and Larry were always passionate about narrative. There was almost always a macho edge that Nick provoked and used challengingly in groups or individually. This was something I myself found increasingly difficult to put up with, and it seemed inevitable that he would clash with Ken and Larry. In the end he couldn't have been a fit for any institution.

One of the things that was most interesting about Nick is that by the time he got to Binghamton, he was wildly radical—not only politically but aesthetically. He had no interest in telling a *linear* narrative, anything conventional by Hollywood standards; he was thinking in terms of self-reflexive devices within his films; he was thinking fragmentation; he was thinking of approaches to narrative that even today would be ahead of their time. I have to give him credit there.

The film we were making never seemed to be taking shape and leading toward coherence. Plus Nick was increasingly into wine and drugs. I remember more than once passing him and several students lounging in one of the corridors with a gallon jug of Almaden white wine dangling from one of Nick's fingers.

I had pulled away from my involvement with Nick Ray long before things got to the point of true acrimony, and graduated in the spring of 1972.

Helene Kaplan Wright: It took us a long time to realize just how many drugs Nick was taking. And after a while, some of us began to wonder how much of what Nick had accomplished in Hollywood was collaborative. How many people had been making Nick look good? Some of the scenes that we shot with him were inspired, but much of it was piecemeal and all over the place.

At some point most of us realized that Nick was beyond doing what he had once been able to do, and this was sad and upsetting because we all had given him so much time and energy—staying up all night in the sound transfer room, and Ken Ross, Phil Weisman, Steve Anker and me working twenty-four hours a day. Nick and his way younger wife, Susan, were always working in a kind of frenzied, deadline-is-approaching fashion, but at the end of the day there was never anything that was cuttable into anything else so that it *meant* something. A picture that was recently published in the Binghamton alumni magazine shows me and Steve Anker behind the camera, and the camera dollying back and David Cohen and someone else in front of the camera—a production still from this purported Nicholas Ray film we were all working on.

Tom Farrell stayed with Nick to the very end—he and Richie Bock had the footage, and, long after Binghamton, were trying to make something out of it. But Nick was crazy, addicted to shooting speed and staying up all night. He had pieces of the filmmaker that he once had been, but when all was said and done, he was a nightmare.

Those were the days when Ken lived upstairs from me on Elizabeth Street. Nick used to come over to my place with the rest of the cast and crew to eat scrambled eggs at four o'clock in the morning. I think Ken must have been quietly seething because so many students he cared about had gone over to Nick. I'm sure Ken could see that what Nick was doing wasn't working and that Nick was in some kind of fantasyland, that he wasn't teaching us much about filmmaking, that we *weren't* making a film, but just going through the motions, looking at stuff on a Moviola, throwing out this shot and adding that shot and syncing up dailies and looking at rushes—doing what you were supposed to do when you were making a feature film, except that there was *no film*; there was just a mess. Ken thought we were being exploited, and he was right. (See fig. 25.)

We all took the film to New York and showed it to David Brown, a producer who had an affiliation with one of the studios, and I remember Nick calling all of the directors that he had any relationship with to borrow money. The whole thing was crazy—and sad, ultimately just really sad. Wim Wenders put some of our footage into *Lightning Over Water* [1979].

Much later, after Nick died, I worked for Susan; she was still trying to function as a film producer. I quite liked her. We worked on a documentary about Tiny Tim for some Australian philanthropist who was obsessed with Tiny Tim. Susan was thirty years younger than Nick

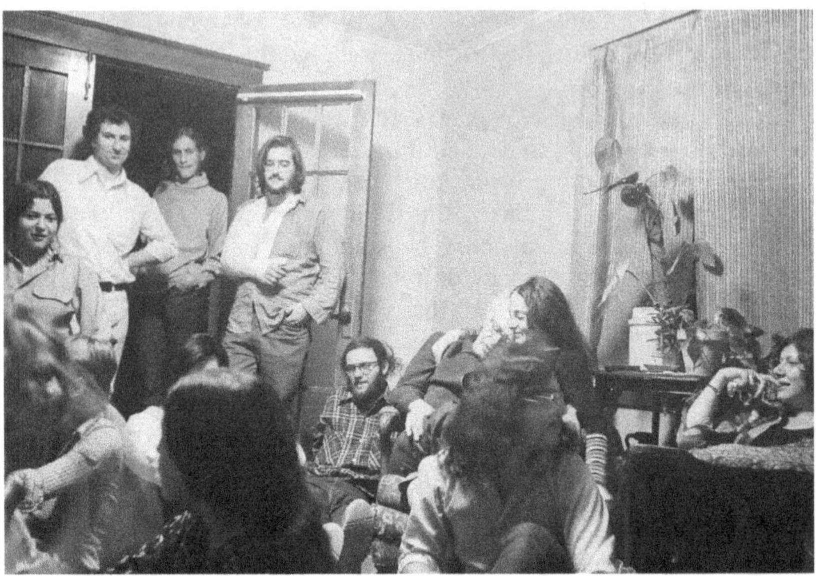

Figure 25. Gathering at Nick Ray's place: on the far left, Helene Kaplan (Wright); on left in doorway, Ken Jacobs; sitting center in beard and glasses, Tom Farrell; on chair Nick Ray and, on his lap, Susan Ray; far right, Jane Heymann. Courtesy Mark Goldstein.

and trying to keep it together when we were in Binghamton, trying to keep *him* together.

Richard Bock: The *We Can't Go Home Again* crowd was focused on dramatic film, whereas Ken and Larry focused more on poetic nonnarrative work. These two schools were in conflict, but I believe that Nick Ray was intrigued with the art films that we were shown, as he had done many experiments with color in Europe. In fact, *We Can't Go Home Again*, as messy as it was, and is, is decidedly an "Underground movie." I suppose many thought Nick was taking over. But what do you expect when a major Hollywood director who lives and breathes film is hired?

Nick brought a few of us to Hollywood to finish *We Can't Go Home Again*. He had flown to Los Angeles at the end of the school year—I believe it was 1973. Phil Weisman, Charlie Bornstein, Luke Oberle, and I think Danny Fisher, and myself got a drive-away car (a gold Cadillac Coupe de Ville!), piled the entire editing room with all the footage into the trunk and drove cross country, straight through without stopping until the suspension broke on the car, I think in Denver—the enormous Caddy trunk was filled to the brim with film cans and boxes.

We arrived in Los Angeles to meet Nick at the California Institute of the Arts. From there we went to an editing room at the AFI mansion, where we worked and lived. We were a dilapidated looking bunch of longhairs alright, but we worked in some of the major Hollywood studios, meeting all sorts of technicians, writers, producers, and actors.

Eventually they kicked us out of the AFI's marble palace, and we moved into *better* digs at the Chateau Marmont, in the same bungalow where Nick stayed while shooting *Rebel without a Cause*. Nick knew lots of people, and some of them, like Ken Kesey and Philip Yordon, came by. I remember one guy saying, "Nick's a good man," meaning, I think, that Nick was a great humanist and had made lots of friends among the Hollywood craft workers.

We shot all the multiple image material for *We Can't Go Home Again* on 35mm film in Hollywood, processed it, and edited at one of the studios, working day and night for two weeks to prepare the film for the Cannes Film Festival. We mixed the film at Glen Glenn Sound in Hollywood, a two-days-straight affair. As the mixers and technicians were all union, an astronomical bill ensued. Nick was charged what they call "double golden time"—meaning three or four times their hourly rate for each worker. I don't believe he ever paid the bill—as was also the case with the Chateau Marmont.

An exciting "field trip" for young college kids! Nick took the results of this grueling month's work to Cannes.

Peer Bode: Meryl Blackman was a student at Binghamton, and my girlfriend for a number of years. We met up at the New York Film Festival recently when *We Can't Go Home Again* was premiering, and she said, "I had no idea you were doing so much stuff with Nick! I thought you were working with Ken!" I was involved pretty much at the beginning of Nick's time in Binghamton. Then there were one or two semesters when I was not involved, then I jumped back in again. But even as I was working with Nick, I was taking classes with Larry.

Nick was clearly connected to the film industry and students were excited to be part of that. Through my brother Ralf—he did the cinematography for *Saturday Night Fever* [1977], *Coal Miner's Daughter* [1980], *Dressed to Kill* [1980], as well as a lot of television commercials and music videos—I had already been a production assistant on some industry productions and I didn't think the process was all that fantastic. What *I* experienced was wonderful people working amazingly hard on films that usually turned out to be uninteresting. Compared to the commercial projects I worked on, Hollis Frampton's films and Brakhage's, all the work we were looking at in Binghamton seemed so advanced, and I was thrilled to be engaged with this amazing new world of personal film, experimental film—and video.

My father, Harald Bode, was an electronic music pioneer, and I'm director of his archive. In the early sixties I was hearing proto-techno music coming out of my father's workshop, which was right below my bedroom. When I saw the Experimental Television Center, I felt a connection with my background, so though I was really in a film head, it wasn't a big leap to realize that video synthesizers had amazing potential.

It wasn't until I was working with Nick Ray and Nick booked some time at the Experimental Television Center to make video recordings that I actually had hands-on experience with video and synthesis. Nick felt that we *had* to use video; it might not be pretty but it was going to be really important: "You have to use every trick in the book."

Bill T. Jones: I remember that the morning we had our fight with Ralph Hocking at the then-new Experimental Television Center about our moving to Amsterdam, Nicholas Ray was there. Ralph was angry—and he was *right* to be angry: we were young irresponsible artist wannabes. So Ralph is castigating us, and there was Nicholas Ray like an old craggy eagle, watching it all.

I remember another day, when Ken Jacobs was at the Center. He had made it very clear that he had *no* love for the *coldness* of video; he was still in love with the sensuality and honesty of light moving through a medium. But he was at the ETC to borrow one of those cumbersome early portable video cameras, saying that he was going to try to look this beast in the eye. He was skeptical about video. But everybody *we* knew, and we very much ourselves, were *very* interested in video.

Danny Fingeroth: I took Cinema 101, the survey course taught by Larry Gottheim. Ken Ross and Hali Breindel were TAs for that class. It included art house movies and some classic noir films and westerns, and there was plenty of Brakhage, and of course Ken's and Larry's own movies. Nick Ray was still a presence—1972–73 was the second of his two years in the department. I didn't study with him, but I did work on the crew of a movie codirected by three senior cinema majors who had studied with Nick. They were making a narrative movie, and in retrospect I can see they were running the set the way they imagined Hollywood directors of the Golden Age had done. That was fun. Since the crew sometimes doubled as extras, I lost a few bucks one night when we were filming at a local bar: my role was, take after take, to walk up to the bar and order two beers that I paid for each time. I also remember that when they wanted to imitate a car coming up a driveway at night, I carried a spotlight that was supposed to show up on film as a headlight. To this day, whenever I wrap electric cords up, I loop them around my forearms the way movie crewmembers do.

Since Cinema 101 was a survey course open to majors and non-majors, most of the students taking the course weren't interested in the independent *Man-with-a-Movie-Camera* type cinema. While it took me a while to get what that kind of filmmaking was about, there was something about it that I was soon able connect with, that appealed to my own personal sense of mythology. The things that I'd been drawn to over my life—baseball players, rock stars, cowboys, private eyes, comic book superheroes—all glorified one-man-bravely-against-the-world, as did the romantic idea of one-person-boldly-making-a-film, exemplified by the classic shot of Brakhage with a Bolex in Lenny Lipton's book, *Independent Filmmaking*.

I remember somebody (I wish I could say it was me) coming up with lineups of baseball teams composed of avant-garde filmmakers, as well as the imagined avant-garde films that major league baseball players would make: for instance, Thurman Munson's *Anticipation of the Night Game* (I believe I did think that one up) and Catfish Hunter's *Metaphors on Pitching*.

Lloyd Bruce Holman: New students who signed onto the Cinema Department were advised that they were more nearly employable *before* studying at Binghamton than they could expect to be upon graduation after years of cinema study. On the whole this was true if one was thinking of conventional employment. However, Nick Ray's students were receiving special training in acquisition and perseverance, which would serve them well if they ever joined a gypsy troupe or took up careers in burglary.

Equipment, supplies, and film stock vanished into the black hole of Nick's studio. Some parts of the hole were blacker than others. For example, there was the coffin in the corner. The film that Nick was improvising seemed to be autobiographical and appeared to conclude with the death of the director, so possibly the coffin was on standby waiting for the final day of filming. (See fig. 26.)

Nick and his crew were persistent: when they ran out of 16mm color film, they switched to 16mm black-and-white; when the 16mm gave out, they were able to continue using Super-8mm, then Standard-8, then they soft-soaped Ralph Hocking into letting them utilize videotape at the Experimental Television Center.

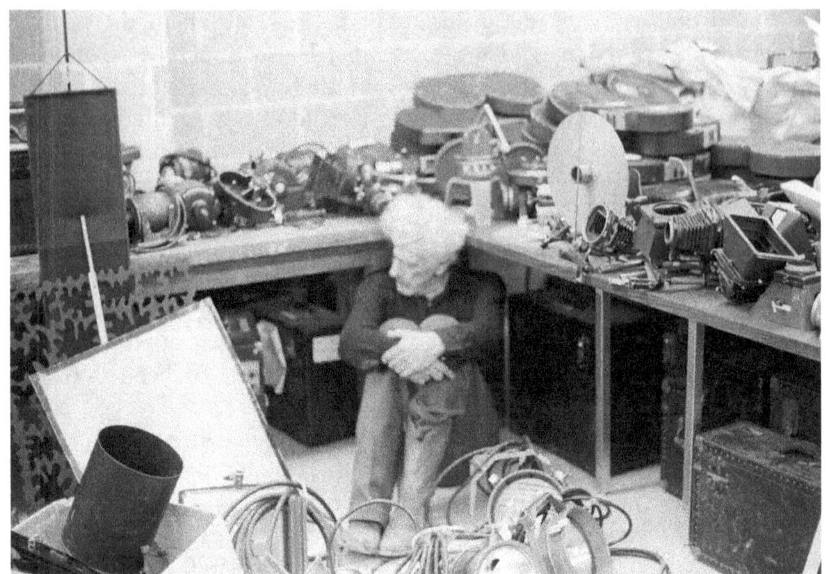

Figure 26. Nick Ray in "the black hole." Courtesy Mark Goldstein.

Sherry Miller Hocking: I think Nick Ray was the first filmmaker on the faculty who was interested in video.

Ralph Hocking: But his interest in video was how it affects, or *infects*. He didn't care about the *concepts* of video. Basically he wanted to see if you could put multiple images on the screen at the same time. You could do that with film, but Nick didn't have the money to do it that way and figured out that video was the cheap alternative.

Tough dude, Nick. Ken hated him, wanted to kill him and *would* have killed him if he'd had the chance. He tried to get Nick fired, did everything he could to get him out of Binghamton.

Sherry Miller Hocking: That was a very tumultuous period in the department . . .

Ralph Hocking: When *wasn't* it a tumultuous period in that department!

Sherry Miller Hocking: When we got older, it got less complicated.

Susan Ray: Nick worked with multiple image way before he made *We Can't Go Home Again.* You can see hints of that even in the Hollywood films, in *Bigger Than Life* [1956] and *Rebel,* for example. The beginning of *55 Days at Peking* is multiple image *and* multidimensional sound. Nick and others with firsthand knowledge have told me about a reel of experiments in multiple image that he shot in the early sixties with the cinematographer Novotny in preparation for something called "Doctor and the Devils," a film based on the Dylan Thomas scenario (the reel was stolen off a luggage rack on a train and the film never got made, at least by Nick). And he had very specific plans for the use of multiple image in the film he began but never finished about the Chicago Seven. During some of the first conversations we ever had, Nick talked about what he called *mimage*—multiple image.

Nick did not intend multiple image as a gimmick; I believe it's truly the way he saw things. Fifteen or so years ago I was in Madrid with an old friend, and we went to the Prado. I wanted to revisit the paintings that Nick had introduced me to in 1974—the black period Goyas, El Bosco [Hieronymus Bosch], Velázquez. As I looked at *Las Meninas* [1656], I understood as I hadn't before what Nick had been trying to do. It seems we are growing into this multidimensionality of perception, however slowly.

Lloyd Bruce Holman: Eventually Nick's film project became so disruptive that it threatened the existence of the Cinema Department. Students who were working on Nick's crew were not attending classes, and two fistfights had broken out between members of Nick's crew and other film students. Technical support was nearly impossible—equipment that was handed to the crew came back in pieces.

Larry came to me and said that it was past time to shut Nick down. He was preparing a memo to the administration, and asked if I would write another, describing the influence Nick's film was having on the technical aspects of the department. I spent two days writing the memo, citing chapter and verse explaining why Nick's project could not be continued.

I decided that it wouldn't be fair to blindside Nick, so I made a copy of my memo and took it to his studio. Nick was not there. I asked the students where he was. France. Nick and a student friend had departed to carry the jigsaw pieces of his film to the Cannes Film Festival. Nick's expectation was that if he screened as much of the film as would go through a projector, important people would recognize it as a work of genius and they would invest in the film's completion. Unfortunately that did not happen. Parts of the film *were* screened at Cannes, but no one invested. I heard that Nick's student friend danced on street corners to raise money for plane tickets back to the U.S. Nick returned briefly to the college but his contract was not going to be renewed.

Susan Ray: Nick had a two-year contract, and by the end of the two years he had definitely alienated a lot of people and his contract wasn't renewed.

I've been trying to finish *We Can't Go Home Again* and get it into the world for the thirty years since Nick died, and until the 2009 Torino Film Festival decided to do a Nick Ray retrospective and asked me to write a piece about the film, I felt I was just banging my head against a wall. I went into debt and lost many hours; I often wondered if I was on a fool's errand. At times I tried to be "objective" and imagined just letting the film go, but that always felt like burying a baby, a fresh young life. I couldn't do it, though it would have made my life much easier.

Writing my piece for the Torino retrospective convinced me that I was correct in staying with the film. As kind of a last-ditch effort I wrote Marco Müller, the director of the Venice Film Festival and said, "Is there any chance you could take this film under your wing," and he said, "Yes, as long as you have the premiere with us." And from there, everything has worked very nicely.

Particular students were crucial to the film: Tom Farrell, certainly, and Leslie Levinson. There were different students at different stages, but certain students hung in for the whole time Nick was in Binghamton, and Tom is still hanging in, god bless him.

I've been reading books about the seventies to see if I can get some kind of perspective on what happened in Binghamton. I think the early seventies were a critical moment in our cultural history, a moment when we failed a test. I think that what happened in the Cinema Department is a microcosm of that.

Larry Gottheim: In the spring of 1973, I took time off to finish *Horizons*, and Ken took over as acting chair. That was the period when Ken and Nick collided: without me killing myself to moderate, they were in continual conflict. Nick's contract wasn't renewed. Then *Ken* took a year off and we were able to get his salary, or part of his salary, to do other things.

5

New Directions

Ken Jacobs: In March 1973, we had this horrific run-in with some citizens of Binghamton, just as Flo had feared we might. The students had scheduled a showing of Sergei Parajanov's *Shadows of Forgotten Ancestors* [1964].

Flo Jacobs: Yes, with *Nissan Ariana Window* [1969], which includes some nudity.

Ken Jacobs: You see Flo nude and pregnant.

Binghamton has a Ukrainian community that, I was told, had emigrated from the Carpathian Mountains where *Shadows* had been filmed. When the screening was announced, a church group considered bringing parishioners to see the film, but they wanted to preview it, which I was against, though the students running the Film Society agreed to the demand. *Shadows* was judged okay, but then they asked to see the short film that was going to be shown with it. The priests decided that *Nissan Ariana Window* was pornography, and the students agreed to show the short *after Shadows*.

I thought, after the grand opera of *Shadows*, people are going to see my little, silent, meditative film! Impossible. At my insistence, the students decided to show *Nissan Ariana Window* first, following it with an intermission (for those who wanted to skip the short and then come in) and then *Shadows*. The church said this was unacceptable, but the students stuck to the program.

The night of the screening, the parishioners show up, and some of them go into the theater to see both films. In the middle of my film, a priest comes in and begins berating the parishioners by name! And I see grown people get up like chastised children and, heads hanging, leave the screening. Grotesque!

And there's a tumult in the lobby. I step up and one woman from the church who worked as a secretary at SUNY turns to me in a fury and says, "Go back to New York City! This was a nice place before you Jews got here!"

The local papers were full of the incident for months.

Flo Jacobs: During the controversy someone dredged up our arrests for showing *Flaming Creatures*,* and in the local paper Ken was called a pornographer.

Ken Jacobs: Yes, now we were "New York Jew pornographers"—it was openly anti-Semitic. We were getting threats on the phone and felt we were in physical danger. We kept our shades down. I even carried a weapon, usually a small hammer.

Larry Gottheim: Ken had decided to have a special showing of *Shadows of Forgotten Ancestors*, which was advertised to the large Russian community in Binghamton. The screening was crowded. For some reason Ken also decided to show one of his own films, *Nissan Ariana Window*, that included Flo nude, which had nothing to do with *Shadows of Forgotten Ancestors*. The deeply conservative and religious Russian audience was outraged, and there was a big demonstration.

Ken urged me, as chair, to get involved in this, but I chose not to. I felt it was Ken's problem that he had pretty much brought upon himself, and I was sick of having to devote myself to his personal issues. Eventually nothing came of it—I never heard anything from the administration—but Ken felt I had betrayed him.

Ken Jacobs: Very few people from the school said anything in support of us—Larry never said a word. I felt very alone. One person who did write in support was Dan Barnett.**

---

*For information about the controversy and the arrests surrounding a screening of *Flaming Creatures* in New York City, see Brian L. Frye, "The Dialectic of Obscenity," 35 *Hamline Law Review* 229, Hofstra University Legal Studies Research Paper No. 11–10—available at http://ssrn.com/abstract=1792810.

**The *Nissan Ariana Window/Shadows of Forgotten Ancestors* event instigated many letters to local newspapers. A citizens group called CURE (Committee for a University Return to Education) called for the firing of Jacobs. One of the few supportive letters was from

In 1973–1974 I took a year's unpaid leave—I was so depressed. We were back in our loft in the City and, after that incident, there was no way Flo would return to Binghamton with the kids.

Larry Gottheim: In Ken's absence I was able to arrange for a series of visiting artists to come for extended visits. Kubelka came for the entire fall [1973] semester, during which he did various things, one of which was a big cooking event. Other visitors included Morgan Fisher, Tony Conrad, and Alphons Schilling. Each came for a period of time, two weeks or so, both to do some of their own work and to teach as part of an ongoing seminar. That was fantastic.

Peter Kubelka: Binghamton was the beginning of what I think of as my despecialization phase, when I thought to myself, "I live only once and I know so little about so many things: I don't want to be a specialist in one field." I've remained a filmmaker all my life and my thinking has been structured by the fact that slices of time are stored on the filmstrip. But at Binghamton I began to educate myself in other interesting fields: ethnology, the behavioral sciences, archaeology—and cooking.

The university library at Binghamton was pivotal for me. In Vienna when you went to the National Library, you had to look up title and

---

a group of Binghamton students; it was published in the Binghamton *Evening Press* on Sunday, April 1, 1973:

> To the editor:
>
> Reading the letters to the editor as well as an editorial and an article by David Rossie we have been outraged by the abusive and derogatory remarks directed at Ken Jacobs and his film "Nissan Ariania Window." This work is not a "slopped together 'home movie' having worth only to Jacobs and his family," but is a complete film made by an artist.
>
> Let it be known that there are people not related to Ken Jacobs who find the film meaningful, sensitive, and pleasurable. We revel in his manner of personal expression and find it slanderous to accuse him of forcing his ego on a 'captive' audience. The film has never been shown behind locked doors.
>
> We feel that for an editor to publish damaging remarks about a film-artist is to influence public opinion in such a way as to effectively censor works of art. It is horrifying that a handful of people who cannot think for themselves should be so quick in attempting to dominate the opinion of a larger group of people in an effort to stifle and degrade a creative thinker.

The letter was signed by Charles Levi, Ken Ross, Hali Breindel, Renée Shafransky, and Mark Graff.

author, then you had to submit a request for what you wanted, then wait two or three days before getting the book. The university library in Binghamton was open twenty-four hours a day, and I could explore the shelves myself. When I found one book, other related books were next to it! For me this was paradise and it helped enormously to advance my autodidactic studies.

It was in Binghamton where I first did a big cooking event. This event, which happened at the end of a course, was memorable for all of us involved, I think; but for me personally it was the beginning of my taking the history and theory of food preparation seriously.

That first cooking event was an adventure because I realized at the last moment that we had no access to cooking facilities at the university—I thought this had been arranged in advance. The students and I met in the late morning, then we had to look for a place to cook and when we found one in the recreation area of the local fire house, it was already late afternoon, and the equipment there was in a horrible state of dirtiness. We started shopping for food just before the stores closed and met again as a group late in the evening. By the time I started to cook, it was already midnight, and I was not ready to talk about the cooking until some things were prepared, and by then a number of students had fallen asleep—they'd been running around for more than twelve hours! The real lecturing started at 3:00 a.m. and went until 7:00. (See figs. 27 a, b, c.)

After the lecture the students were very enthusiastic and wanted to take me to the Binghamton zoo: a zoo is *about* animals and we had just *eaten* animals and they wanted to feel this relationship. The zoo was not open so early, but we saw some ducks on the other side of a wire fence. I tried to establish contact with the ducks and one of them tried to eat my finger. After the zoo, *I* fell asleep in the car. The students brought me home.

Larry Gottheim: The strongest filmmaking students who had major careers after graduating were able to absorb the best that Ken had to offer, while also absorbing what they could get from other faculty and visiting artists. I think this was the case with Alan Berliner, Dan Eisenberg, Phil Solomon, Phil Weisman, Ken Ross—all of them and many others were very much influenced by visiting artists and faculty. Most of those who worked with Nick also had classes with Ken and others, and there was another group of students who, while taking some classes with Ken, gravitated to Ralph and became video students. Each of the faculty or visiting faculty or visiting artists greatly influenced students. What angered me about the chapter on Ken's teaching in *Optic Antics:*

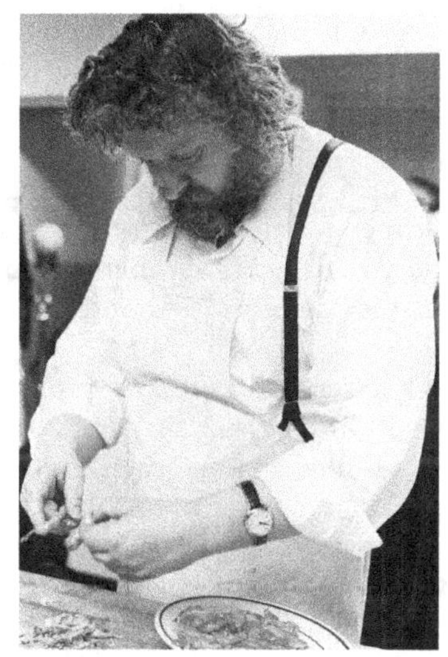

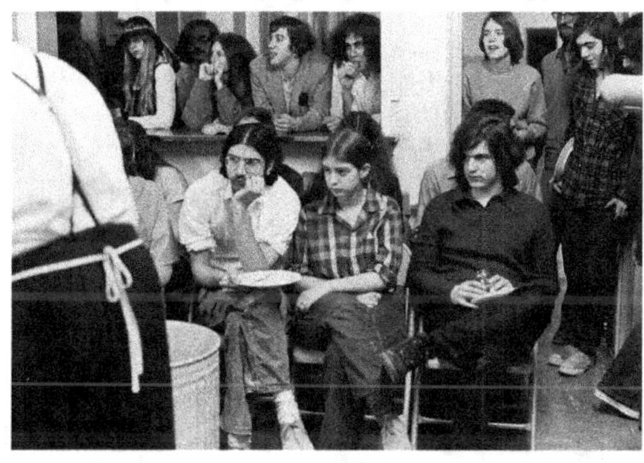

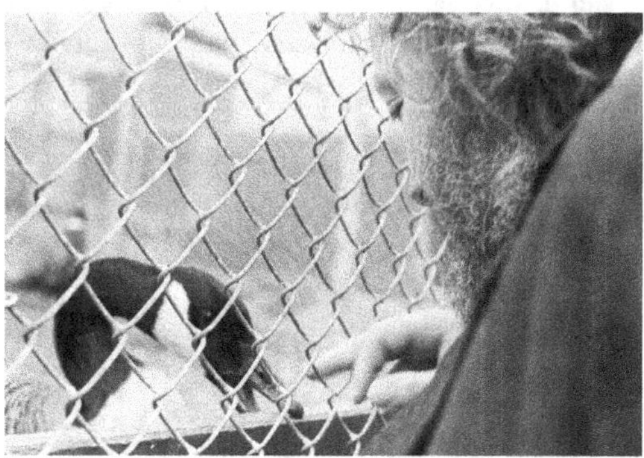

Figures 27a, b, c. Peter Kubelka cooking; class watching the cooking performance; and Kubelka and goose at Binghamton zoo. Courtesy Mark Goldstein.

The Cinema of Ken Jacobs was that it not only didn't give me what I felt was appropriate acknowledgment for my role as chair and teacher, but also didn't give nearly enough weight to role of the other faculty and visitors.*

By 1972–73, it seemed as if we were expanding. Ken and I were the old guard of the department. Dan Barnett, then Saul Levine, came in as the new, younger faculty with different energies and different interests. That was also when Ernie came back—though he didn't want to stay.

Dan Barnett: Before I started working as a professional editor, when I was living in Cambridge, working as a machinist and making my films, I started going to the MIT film society, when Fred Camper was running it. I met Jon Rubin there; he was more social and more connected than I was. We visited and showed each other our films. Jon told me about Ken and Binghamton and said he thought Ken would be interested in seeing what I was up to. Somehow or other, I sent a couple of pieces to Ken, and I was stunned when he sent me a quarter-inch tape of the class he'd taught around my work.

I'd recently seen *Tom, Tom, the Piper's Son* and had left the screening absolutely blasted by it and floating; so the fact that *Ken* was interested in my work was extremely flattering. I remember writing him and the class a long letter in reply to his tape. When Larry subsequently asked me to come do a show, I wasn't quite clear that it was a job interview as well. After the screening and my talk, they took me out to dinner at this Italian restaurant. I remember it had booths and a phone in every booth.

Ken and Larry were enthusiastic and really seemed to want me to teach at Binghamton. My situation in the Boston area at the time was great: I was living in a wonderful house next to a town forest, had an interesting girlfriend, was happy with the personal film work I was doing, and was making a decent living as a freelance worker on documentaries. I wasn't eager to ditch all that to come to a depressed valley in New York State.

When I resisted their offer, Ken looked hard at me and asked, "Are your parents alive?" When I affirmed they were, he reached behind me, grabbed the phone at the back of the booth and said, "I'm calling your mother right now and telling her what a schmuck you are for turning down this opportunity!"

---

*See Michael Zryd, "Professor Ken," in Paul Arthur, David E. James, and Michele Pierson, eds., *Optic Antics: The Cinema of Ken Jacobs* (New York: Oxford University Press, 2011): 249–261.

If I recall, I started at Binghamton in the spring semester of 1973. I joined the faculty in the middle of the academic year to cover for Larry's sabbatical and took over the second semester of his introductory lecture class, Cinema 102. Halfway through that semester, they offered me a three-year contract.

I was hired in the middle of the battle between Ken and Nick Ray. Very early in the semester, Nick strode into my class with a cohort of his entourage in the middle of a sentence I was struggling to form and introduced himself: great shock of white hair, eye patch, one hand jammed into the pocket of his jeans. My image of that moment seems very clear to me now—but perhaps it's become distorted over the years.

I was only dimly aware of who Nick was—I was a philosophy student and not particularly interested in narrative film—but his chutzpah amused me, and obviously I was the junior figure in this encounter. He invited me to visit him in his office for a chat. At that moment I was not aware that there was a fierce intradepartmental struggle going on around this guy. No one had bothered to inform me until, puzzled, I began to inquire.

I did go to Nick's office, which was also his production studio for the film he was making with his students. He was posed on a high stool at an upright Moviola, and a jug of cheap wine was on the floor at the foot of the machine. Nick gave me a lecture about the superiority of the Moviola as an editing tool over the increasingly popular (in the industry) flat-bed editing machines. I had worked on both and tended to agree with him, but didn't think it warranted a disquisition. At some point a student came in and Nick introduced him as a writer on the project he and the students were working on. The student was extremely upset about something, close to tears, and began a tirade at Nick that ended: "You're not a Hollywood director, you're just a perverted old has-been!"

Nick's reply: "I am still a Hollywood director and will be until the day I die!"

Danny Fingeroth: Larry was on sabbatical in the spring of 1973, so I took Cinema 102 from Dan Barnett, who they had just brought in. I got along well with Dan. Cinema 101 was the shake-out class, and by 102 only the majors and the people who weren't scared off by 101 were left. Then, the next year, Saul Levine came in and I studied filmmaking with Saul. Throughout the spring, I would often sit in on Ken's classes because they were fascinating.

Somewhere in there I took an animation course with L. Bruce Holman, who was an animator and also the guy who took care of the equipment. Bruce was unflappable, no matter what craziness was going on. And accessible: if you were there while he was fixing a piece of equipment, you'd sit and chat with him. I recall Bruce's sonorous voice and his aura of great competence.

Art Spiegelman was around, but I didn't get to know him then—though some students did: David Kasakove, for example, who with Spiegelman and John Benson cowrote a famous article on a classic EC Comics story, "Master Race," by Al Feldstein and Bernard Krigstein. At the time, I had only the vaguest notion of who Spiegelman was. This is before the full-length *Maus* and even before *Arcade* magazine. He gave a series of lectures at Binghamton over the course of several days in 1972, I think—but I only got to know Spiegelman in New York in 1980, when Ken gave a course at the Collective for Living Cinema, an in-depth study of Frank Capra's *Meet John Doe* [1941]. Over the years I've come to know Art, especially since I've become more and more involved in comics academics and comics museums. (See fig. 28.)

Richard Herskowitz: During my third year Ken took a sabbatical and a parade of filmmakers came through. Jack Smith!—he didn't speak to us, but did a performance. And Carolee Schneemann and Brakhage, each for a few days. Peter Kubelka came for a week, and just blew everybody away; then came back for a full semester. I just sat in my place and the avant-garde film community came to me.

Ralph Hocking: We never had the kind of coagulation among video makers that the filmmakers had. I think part of this had to do with the fact that people get together to watch film, but you tend to watch television by yourself.

Of course, Woody and Steina Vasulka were very much tied to video as a social medium. Nam June certainly was, and other people too, but lots of people weren't. I was never interested in a social scene around video. I didn't give a shit about video installation or video performance. My ideal setup would have been for everybody to take video work home and sit in their chairs or lie in bed and watch it. That way you can control everything, the way you're in control if you're reading a book.

At first we were always fighting with dancers who got a lot of the video money from NYSCA [New York State Council on the Arts], and then as time went by, the other moneys were slowly eased towards social change media. Pretty quickly it became almost impossible to find money for anything that had to do with working with the *stuff* of video.

Larry Gottheim: Taka Iimura taught a video class when Ralph was on leave. One of my proudest moments as chair was when one of Taka's

THE LANGUAGE OF COMIX

LECTURES AND DISCUSSIONS WITH art spiegelman

S.U.N.Y. BINGHAMTON, DEPARTMENT OF CINEMA, APRIL 1,2,3 1974.

THE COMIC STRIP, LIKE FILM, WAS BORN AT THE END OF THE 19TH CENTURY. UNTIL VERY RECENTLY BOTH MEDIUMS HAVE OFTEN BEEN ASSIMILATED BY THEIR AUDIENCES BENEATH THE LEVELS OF CRITICAL AWARENESS.

UNLIKE FILM, COMICS NEVER HAD A D.W. GRIFFITH OR A SERGEI EISENSTEIN TO HELP FORMALIZE THEIR GRAMMAR.

THE LANGUAGE OF COMICS, EVEN MORE SO THAN THE LANGUAGE OF FILM, HAS BARELY *BEGUN* TO BE DISCOVERED.

THESE TALKS WILL EXPLORE THE WORK OF A FEW COMIC ARTISTS, PAST AND PRESENT, WHO HAVE STARTED DEVELOPING THIS LANGUAGE.

"GOOD COMIX ARE NOURISHING COMIX— UNLIKE THE HOSTESS TWINKIES TO BE FOUND IN THE DAILY NEWSPAPERS OR IN MOST CHILDREN'S COMIC BOOKS.

GOOD COMIX CAN BE READ SLOWLY AND OFTEN. HOPEFULLY EACH RE-READING SERVES UP SOMETHING NEW!

IN MY OWN WORK I TRY TO MAKE EVERY PANEL COUNT, AND SOMETIMES WORK AS LONG AS A MONTH ON A PAGE.

IT'S LIKE.... CONCENTRATED ORANGE JUICE!"

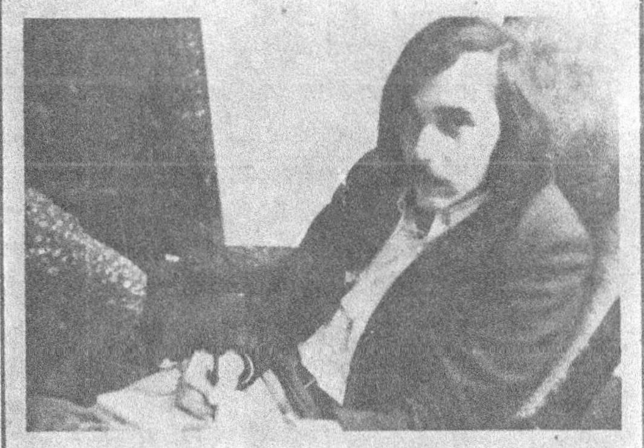

THE COMIX IN THIS BOOKLET ARE FROM THE FOLLOWING SOURCES: "MAUS" FROM FUNNY AMINAL COMICS #1, "PRISONER ON THE HELL PLANET" AND "ZIP-A-TUNES" FROM SHORT ORDER COMICS #1, "REAL DREAM" FROM SHORT ORDER COMICS #2, "DON'T GET AROUND MUCH ANYMORE" FROM SHORT ORDER #2. AUTO-DESTRUCTO FROM SELF-DESTRUCT COMICS, PHOTO - KEN JACOBS,

Figure 28. Poster for an Art Spiegelman event, hosted by the Cinema Department.

students complained to me that Taka had opened a book to read something to the class and became so engrossed in the book that he continued to read it silently to himself, forgetting the class was there. I told the student that was the best lesson he could ever have!

Phil Solomon: I was at Binghamton at a fortuitous time, from 1971 to 1975, right at the tail end of that initial huge endowment of sixties-era SUNY Rockefeller money—so there were a lot of new faces coming in and out of the newly established Cinema Department. Partly because I'm a New York Jew, my father had the usual doctor expectations for me. *I* never thought I could be a doctor, but I always loved animals, so I thought maybe I'd be a veterinarian—though from early on, I also loved the movies. In my high school yearbook people wrote, "Good luck with directing animal films, or *Lassie.*"

When it came time to look for a college, I was searching for a place with a premed *and* a cinema program—covering my bets—and at that time, Harpur was, so far as I knew, the only SUNY school besides Buffalo and the brand new SUNY-Purchase (the SUNY schools were the only ones my parents could afford) that offered a program in cinema. I expressed an interest in the Cinema Department in my application, and I received a form letter (an advance warning!), signed by Ken and Larry, explaining that their department focused on "cinema as art." I thought, "Right: Bergman, Fellini, European art cinema"—I was a semihip suburban high school kid; I'd often take buses into New York to go to the Thalia, the Bleecker, and the Paris—the repertory cinemas that often featured European art films. I was also interested in the American "art films" of the late sixties and early seventies—Frankenheimer, Penn, Altman . . . So "art cinema" sounded fine to me.

My first semester, I took calculus, chemistry—and Cinema 101 with Ken Jacobs. The first day of class—if memory serves, Ken wasn't actually there that day—the teaching assistant, Helene Kaplan, shut the lights off in this large lecture hall and showed Tony Conrad's *The Flicker* [1966], along with other "structural films" that were in vogue at the time, like Hollis Frampton's *Lemon*. Now, I had no background whatsoever in the aesthetics of modern art—I had mostly grown up with TV and the movies, pop culture and rock and roll—so when the lights came back on, I thought, "What the hell was *that*!" I was initially very suspicious and thought these films were put-ons, conceptual jokes. Later, when I began teaching, I discovered that a lot of my students felt similarly, though MTV and other pop culture sources have clearly absorbed elements of the syntax that for us in the early seventies was the modernist shock of the new.

I continued to be suspicious and skeptical about what I was seeing, and about two weeks into the course, I screwed up my nerve—there were probably a hundred or a hundred and fifty people in this class—raised my hand, and asked Ken, "When are we going to see some major motion pictures in this course?" Long silence. Ken took the question seriously without getting offended and very calmly explained the nature of what he was trying to do; and in fact, during that semester, he *did* show several "major motion pictures" and had fascinatingly original, often quite humorous takes on the movies.

By the end of the first semester I was opening up to avant-garde music and I began to discover the educational uses of marijuana and acid—and then I saw Brakhage's *Blue Moses* [1962] and had a revelation: I began to understand the simple, but important notion of modernist reflexivity, that, yes, this film is about cinema, and narrative cinema was essentially this false front where "behind every camera there's a cameraman" and so on. In the excitement of my "deconstructive" breakthrough, I remember going up to Ken and saying something like, "Do you think one can really *learn* this kind of cinema?" And, with one eyebrow raised, he said, "Well, what do you think I'm *doing* here?"

Little by little, as I was becoming disenchanted with premed science and math, I found that I was—much to my parents' dismay—becoming completely committed to this exciting and weird little scene of poetic filmmaking, mostly because of the passion and intelligence of the teachers I had the good fortune to study with. Like some of my peers, I became a film artist *because* of academe, not despite it.

Ken Ross: We used to say, "What the hell are we gonna do after we graduate?" We realized that we were living in a dream, that we had found ourselves in the right place at the right time for this dream. We didn't want to stop making films; we didn't want to stop seeing the kinds of films we were seeing; we didn't want to end the kind of engagement we had developed around film.

One day—I remember exactly where we were—Phil Weisman, Mark Graff, and I were sitting outside of one of the lecture halls and it just came to us: let's have a place in New York where we can offer film workshops, where we can show our films and the films by all the new filmmakers that are coming in; and let's show cool stuff, stuff from the history of film, and personal films in every shape and form. This was really the Ken Jacobs aesthetic—the embrace of the personal and the socially relevant and unique in film, as well as the experimental.

We felt that Anthology Film Archives and Millennium Film Workshop weren't doing what we wanted to do: Anthology felt like an elite club that you had to earn some kind of membership in; and Millennium was basically a series of one-person shows. We were going to create *events* and they were not going to be limited to film, but would include para-cinema, dance, performance . . . At some point, we decided to call it the Collective for Living Cinema.

I had been working for the *Village Voice* during summers when I was at college, and I got Phil Weisman a summer job there too. After graduating, Phil and I worked in the circulation department, and that was where we organized the Collective. We had our first events in the fall of 1973.

Phil Weisman: In most ways the Collective was a Binghamton spinoff. We were no longer under the direction of our teachers—we did this ourselves—but of course, without the contribution of their work and their thinking, the Collective wouldn't have occurred to us.

When Ken Ross and I, and at the very beginning Lushe Sacker and Andrea and Mark Graff, were establishing the Collective, my generation of filmmakers was at a low point. We didn't have outlets for our work; Anthology and Millennium seemed closed to us.

We came out of Binghamton extremely idealistic, interested in doing a *cooperative* thing, something socially active. We weren't particularly into our own careers. This was an extension of what Ken and Larry had taught us, particularly Ken, because he gave us a real education in B movies and early ethnic films, all kinds of film, and we wanted to expand film culture in New York City. We wanted to find the people who were trying to do new things, wherever this took us. We didn't have much money—we were all working other jobs during that period—but we were devoted.

Ken Ross: Mark Graff and his wife Andrea became involved early on, and Renée Shafransky: she was a friend of ours—when I went off to teach at Bard College in 1978, she took over as program director. That started the tradition of new program directors coming in to curate, which was one of the things that helped separate the Collective from the other venues. Neither Phil nor I wanted to be the figurehead of the place, as Howard Guttenplan was at Millennium and Jonas, at Anthology, and as Karen Cooper was at Film Forum. We were into a much looser and freer thing. Later, Alf Bold, then Simon Field came to do the programming. (See fig. 29.)

Amy Halpern-Lebrun: I dropped out of Binghamton after a year because I wanted to make movies right away, and I didn't want to work in the

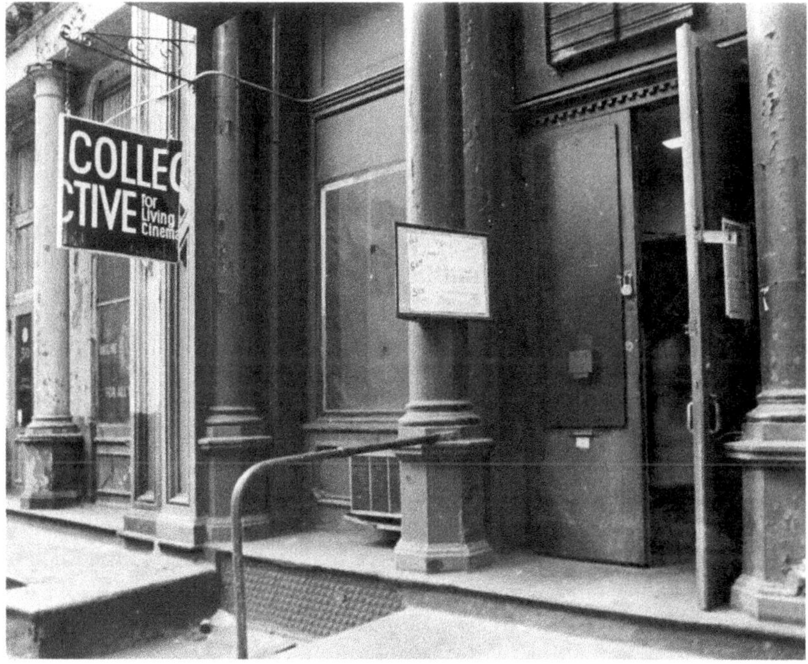

Figure 29. The Collective for Living Cinema on White Street in Manhattan. Courtesy Anthology Film Archives.

hothouse of the Cinema Department. I was aware of my fragility as a young artist, and Ken and Larry were *so* forceful.

I moved to New York and worked with Ken's Apparition Theater when they came to town. I typed for a living full-time at *Woman's Day* magazine, and when Ken Ross, Phil Weisman, and Mark Graff graduated and came to town, we started the Collective—though I've been written out of that history. I was there for several of the early years; I set up the chairs and projected and programmed with everybody else, and I remember when we decided to show our own work for the first time. Jonas wrote us up, though he misnamed my film as *Slush Flush*—it was *Slow Flush*. Basically he saw us as "children of Ken."

I had the opportunity to shoot Mikis Theodorakis performing in Philadelphia—the first real film shoot I had to arrange. I was working full-time and didn't have camera equipment, and I remember calling Kenny Ross at midnight and saying, "I know you have this new Beaulieu and I know it's midnight, but I have to borrow your camera, and for every reason we founded the Collective you *have* to lend it to me!" I took the camera and three different kinds of black-and-white stock and shot *Filament* [1975]. Later I came out to Los Angeles, where my parents had moved, went to UCLA and over time finished my BA, then my MA while working film shoots.

And I helped form the Los Angeles Independent Film Oasis with Bill Moritz, Pat O'Neill, the astonishing scholar Beverly O'Neill, and David and Diana Wilson of the Museum of Jurassic Technology—both were making films then—and Roberta Friedman and Grahame Weinbren, when they were still a couple. Morgan Fisher soon joined us. Oasis ran for five years. Basically, as at the Collective, we were a group of desperate filmmakers who needed to see work.

Richard Herskowitz: Recently I was reminiscing with Richard Abramowitz, the distributor who runs Abramorama (Richard was at Binghamton at the same time I was), about our experience there. I was telling him how intimidated I was by Ken and how tongue-tied I'd get in those moments when I was in Ken's presence and had to speak; and Richard told me a story about how Ken suddenly came up behind him one day on the street and said hi, and Richard got so flustered that he walked out into the street and almost got hit by a bus—Ken had to yank him back.

Renée Shafransky had a more direct relationship with the professors than the rest of us did. Renée didn't seem to have our sense of intimidation; she could talk comfortably to Ken and the others—I remember that very clearly.

There were communities within the larger community of the Cinema Department. There was an incipient video community that drifted towards Ralph Hocking, and Peer Bode was at the forefront of that. I remember Peer and his girlfriend at the time, Meryl Blackman, always sitting in the same place together, a little apart from the rest of us.

And there was the whole Nick Ray gang.

For me the major influence was Ken, although I took film production with Larry, then later with Dan Barnett. When Ken left on sabbatical, I had almost no interest in Binghamton anymore. I rushed through my BA and went on to the University of Pennsylvania where I met Amos Vogel and became his assistant—but that's another story.

Though I've become a programmer, I didn't do any programming while I was at Binghamton. I wanted to be an experimental filmmaker and particularly loved making found-footage films. But increasingly I was feeling that there were *incredible* filmmakers making far better work than I could dream of making, who were not getting seen; and maybe it would be a more valuable use of my time to help these filmmakers find an audience than to put the films that *I* would make out into the world.

Peer Bode: I met Meryl Blackman during my sophomore year. I was living off campus in a house on Main Street in Johnson City, across from what I remember was a General Electric Company building. Around Halloween, Meryl, a Cinema Department student, came by the Johnson City house—she'd heard that someone was projecting films onto the windows. She had just come back from horseback riding and smelled of horses. She became my first serious girlfriend—we had a lot of fun together. Meryl was also on the film crew with Nick Ray in 1972.

I met Arnie Zane, of what became the Bill T. Jones and Arnie Zane dance duo, when I picked him up near the house, hitchhiking to the university. Arnie was colorful and exotic looking, wearing various layers of wool leggings, sweater, hat. In 1974–75, after graduating, Meryl and I took dance classes at the American Dance Asylum space in downtown Binghamton. We were in dance performances with Bill and Arnie, and Lois Welk, Jill Becker, and others.

We used video in several performances. Together with Meryl I choreographed a dance with video called *Matrix Dance*. It was part of an evening of video and dance pieces at the Experimental Television Center. *Matrix Dance* expanded and became *Movements for Video, Dance and Music*, which was performed in 1975 at the Johnson Museum of Art in Ithaca and the Everson Museum in Syracuse. Meryl and I did the choreography, and Bill T. Jones, Arnie Zane, Cara Brownell, Bob Warren, and Charlie Seltzer were the dancers; David Jones did the video engineering.

Meryl is presently a real estate agent in Brooklyn, and she's involved with an organization that takes care of and finds homes for stray New York City dogs.

Bill T. Jones: Phil Sykas was a new friend of Arnie's and mine. The three of us spent a lot of time together reading *The Autobiography of Alice B. Toklas*, exploring the wonders of kitsch, stoneware, and the pinhole camera. (See fig. 30.)

The magic lantern was very important to Arnie. Phil Sykas and Arnie dug through junk shops, and I still have some amazing lantern slides that they found. One is called *The Elephant's Revenge*, which is pretty racist: a caricatured black native shoots an arrow into an elephant's ass and the elephant chases him and does all these terrible things to him, ostensibly to teach him a lesson. Arnie and I made a performance work

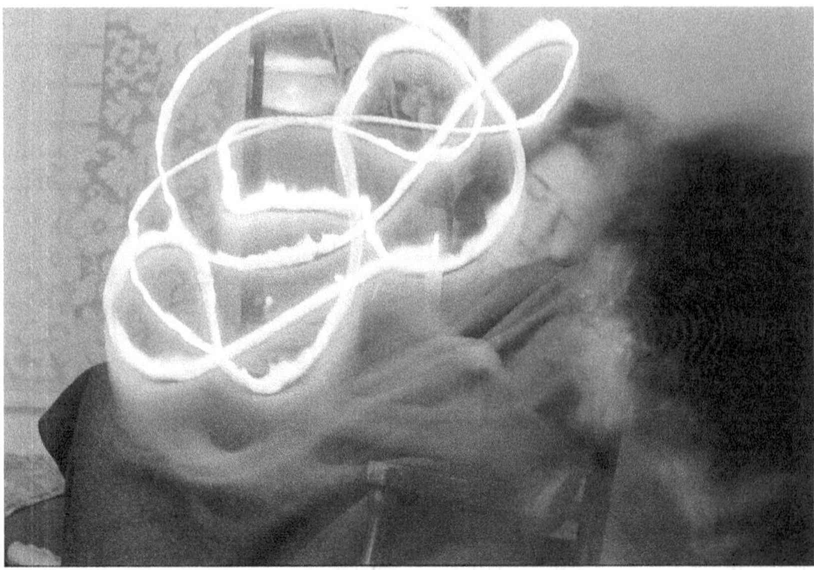

Figure 30. Photograph of light-play and Arnie Zane sleeping, by Philip Sykas. Courtesy Philip Sykas.

where we played James Brown's "The Big Payback" while projecting a magic lantern show of *The Elephant's Revenge*.

Arnie went so far as to begin making his own slides and he made a whole body of work. I still have the magic lantern and the slides that he made for it—some of them are quite beautiful and a wonderful extension of photography. His interest in these antique image technologies was a result of our connection with the Cinema Department.

Philip Sykas: I cannot remember when I began to study precinematic devices and to make serial-image works, but I took it up as an independent study in the fall, 1972 term. I remember making thaumatropes, and being quite proud of a single-frame "film" I devised using a cylindrical Quaker Oats carton. By turning the top of the carton, the face of the eponymous Quaker journeyed around the inside of the carton until he appeared once again in the opening I had cut.

My final project was a magic lantern show. I remember always being worried by the complexity of cinema and its expensive high-end gadgetry. I knew that if I was going to make films, I'd have to start with the basics and make my own equipment. So I began by making a magic lantern. I studied elementary optics and constructed my own condenser lens. I made slide carriers from hardwood veneers assembled with tiny brass screws. And glass photographic plates were specially ordered and processed to be employed alongside antique painted slides purchased in Binghamton and New York City antique shops. I still have these slides. One is a classic skipping rope effect, and another shows the moon emerging from clouds. There are processions of comic figures, a farmyard scene with a sequence of domestic fowl, and a Dutch slide with a duck playing the piano. Painted in a continuous strip but having four or five "frames," they come alive when projected with the rhythm created by gently pushing the carrier.

On the 30th of May, 1973, I moved to the former Elks lodge ballroom space at 137 Washington Street in Binghamton that would provide the venue for the performance. It was quite derelict: glass needed installing in the windows to keep the pigeons out and mounds of dung had to be cleared away. There was no running water or toilet, so water was collected in a five-gallon jug from the antique shop across the road, and the toilet in a local hotel was used discreetly when needed. Perhaps this sounds mad now, but I didn't think much beyond my delight in renting, for a fairly nominal sum, this huge and evocative space with its chandeliers and stained glass. The floor below was used as a rehearsal studio by a rock band, and after the band moved out in 1975, that lower floor became the home of the American Dance Asylum.

Bill T. Jones: Phil was working on his thesis project for the Cinema Department and the three of us decided to make his presentation a real performance event by adding music and dance and even a little magic. We dedicated the evening to a fictitious character, "Babar Rebus, The Dunwich Horror" (Babar the elephant, Merce Cunningham and Robert Rauschenberg's *Rebus*, and H. P. Lovecraft's *The Dunwich Horror*), and performed in the shambles of Binghamton's old Elks Hall, where Phil was living—later to become the American Dance Asylum, the collective led by Lois Welk that we would join in a couple of years.

Philip Sykas: For the final thesis presentation, I invited staff and students of the Cinema Department to the ballroom space. Music for the show was to be provided by a portable wind-up Victrola I'd purchased in an antique shop. My tiny music collection included Artie Shaw's 1938 recording of "Begin the Beguine," and Shaw's clarinet was to re-create the ballroom atmosphere for the show. I can't remember exactly how it came about—I must have played the disc while Arnie and Bill were visiting and they began dancing somewhat playfully. But something unexpected happened in those three minutes that was to crystallize into a pas de deux performed as part of my magic lantern show. Of course, Arnie and Bill would eventually have partnered each other without my intervention, but I like to think I had some small part in their later duets, as they both did in my artistic development.

The night of the show, a considerable group of friends and fellow students assembled at the ballroom, but we had to do the show without Larry Gottheim and Ken Jacobs who were held up at critiques taking place on campus. Standing on the balcony above the space with my home-made magic lantern, I began, nervously. Turned on, a disc of light illuminated the screen, and I slowly moved the objective lens to focus on the lamp filament—the source of the magic—and then beyond. The found and made slides followed. Then the dance performance. The next day apologies were received from Larry and Ken, and I was awarded an "A" grade.

Bill T. Jones: Arnie and I created a duet—our first—for Phil's thesis show. We called it *Begin the Beguine* after a record we'd found at the Salvation Army store. Our *Begin the Beguine* began with the lights out. When the needle touched on the record, the lights came up along the opposite sides of the long narrow room, and we appeared shirtless, wearing matching navy pants, swaying—*Right, left, turn, turn, turn. Right, left, turn, turn, step*. The piece grew into a parody of thirties show dancing as the stepping and turning expanded to include pedestrian gestures like brushing our teeth, combing our hair, smelling each other's armpits, mock fighting.

We weren't sure what we were doing beyond thumbing our noses at the "avant-gardisms" of the Cinema Department, so enamored of the outrages of Andy Warhol and the performance sacrileges of Jack Smith. We wanted to show the audience our own brand of nostalgic outlandishness.

Philip Sykas: Arnie arranged for us to have another showing at the Collective for Living Cinema, then located at 4 West Seventy-Sixth Street in New York. This took place on Sunday the 10th, November 1974, and was a much more elaborate program of lantern slides, cinema, and dance works, created together with the American Dance Asylum.

Bill T. Jones: Phil's project was a success, and we gained a rather notorious reputation in the Cinema Department. Arnie still felt himself to be more of a photographer than a dancer and had danced *Begin the Beguine* as a kind of lark, a way of taking part in the spirit of the evening. But afterward, he began to create his own solos. His first, *Self Portrait*, had a sensibility similar to *Begin the Beguine*, though less camp. To Caruso's "La Donna è Mobile" [from Giuseppe Verdi's *Rigoletto*] and against a backdrop of sepia-toned magic lantern slides of himself, Arnie—with a shaven head and wearing an antique dressing gown—stood up on a chair. Every time Caruso hit a high note, Arnie would fall violently to the floor, bruising his buttocks and lower back. It was charming, enigmatic, and painful to watch. We saw great value in these qualities.

Arnie was an avid collector and part of his ongoing research into life and creativity was his attention to kitsch. He came in to Ken's class one day with a treasure trove of broken dolls. I remember the crowded classroom with Ken lecturing and Arnie sitting there with his lap full of these demented antique dolls—Ken made some comment about them. Arnie was already a little different—and by this time neither of us was a student; we were working artists living in Binghamton—already living a kind of East Village experience. (See fig. 31.)

We sometimes did events that students and faculty from the Cinema Department would attend. The Cinema Department had invited Anthony McCall to present his Cone films, which were made visible by a smoky cloud of incense and cigarettes and joints, at our American Dance Asylum on Washington Street. That screening was an *event*; people were allowed to lie on the floor, move through the cone of light—the audience became the performers.

Daniel Eisenberg: I started at Binghamton in 1972. I arrived as an English major, and remained one: I graduated as a double major in the English Department and the Cinema Department. I was the *only* one of my classmates in cinema to take the cinema analysis track, rather than the production track; and the irony is that I became a filmmaker while many of those who took film production did not.

I hung out with Mark LaPore, Alan Berliner, Steve Weisberg, and Lee Krugman. Phil Solomon was there, too. I did start making films during my third year, but at Binghamton I was never more than a beginner.

My first exposure to the Cinema Department was with Larry Gottheim, and at first I didn't know what to make of him. Larry was the first teacher I'd ever had who would think out loud in front of a group of people. He was performative in a certain way and interesting to watch. Larry had a quiet brilliance; I learned to love the way his mind unfolded things. He taught me how to think analytically about film, but also about literature. Even in front of a group of 200 students, he was playful and often inspired and inspiring.

I remember that when Larry showed us Godard's *Vivre sa vie* [1962], my whole conception of film just blew open. The two films

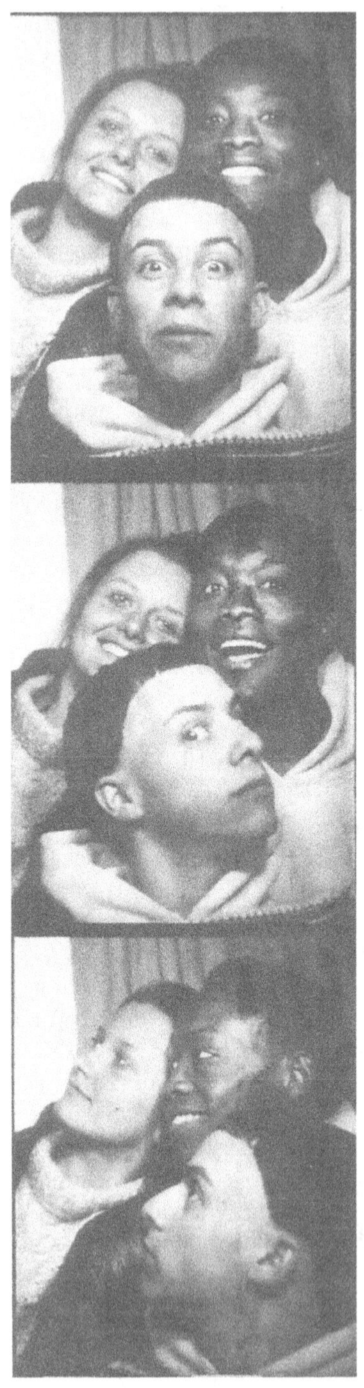

Figure 31. Arnie Zane (in front), Lois Welk, and Bill T. Jones, © 1976, in Binghamton photo booth. Courtesy Bill T. Jones.

I remember most distinctly from that first year were *Vivre sa vie* and *Wavelength* [1967]. This pairing of two modes of filmmaking—film as writing and film as time and space—is still important to me. And I loved *Larry's* films, and learned a lot by looking at *his* work. For whatever reasons Larry never sought attention, or maybe he just wasn't good at getting it. I thought that some of his works were masterpieces and they're memorable for me to this day.

Another important teacher for me was Kubelka, whose lectures were also very performative—but in a very different way from Larry's: Kubelka seemed very polished, finely tuned.

I never took a class with Ken. Maybe that's one of the reasons I continue to make films. I say that because Ken was an overwhelming presence and in some ways his coterie of students was very cultish: he was the leader and they were the followers. Ken was both wonderful and awful. From what I saw, he had a tendency to either celebrate you or berate you. Although I was deeply impressed by his film work, I learned very early to keep my distance.

Phil Solomon: Many filmmakers came to campus while I was a student and each brought something special: Ernie Gehr taught an advanced production class and played us the music of Charles Ives and Philip Glass. Klaus Wyborny was talking to us about D. W. Griffith and algebra; Tony Conrad brought his "yellow movies" and rigged up an installation [*Film Feedback*, 1974] where the film that was being shot would come out of the camera, go through a development tank, and wind up on the projector—all in real (and reel) time. Alfons Schilling was doing his 3-D paintings and experiments, the primary inspiration for Ken's Nervous System.

Larry Gottheim: Speaking of visitors I invited, there is also Ondine. When I had an early screening at the Carnegie Institute, organized by Sally Dixon, I learned that Ondine had moved to Pittsburgh. As a Warhol fan, I went to visit him where he had an apartment with his then-partner Roger Jacoby (at the time, one of the few filmmakers who developed his own films). They started to play opera records by Maria Callas, and this went on so long that I missed my flight, and stayed with them for an all night session of Maria Callas.

I invited them to Binghamton. It turned out that Ondine had a print of *Chelsea Girls*, which he showed in a double projection. And he and Roger gave a session on Maria Callas. I think this started Ondine on a short career traveling the film art circuit with his print.

Phil Solomon: I studied with Peter Kubelka for a semester, in a course that focused exclusively on his own films (and on cooking!), which was very important for me, especially in learning to think about formal economy and integrity. Dan Barnett and Saul Levine were key figures for several of us, including Mark LaPore and Dan Eisenberg. Larry, Ken, Saul, Dan, and technician/animator Bruce Holman were on the regular faculty; Kubelka and the rest were visiting artists. Even Nick Ray was there during my first years. I sat in on Ray's public lectures, as I was too "fresh" to be included in the more senior group that collaborated on what became *You Can't Go Home Again*—nor was I part of the senior group that would go on to form the Collective for Living Cinema.

I studied critical analysis with Ken, and his courses and syllabi were imaginative and inspiring. He turned out to be a great model for my teaching. His classes were very present tense; he didn't do packaged lectures. He thought and reacted on his feet. He legitimized difficult films for me through his enthusiasm and passion and his peculiar and uncanny nonacademic intelligence and wit. I find myself channeling him all the time when I'm teaching, and to this day he remains a giant figure in my life, as an artist and a friend.

Larry was a very sensitive thinker—I think I learned a great deal from Larry by just watching him muse in class, working out aesthetic problems. He had what I would call a chamber sensibility—I think of hearing the Brahms clarinet quintet on his excellent turntable played through a McIntosh amp, as the sun was setting at his house on the hill. His films at the time were quite minimal, very beautiful and bucolic, an interesting counterbalance to Ken's urban stabs at happiness. They were quite the pair, those two, and when the money finally ran out and the tent was taken down and all the other colorful characters left the circus, the department shrank back to the two of them, and Ralph.

Lloyd Bruce Holman: Larry arranged for a substantial number of filmmakers to come to Binghamton to present their work. Tony Conrad came and brought *The Flicker*. He and I discussed the fact that *The Flicker* had never actually been seen in the manner Tony had planned. He wanted the alternating white and black frames to appear *bang* on the screen, but all movie projectors were equipped with two- or three-bladed shutters to reduce flickering. "What the hell," I said. "We have two hours before the screening, let's convert one of the projectors to a single-bladed shutter." We removed the three-bladed shutter from one of the machines and replaced it with a one-bladed shutter fabricated from a coffee can lid. When the film ran that night, the whole theater seemed to rock back and forth. The audience cheered—and no one went into a seizure.

Larry tried to get Andy Warhol to visit, but Andy sent a gentleman who billed himself as Ondine. We asked Ondine what he planned to talk about at that afternoon's presentation. "I'm a professional," Ondine said,

"I can talk for an hour about the darns in my socks. What if I narrate whatever film you have on hand?" I pulled out the two reels of the 1931 *Dracula* and took them to the booth, where a surprise was waiting—the short focal length projection lenses were missing. Nick's crew was later implicated, but for the moment it was impossible to fill the screen.

Larry was talking with Ondine when I came to tell them about the problem. "Not to worry," Ondine said. "Let's project both reels simultaneously, with one image beside the other; *that* will fill the screen—and that was the way *Dracula* was presented: reel one on the left; reel two, on the right. Center stage, Ondine ignored both images while he improvised a lecture about the career of the soprano Maria Callas whose singing he admired.

Dan Barnett: The Binghamton job was practically my first time teaching, and definitely my first experience of teaching a huge lecture class (150 students) that met three times a week for three hours a meeting. Preparing for these classes was intense. My stomach was always in a knot and I could never eat before class on the days I taught—I'd be near fainting when class finished at four. I thought that many of the films we were showing were expressive in unique ways that were beyond verbalization—I knew there were likely to be techniques for opening students up to these ineffable qualities, but knew that I hadn't yet learned them.

The students in the class were *extremely* smart and they could be intellectually very aggressive. Early during my first semester, in a kind of quixotic gesture, I decided to try to make personal contact with everyone in the class. I asked people to raise their hands when I called their names so I could see who was who and begin to get to know them individually. I looked intently at each person, trying to memorize the name/face relationship. One young woman sitting in the last row had her feet up on the backs of the seats of the row in front of her, legs spread, crotch aimed at me for maximum effect. I acknowledged her, like the others, and moved on. The next class day, I arrived, as usual, an hour ahead of time to get my shit together and brief the projectionist, and this same student was waiting in ambush.

In a thick Brooklyn accent, she asked, "Why were you looking at me like that the other day?"

I drew a blank. She steamrolled right ahead: "Was it because of what I said about you?"

"Uh, no . . . what did you say about me?"

"I called you a pompous prick and a condescending asshole!"

Apparently, half the students in that first lecture class *hated* me and half of them *loved* me. I wasn't really aware of this until much later, when my wife told me how she remembered meeting me—an occurrence

I don't remember and that Gail [Currey] teases me about. Gail was the roommate of a woman who was in my class. This roommate would return after my classes and complain bitterly about my teaching, so bitterly in fact that Gail thought, "Hmm, there's got to be something else going on here; I've got to meet this guy." Gail left Binghamton after her first year, and went on to study with Tony Conrad at Antioch and then got an MFA in photography at the School of the Art Institute of Chicago. Currently, she's head of studio at PDI/Dreamworks Animation in Redwood City. But she credits Ken as a major influence.

I suspect the complaints about me had to do with my take on the Binghamton students. Their way of being students was to psych out the professor: figure out who he was and what he wanted, then feed him back what they assumed would satisfy him. My idea of education is the old Latin root, *educere*, to draw out; my idea was that I should be drawing out of them what *their* thoughts were. I was interested in getting them to formulate impressions and ideas of their own, rather than feeding them mine, and some kids loved that and some hated it.

The student, besides Phil Solomon, that I remained closest to for a long time, Steve Weisberg, went on to become a well-known and sought-after feature film editor (*The Cable Guy* [1996], *Men in Black II* [2002], *Harry Potter and the Prisoner of Azkaban* [2004] . . .). Steve was a bit of an anomaly at Binghamton, as I felt I was. I recognized him as an autodidact and just got out of his way. I think he was grateful for that.

Steve Anker, who I came to know later, was a legendary character from the past—he had graduated by the time I arrived.

I was not big on the history of film. I *was* interested in how you have to change your perspective in order to understand what's going on in a work: What do you have to do to change *your* thinking in order to figure out why this person was doing what *he* was doing?

Alan Berliner: When I arrived in Binghamton in the fall of 1973, it didn't take long to realize that the Cinema Department was *the* most dynamic place on campus. It made the Art Department seem like a Rotary Club. There was an incredible energy all around, an astounding visiting artists program, people coming from all over the world to study, or in some cases, just to hang out and absorb the scene. Imagine: I was taking classes with Peter Kubelka as a freshman! Even though I didn't know exactly who he was or what he represented, I *did* know that something really exciting was going on and I wanted to be a part of it.

I had just come from a very difficult high school experience, not to mention a very painful experience at home, culminating in my parents' ugly divorce. I remember during the summer just prior to entering college, sitting alone for hours in the middle of a stretch of rapids on the Delaware River, making a kind of pact with myself, and thinking, "It's time to refocus now, time to stop getting high all the time, time to get serious." I was just sixteen years old and primed for a transformative experience. For me, finding the Cinema Department that fall was pure synchronicity.

At their best, Larry and Ken represented a dialectic of two altogether different temperaments and aesthetics. In the collision of their personalities and sensibilities—and we're talking about two *brilliant* people here—was a tension that became fertile, dynamic, and stimulating for everyone. Both were charismatic teachers and *totally* dedicated to the art of cinema.

Larry had grown up in New York City, but in Binghamton he lived with his family in the lush green rolling hills behind the campus. Several of his films—*Fog Line* [1970], *Doorway* [1971], *Barn Rushes*, and *Horizons*—were inspired by his love for the Upstate New York landscape that enveloped his daily life. Larry emanated a kind of gentle wisdom—he was the pure blend of artistic soul and intellectual passion, someone who could talk deeply and eloquently about everything from Dostoyevsky to Schoenberg, from Heidegger to Cezanne, from Orson Welles to Michael Snow (to name just a few of his favorites).

Ken, on the other hand, was a uniquely urban creature, also a big reader, but with darker edges. He was more neurotic, more politically agitated, more prickly, perhaps you could even say more "Jewish." In the vernacular of the era, if Larry was *mellow*, Ken was *intense*. Ken exerted a powerful hold over students. He was incredibly demanding, both as a person and as a teacher. Some students idolized him to such an extent that when they didn't get the follow-through of his encouragement, it seemed as though their spirits were broken. But the truth is, if you had the strength to handle it, Ken's demanding approach could bring out the best in you. It's just that not everyone is ready—or even able—to be challenged so completely so early in their lives or in their artistic development.

Ken was also a pack rat. He and I both savor and tinker with the odds and ends, the detritus of culture. We both like surrounding ourselves with lots of *stuff*. I remember visiting Ken's loft when I was a student and being amazed at all the fascinating things there were to look at, touch, and read. There was very little separation between life and art, which is true of my own home/studio environment as well. I can't say that I emulated him in this, because I've always been a bit of an obsessive collector, but seeing his New York space definitely made a strong impression on me.

During my years at Binghamton, Ken took the bus up from New York to Binghamton every Monday, arriving in time for his evening class, and stayed through Wednesday, always carrying books, films, objects, or some kind of contentious notion to challenge us with; he always had something provocative up his sleeve.

6

Younger Colleagues and More Visitors

Dan Barnett: Ken and Larry were older than I was and had opinions and attitudes and an organized sense of the history that mattered to them. Theirs was a mantle that I was expected to adopt, but that I didn't feel comfortable with. So I didn't try to adopt it. I think that led a lot of the students to feel like they were wasting their money: they weren't getting *professed to*. But I felt I was getting them to reflect in their own ways on the things that *I* thought mattered.

I recall Phil Solomon being in one of my first classes, maybe the first one. I remember many of the people from that first semester, some of them quite well. There were a number of very strong personalities. Ken Ross. Certainly Renée Shafransky. There was Brandi Dawn Scheiner (at one point I asked the class to think for a moment about how they experienced time and what was the first thought that came to mind; Brandi: "Time is what happens between orgasms"), Bob Israel, Lee Krugman, Danny Fingeroth—and, of course, Phil, Mark Lapore, and Danny Eisenberg, though I remember those three mostly because they continued on with me at Massachusetts College of Art in Boston after I left Binghamton. David Marc was a satellite figure, since he was, I think, a graduate student.

One character who deserves a shout-out is the then dean of faculty, Peter Vukasin. When I negotiated salary with him, he impressed me as the savviest college administrator I'd ever met. I remember bumping into him on campus during the summer after my first full year of teaching—I was living in town and working on *White Heart* [1975]—and him asking how I was enjoying teaching there: at the time I was ecstatic to be paid over the summer to work and read.

I had the opportunity not only to do film work, but to continue to read and to think about my real interests, which related to abstracted language studies. This thinking, in the end, resulted in my book, *Movement as Meaning in Experimental Film.* Binghamton gave my ideas the time and space to flourish and me, the sense of legitimacy that an assistant professorship confers. Years later, when I finally started writing, it was amazing to me how fluidly and coherently I remembered what I had been thinking about during that summer in Binghamton—even though over the intervening twenty-five years I'd been too busy making a living to have had much room in my head for theoretical writing.

Saul Levine: I got to Binghamton in 1973. I always remember the date because of the Watergate hearings. I had just gotten my MFA from the Chicago Art Institute. Somewhere I saw an advertisement for the Binghamton job, and I knew Ken taught there. I'd seen a lot of Ken's work, and had met him at a show in Boston where he did shadow play—kind of an avant-garde vaudeville show. He may have come to the Art Institute when I was studying there; we certainly had seen *Tom, Tom, the Piper's Son*, which is not a big favorite of mine actually—I'm in the minority about that.

Dan Barnett: I'd met Saul Levine at the MIT film society. That was the only place in Boston where you could regularly see experimental film, and Saul was an outstanding member of the audience. We fell into conversation and showed each other what we were working on, and an increasingly intense conversation developed. I'd briefly been a graduate student at the Art Institute of Chicago—I left after a semester. Saul asked me what the Art Institute School was like, and I told him the pluses and the minuses of the personalities involved—but he still decided to go there.

Then, later, when I was at Binghamton, a new faculty line opened up and I recommended to Ken and Larry that they interview Saul, and they did; he was an obvious choice, so they hired him. Once Saul got to Binghamton, we shared a house and a studio.

Saul Levine: I applied for the Binghamton job because I liked teaching. Before going to the Art Institute, I'd taught at Tufts as an adjunct. At the time, my wife was an occupational therapy student there, and because the university wouldn't start a film program, the Tufts film society approached me to teach for them: the students got Tufts credit, but the film society paid me. Then I got fired because I was a political activist.

I'd been banned from the Tufts campus, and I could see that if I was going to get a job teaching anywhere, I needed to have an MFA. I knew Dan Barnett from film screenings around Boston. He and I were friends—not as close as we were to become at Binghamton—and Dan had studied at the Chicago Art Institute. He told me, "Oh, you could get in, and they'll probably give you money." It was such a different time: nobody paid to go to the Art Institute as a graduate student back then; you got a tuition waver. They accepted me right off—apparently John Luther Schofill knew who I was.

I went to the Art Institute partly because Marjorie Keller, who had been my student at Tufts, then my lover—one of the many things that broke up my marriage—wanted to go to there. At Tufts Margie had learned everything I had to teach her in about three weeks, but I was in love with her so I followed her to Chicago—although the idea of studying with Brakhage was very attractive too; I was already an informal disciple of his. I knew being a student at the Art Institute had to be as good as selling pretzels, which was my only option in Cambridge!

Brakhage was there. George Landow was there—I knew him from high school. And a lot of people came through: Lucy Lippard, Morgan Fisher, who I also knew from Boston. It was a very exciting period, and Chicago was a great place for a political activist—I got arrested that summer. Both Margie, who was also a political activist, and I left SDS [Students for a Democratic Society] at around that time because of political differences with the organization.

Brakhage did his lectures. Bill Brand, Louis Hock, and Coleen Fitzgibbon were my colleagues and I learned a lot from them. Margie was becoming a deeper and deeper filmmaker, and a scholar. And I met Ruby Rich, who had a love affair with Margie. Ruby's *Chick Flicks* includes her well-written essay about this period and, to my surprise, a flattering portrait of me.*

Margie's brother had commissioned her to make a film about the birth of their second child, which became *Misconception* [1977], and I was part of the team that worked with her. It was a double-system, Super-

---

*Rich: "She [Marjorie Keller] lived with Saul Levine, a filmmaker who is now a part of 8mm history but then was merely a graduate student at the School of the Art Institute (though he already looked way older than his years, a Talmudic scholar born into the wrong time and place)"—B. Ruby Rich, *Chick Flicks* (Durham: Duke University Press, 1998): 116.

8mm sound film. The experience was significant in my own development because I was making a transition from silence to sound.

So anyway, I applied for the Binghamton job—didn't expect to get it. I assumed Ken and Larry (I didn't know Larry yet) would hire one of the New York structuralist filmmakers. There were many outstanding people: Ernie Gehr, for example. Then they lost my application, which included the only copy of my Regular-8mm film, *Big Stick* [1973].

I remember calling them from Wilkes Barre, where we were working on *Misconception*—that's where Marjorie's brother lived—and asking Larry, "Hey, did you find my film?" Larry said, "Yes, it was lying on the floor in my office!" And he asked me to come up for an interview. Larry picked me up at the airport, and we had a nice time talking. Like Larry, I was coming from an English major background: our first conversation was about the difference between filmmakers like Larry and me (and Brakhage and to some extent Maya Deren), who were coming from a literature background; and people like Ken, Carolee Schneemann, and Bruce Conner, who were painters or sculptors, and for whom film was an extension of these visual art practices.

I stayed at Larry's house and we had a great dinner. The next day was the formal interview. They said they were interested in me, and I said, "Why?"—because they didn't know me or my work. "Well, we think it's interesting that you've done a lot of shows, even though you work in Regular-8." I'd had a show at Millennium and at the Cinematheque in San Francisco; I'd shown around Boston, and I always put my stuff in the Coops—so they could see I was serious. I'd taught production for three or four years in Boston and in Chicago. As it turned out, I think that it was an advantage for them that they *didn't* really know me: by hiring me they were insulting *everyone* else and not hiring one of their friends over another.

Funny story about the interview: we do the normal interview things, then Ken says, "I'm teaching a class, why don't you come along," and I say, "Oh, that sounds like fun." So we go to the class, and Ken gets up and says he's going to show this film by Victor Faccinto, who he calls "Video Vic." He shows the film, then turns to me and says, "Now, Video Vic, you take over the class." So I said, "Hi, I'm Video Vic, what do you think of my film?" We talked about the film, and eventually I revealed that I wasn't actually Video Vic. I guess I handled it well enough—they hired me.

The teaching load was two classes a semester—fucking amazing. At MassArt my load is four! Ken and Larry taught Film 101, which everyone had to take before they could take production, and that class always enrolled a hundred people. You needed someone who could hold the interest of large group. Dan and I would teach the much smaller production classes. I also taught film analysis, which enrolled thirty people or so. At Binghamton I even had *two* projectionists, which may not seem like much, but at Mass Art, I still have to do my own projecting.

Lloyd Bruce Holman: I liked Larry Gottheim. He gets the credit for founding the Cinema Department and for sustaining it during very difficult times. Larry was well liked by the students. He had a sense of humor—he would introduce me to visitors as being the only person in the Cinema Department who actually had a degree in the subject we were teaching. And since I was the only non-Jewish person in the department, Larry haled me as "our token goy," which I still find amusing.

I can't say the same about Ken Jacobs. The arts are conducive to egocentricity—dancers, painters, writers must believe in the validity of themselves and their work—but Ken went beyond our usual bounds. A self-proclaimed genius, Ken held everyone else in contempt. A book about independent filmmakers had commented that "Ken Jacobs is a violently opinionated person"—*understating* the point!* Ken was a petulant child. It also annoyed some of us that Ken was publicly dismissive and verbally abusive to his wife, Flo.

Others came and went. I remember Saul Levine and Dan Barnett, both from Boston. Saul's film work was mainly in 8mm, which put him at the bottom of the pecking order in the eyes of those who worked in 16mm. Saul had been involved with the Students for a Democratic Society and his political stance was evident in his films. It's possible that some of the things he told me about his SDS actions could still get Saul in trouble, so I won't say anything further.

Dan Barnett was an inventive filmmaker. I recall an experiment he tried: working in a darkened room, he removed the prime lens from his movie camera and directed narrow beams of light onto the color 16mm film passing through the camera gate. On screen, the effect was unearthly.

Phil Solomon: I studied *filmmaking* primarily with Dan Barnett and Saul Levine, and would continue with them a few years later at MassArt, where I got my MFA. Saul was a different sensibility from anybody else at the college—much more of an unreconstructed, leftist, sixties, hippie freak. Saul had just arrived when I began to take production courses, so he was my first film teacher.

What I learned from Saul, especially as a beginning filmmaker, was an appreciation of the mundane, of the daily, of the rough-hewn beauty

---

*Sheldon Renan, in a caption for a photograph of Jacobs in *An Introduction to the American Underground Film* (New York; Dutton, 1967): 148.

at the fringes. Saul was into a certain kind of funky, raw, Regular-8 and Super-8, nonglorious, nonheroic, from-the-soul filmmaking. When I think of Saul, I think of the kind of phonograph you had when you were a kid, playing a warped and scratched Champion Jack Dupree blues record—this being part of the soundtrack of Saul's greatest work, *Notes of an Early Fall* [1976].

When I was starting out, I would bring in loose, off-the-cuff stuff, shot in Super-8, and Saul had an ability, rare in a teacher, to find interesting and positive things to say about almost anything. He was open, encouraging, and unpredictable. Like many others, I was going through my imitation-Brakhage phase and showed the class a little out-of-focus roll that I'd shot of my girlfriend, extremely close-up. Saul said it reminded him of Brakhage's *Loving* [1957]—only this was better. I don't know whether that was a put-on or the way he really felt, but I walked out of that class thinking, "I can *do* this!"

Dan Barnett came to cinema from studying philosophy and was essentially applying philosophical models of thinking (Quine and Wittgenstein, primarily) to the language of cinema. I recently took on his dense, difficult and very rewarding *Movement as Meaning in Experimental Film*, and it reminded me a great deal of his musings in the classroom.

Dan was a formidable character for my group. We were somewhat in awe and intimidated by his fierce intelligence, and simultaneously confounded and a bit alienated by his utter lack of interest in popular culture. Dan was working on his Wittgensteinian tour de force, *White Heart*, a stoned-out, whacked out, original and visionary work which influenced the way all of us thought about color, sound and image. *White Heart* lives on in my own work and in the work of Nina Fonoroff, Alan Berliner, Dan Eisenberg, and Mark LaPore. I hope it sees the light of digital day at some point.

Danny Fingeroth: I was a film production major, not a film theory major, and Ken was my senior thesis adviser. I made two films, one that started out as my thesis and one that I saw as a more casual work but that ended up being my thesis. The film that I thought would be my thesis was a narrative (I was so daring!) based on an old Yiddish short story called "Bontsha the Silent," by I. L. Peretz—a profound and ironic story about a guy who lives a self-effacing, impoverished life in a Jewish shtetl in pre-Holocaust Eastern Europe (in my film Binghamton stood in for a Polish town, and Saul Levine played God). I didn't finish that film until after I'd graduated.

The film that became my thesis was inspired by movies like *Pull My Daisy* [1959, Robert Frank] and *Blonde Cobra*. It was unedited reels of just me and a friend clowning around, to a soundtrack of improvised comedy routines in the style of Carl Reiner and Mel Brooks. It was called *Gorillas in a Can* [1976]. It was well regarded by the department and was eventually shown at the Collective on a double bill with Cheryl Gorman's *Trail of Dreams* [1973], a brilliant film that was a sensation around the Cinema Department; it was well made and smart and funny, head and shoulders above other student films—a meditation on the images of women in the movies, but a lot more than that too.

For years after I left Binghamton I thought of myself as a film guy who had a day job in comics. I was working on a Super-8 film opus that I never finished; it was going to be my montage statement on existence. I felt I had a perfect avant-garde title: "Negative Release Trauma Vacation"—don't ask me what it meant. After ten years or so, I accepted that I'm a comics guy, not a filmmaker. Interestingly, I've recently been a producer on some films, including *Irwin: A New York Story* [2011, directed by Dan Makara], a documentary about Irwin Hasen, the cocreator and artist of the classic Dondi newspaper strip, a fascinating guy who just turned ninety-five.

Bill T. Jones: I remember seeing some of the Cinema Department student projects: a Warholian experiment, a pastiche of George Romero–esque horror films, a flicker film . . . And I remember somebody from the Art Department coming to give a critique, and saying, "The first problem is that your films look messy!" We almost laughed him out of the room. The Cinema Department students were young bums, definitely into trash art, into art that was *not* tidy. In general, the Art Department and the Cinema Department had very little to say to each other.

Larry Gottheim: The thing to remember about the cinema program was that cinema was a legitimate academic subject at Binghamton. A cinema course had the same value as a history course or an English course.

In time, the administration changed, and decided they couldn't support anybody who wasn't generating student hours. They approached me and asked if Ralph could teach photography as part of the Cinema Department. Though we were suspicious of photography, we said that he could—but that he wouldn't be part of the regular department: when it came time for us to hire a new person in film, we didn't want them to say, "You've already hired someone." They said, "Oh, no problem about that," but of course in the end that's what happened.

I liked and admired Ralph, who had started to do his video thing and wanted to teach video classes. I was reluctant about going along with the administration, but thought incorporating video was an interesting possibility: at the time, having video production within the program was pioneering. Peer Bode, who was one of our students, got involved with video through Ralph and would go on to develop an important program at Alfred University.

Ralph Hocking: After a certain point, students in the Cinema Department had to take film *and* video in order to graduate. There wasn't much video, just my production course, but it was mandatory.

Sherry Miller Hocking: Because of Ralph's interests, the video students were focused on production, while the film students, although they did a lot of production work, also took theory and history courses, which were always *film* courses not involved with other media.

Larry Gottheim: Another thing that was part of this early visionary era was the School of Advanced Technology, which was originally started as a creative think tank. A lot of the economy of Binghamton was IBM, which had started nearby in Endicott at the Endicott Time Clock Company, and there were all these engineers around. The idea was that there would be a program of creative thinking that would be useful for these engineers. Walter Lowen was the director of the School of Advanced Technology, and it happened that their offices were located down the hall from us. They became supporters of the Cinema Department because what we were doing was right in line with what they were doing. The transformation of computers from whole buildings to smaller, then personal computers was happening at the same time as the development of video.

Heinz Emigholz: I started filmmaking in 1968 and screened the results, shot in Super-8mm and 16mm, at the yearly showcases of the Hamburger Filmcoop. But in 1970 I declared my filmmaking finished; I'd decided instead to study the writings of Hegel, Marx, and Edmund Husserl—and never looked at my sixties films again. My philosophical studies ended in 1972 with a nervous breakdown; and in a reversion to my interest in working with pieces of time, I started filmmaking again.

I wrote a score for a single-frame landscape film, to be filmed in black and white with a 16mm Bolex, in a forest near Frankfurt during the winter of 1972–73. I called it *Schenec-Tady*—from the name of a town (Schenectady, NY) I had found on an American postcard that had caught my eye because of its totally unrealistic color separation. The sound of "Schenectady" related to my film. Klaus Wyborny smuggled an early version of the film into the program of the Hamburger Filmschau in June 1973, where Larry Gottheim had been invited to screen his new film,

Horizons. Larry explained later that he went to see *Schenec-Tady* because its title was the name of a city not far from his hometown. He loved my film and invited me to come to the United States.

In the spring of 1974, I abandoned my university studies for good. I got a DAAD [Deutscher Akademischer Austausch Dienst: German Academic Exchange Service] grant to do films in the US ($400 for ten months), and in August I traveled to New York. The DAAD grant involved visiting a university—otherwise the US could not have granted me a visa. Larry was of great help with this. I settled in New York City, and visited the Cinema Department in Binghamton every now and then to screen films and meet friends—interesting screenings and fruitful discussions that went well beyond cinema.

My visits to Binghamton led to collaborations with David Marc, Art Spiegelman, and Marcia Bronstein, and in some cases to lifelong friendships. I may have met Steve Anker, Renée Shafransky, Richard Levine, Phil Weisman, and Jim Hoberman at Binghamton—though I may be confusing Binghamton with the Collective, which was up and running in New York City: my visits with Larry and Debby Gottheim and to the Collective were my main connections to Binghamton. I also participated in two publications, *No Rose* and *Idiolects*, both founded by Binghamton people in conjunction with the Collective.*

I became friends with Ken Jacobs and Ernie Gehr later, in New York City.

Klaus Wyborny: I met Larry Gottheim in Hamburg in 1973, when he visited to show *Horizons*; and I met Ken Jacobs the same year at the Festival of Independent Avant-Garde Film, held at the National Film Theatre in London. While there, I acted as a living statue in one of Ken's shadow plays. They both liked my film *The Birth of a Nation* [1973], and in 1974 Larry invited me to teach at Binghamton. I arrived in October or November of 1974, and stayed until the end of August.

**Idiolects* and *No Rose* began publication in summer, 1976. Steve Anker, Lee Krugman, and John Maliga were "Production Coordinators" for the first issue of *Idiolects*; Krugman and "Rotating Editors" Andrew Anker and Mark Graff edited the second issue; Krugman, Nick Penkovsky, and Steve Weisberg, the third; Helene Kaplan and Bob Schneider, the fourth. Richard Levine and Renée Shafransky edited the early issues of *No Rose*. Early contributors to *Idiolects* include Steve Anker, Jim Hoberman, Helene Kaplan, David Tafler, and Richard Levine; to *No Rose*, Marcia Bronstein, Helene Kaplan, Lee Krugman, Richard Levine, and Ken Ross. Heinz Emigholz contributed to volume 1, number 2 and volume 2, number 1, of *No Rose*; and later on, to *Idiolects*, no. 7 (1979).

I taught a theory class (I think there were about twenty students) called Elementary Editing Theory (about which I published a 460-page book in 2013 [*Elementare Schnitt-Theorie des Spielfilms*/"Elementary Editing Theory of Motion Pictures" (Berlin: Lit Verlag)]. And a filmmaking class. One assignment was to convert a short Schönberg piano piece into film; and two or three times I brought a few hundred vintage landscape postcards and distributed them so that each student had some: the assignment was to order the postcards in a sequence that could become a film.

During those months I did film shows all over the country.

Dan Barnett: I used to show what I was working on quite regularly when I taught—not just finished films, but experiments. I thought that was a good way to expose students to the process and open them up to the idea that failure might be one path to knowledge.

I had a friend in Boston who made a practice of inviting musicians to her home a couple times a year for a feast (she was renowned for inventive cooking), but they would have to play for their supper. The house—it was right near Symphony Hall—was like a mini–opera house with balconies and boxes arranged around a small stage. The catch was that regularly she would spring a surprise on the musicians, something likely to be unfamiliar, and then have them attempt an unrehearsed sight reading. These were the most interesting musical events for me—because her rule was that no matter how out of sync the musicians got, they couldn't stop playing. The formal tensions that developed were occasionally hilarious, but always interesting. I was, and still am, interested in aesthetic tensions that skate along the edge—in the moment when forms break or fall apart. This seemed a new and unexplored kind of formal tension, begging for a whole different approach to resolution.

At Binghamton I realized that I was in a position to study that very phenomenon, since the university had a great grad school of music that seemed to specialize in chamber music, and the Cinema Department had an Arriflex BL with a thousand-foot magazine. So I got different groups together and tried to recreate the phenomenon I'd seen in Boston so I could film it and really study the effect—it took me quite a while to get the hang of catching the moments I was looking for. The results were interesting but in a different way from what I expected—these were grad students who were more self-conscious about their proficiency, so they never reached the levels of hilarity generated by the pros as *they* struggled. Another unsuccessful experiment.

Like a good deal of my work (in those days and these), that project was intended to teach *me* something rather than to be an addition to my "*oeuvre.*" I have scores of unreleased experiments—interesting maybe to students of the medium, but in my eyes ultimately unsuccessful.

Klaus Wyborny: At Binghamton I attended all Ken's lectures. I remember his doing an analysis of *Scarface* [1932] that lasted a whole semester. What brilliant teaching! Ken and I shared an apartment in Binghamton, where I had access to his fantastic record collection. Larry Gottheim was also very important; I remember seeing his editing scripts for *Mouches Volantes*—very impressive. Saul Levine was there of course, and Dan Barnett, whose film experiment about a string quartet I found astonishing.

Among the students, I remember Renée Shafranksy, and Alan Berliner who I met again later in Berlin when he showed films there. Most impressive at that time was Danny Eisenberg; we shared work in Berlin and Hamburg later on.

Also interesting were events held at the Experimental Television Center that Ralph Hocking had set up downtown. I remember seeing Nam June Paik there.

The weekly film shows put on by the Harpur Film Society were excellent. I did two of those, and Heinz Emigholz, with whom I shared an apartment in New York City, showed his *Schenec-Tady* series.

There's one thing I *failed* to do in Binghamton: the historian Fernand Braudel was teaching there at that time (I didn't even know it!), and I would have loved to attend his lectures [the Fernand Braudel Center for the Study of Economics, Historical Systems, and Civilizations was founded at Binghamton University in 1976]. Well, as Ken Jacobs once put it: Stupidity is God.

My students and I made a music recording for my film *Pictures of the Lost Word* [1975]: I played a 25-minute piece on the Steinway in Lecture Hall 1, and we discussed how it should be recorded. In Binghamton I also finished the editing of that film and did the sound recordings and the elaborate sound editing. *Pictures of the Lost Word* was premiered at Anthology Film Archives in May 1975.

Saul Levine: Ken, Dan, and I once had a discussion about teaching. It was a very strange night, for one thing because Ken and Dan were both going out with Renée Shafransky. We were over at Ken's house—Flo may have been there, I don't know. We were watching *East of Borneo* [1931, directed by George Melford], the film that Joseph Cornell made *Rose Hobart* [1936] from, and possibly *Cobra Woman* [1944, directed by Robert Siodmak]. Ken and Dan were both trying to thread the projector and it became this macho thing, which I found a little horrifying.

Then we got into a discussion about teaching, and Ken put forward the notion that a teacher is a kind of shaman and very interventionist. I had those tendencies too, but had struggled with them, and I said, "Ken, I don't want that responsibility; a teacher should be a *teacher*, not a therapist, not a shaman." As a teacher, Ken was very charismatic; he left a very big imprint on his students. I put forward the idea that the teacher should be invisible. Of course, both of these are ideals that nobody actually lives up to: in fact, Ken and I were both mixtures.

When Mark McElhatten introduced me at Views [Views from the Avant-Garde, from 1997 to 2013, an avant-garde sidebar to the New York Film Festival] a few years ago, he said that he had always been impressed that when he would come across strong filmmakers, filmmakers from very diverse backgrounds, they would all have been students of mine. I made the joke that I leave my fingerprints on my *films* (because I'm kind of a messy filmmaker!), not on my students; my ideal has always been to help students find themselves.

Dan and I taught more production than Larry and Ken, and less history and theory—although Dan was certainly theoretical: Phil Solomon remembers Dan asking the class, "How do you make a film about nothing?" I like to teach splicing. I'm certainly not the technician that Dan was, but I was good at teaching basic filmmaking and getting people excited.

As a teacher, I have something like a psychoanalytic approach. I've often found that when students come to me with problems in their work and I just let them talk, at the end they say, "Saul, you really helped me a lot!" All I've done is say, "Yes," and I might have asked a question here or there.

There's a Hassidic joke about how, when you get to heaven, the judge doesn't ask you whether you were Moses; he asks you whether you were, in my case, *Saul.* I think that in being an artist, you don't have to be somebody else; you *do* have to find your own voice. (See fig. 32.)

Daniel Eisenberg: Ernie Gehr was my first production teacher. I remained close with Ernie for many years. And I learned an enormous amount from some of the visitors who came for short periods: Klaus Wyborny, and Tony Conrad, who was there for a few weeks, and Alfons Schilling, who I had for a semester. Brakhage would come every year. I was in Binghamton at a very fortunate time; there was money in the system and a lot of people passing through. When I first arrived, Nick Ray was still there—like Ken, an overwhelming presence, but strange; I didn't have much to do with him either.

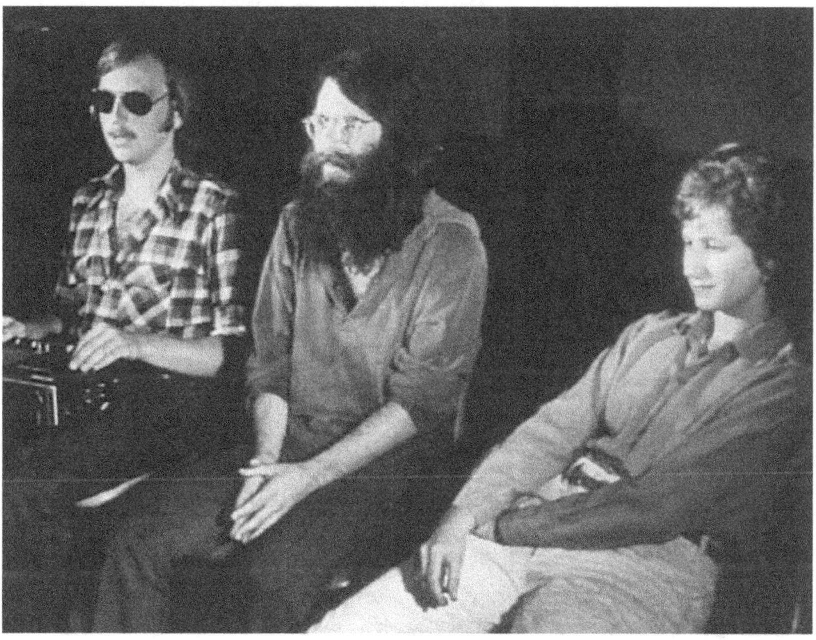

Figure 32. Saul Levine (middle) with Binghamton students in Bill Brand's *Before the Fact*, shot in a Binghamton classroom in 1974. The entire film, which is part of a series of short films called "Cartoons," is available on Brand's website: www.bboptics.com/cartoons.html. Courtesy Bill Brand.

Dan Barnett and Saul Levine were important to many of us. Dan brought in kinds of work that the other professors didn't, mostly current work of people of his generation. Saul also brought in visiting artists, often people he had gone to school with. Saul and Dan were junior faculty members and could turn you on to people who had just come out of graduate school and were making work in a very different way from the older generation. With Dan and Saul, the focus wasn't the New York art scene; it was people from Chicago, people from San Francisco.

From my admittedly limited perspective, both Dan and Ken had powerful egos, and I felt that ultimately Ken couldn't stand having Dan around, and made sure that he would leave—though Dan was a very effective teacher. The younger faculty definitely nurtured us as filmmakers much more than the older faculty. Dan organized a screening of his students' work at the Collective. That was my first public show, a big deal for me. The older faculty expected us to be acolytes; the younger faculty were interested in creating an active film culture of filmmakers, *participants*.

Actually, I didn't learn much production while I was at Binghamton. I absolutely learned how to look at films in a deep way, but there was little emphasis on technique. I distinctly remember saying to myself as I was leaving Binghamton, "Now I need to learn how to *make* films!" And so I went to New York and, being a working-class person, I found a job and learned.

Saul Levine: Binghamton was a great place to see films and to encounter people thinking about film in unusual ways, like Klaus Wyborny, who was using computer programs to get away from individual decision-making. I remember going to Ernie Gehr's class on Eisenstein's *October* [1928] and Ernie saying, "*October* is not about Marxism or revolution or the Russians; it's about circles." I would go to Ken's lectures—sometimes Ken would get upset at me because my face would indicate that I was disagreeing with him or thinking about other things.

Dan Barnett and I were roommates, living together, first in Friendsville, Pennsylvania in a trailer, which was way out in the country, then in a house in Binghamton. Dan was struggling with *White Heart*, making the film on a workbench with a squawk box—sound was important to him and he paid a lot of attention to what others were doing with sound, particularly Michael Snow. I'm *in White Heart*, the figure swimming, and my voice is also in the film.

Tony Conrad: As I remember, I was in Binghamton for about a month in the spring of 1974. Several moments stand out.

Ernie Gehr lectured (I *do* mean *lectured*—in a banked-seat lecture hall) for *a week* on *The Man with a Movie Camera* [1929], endlessly noodling through the film from beginning to end, a few feet at a time, on an analytic projector—to the visible dismay and distraction of the students. Ernie, after all, is a quiet, even unassuming speaker. But as he unfolded one alchemically tangled image after another, I was rapt; Ernie's commentary was full of fire and insight—possibly the most perspicuous and continuously inspired talk I've ever heard on cinema.

I also had a personal comeuppance, when I denounced the film ideas of two outspoken women in my class. We had a memorable confrontation that I remembered later, when I was brought around completely to admire the work of one of them: Coleen Fitzgibbon. This was my first year as a teacher—and at the time I was also following some hot directions in my own work, so I was full of conviction and energy.

But this incident helped me realize how wrong I could be as a teacher, and what I could learn by paying attention to the fresh initiatives of students and younger artists.

Larry Gottheim: Lowell Bodger deserves mention. I got to know him when he was a projectionist at Millennium. He had a wide range of interests and we had mutually intense meetings and correspondence (that I have kept). He was someone whose visits were generally "under the radar." He came to Binghamton once or twice as visiting filmmaker or just to visit me. Once he happened to be there at the same time as Morgan Fisher and helped Morgan work on a film.

Lowell had an early interest in the mapping of space. He went to some of the early NASA conferences, and had NASA space maps on the walls of his studio near Union Square. Like Alfons Schilling's work, Lowell's had an oblique intellectual aspect that was lost on those who were only looking for beautiful surfaces. Alfons turned me on to aspects of Renaissance music and architecture, and the history of memory. My frequent visits to the studios of both Lowell and Alfons were inspiring, and I always left with my head buzzing.

I lost track of Lowell after he had become interested in the history of typefaces. A couple of years ago his wife contacted me to tell me he had succumbed to Alzheimer's. I went to a memorial for Lowell at Columbia University, thinking it would be a small, obscure event and found a large classroom filled with professors and scholars. It seems that Lowell had become a leading figure in the study of typefaces, and he was worshiped by those present.

His wife organized a screening of his films at Anthology last year, but I couldn't go.

Morgan Fisher: I was at Binghamton in the spring of 1974 for, I think, one week. I could be mistaken about the length, though I recall that after I got back to Santa Monica, I went on unemployment, and the woman at the office was incredulous, and I think annoyed, that I had gotten paid what to her was clearly an unimaginably and unjustly enormous amount of money (between $600 and $700, as I recall): "You got that *for one week?*"

I had the idea for my film *240x* [1974] before I got to Binghamton, and it was a stroke of pure luck that at Binghamton I found the equipment necessary to make the film—a xerox machine, an animation camera (an Oxberry, in fact), a cel punch; and of course a 16mm camera that could shoot sync sound (an Arriflex BL, as I recall), and a Nagra—and people willing to help.

The camera operator was Bill Prenovitz, who was a student. The sound recordist was L. Bruce Holman, the technical person in the department. Bruce contributed practical articles to *Filmmakers' Newsletter* that he illustrated with drawings. I still have an issue with an article by him showing how to make a tripod spider, illustrated with a drawing that is technically accurate and at the same time has lots of character. Both Bill and Bruce were very nice guys, although my memory of Bruce is a little more vivid because I spent more time with him.

The production assistant was Lowell Bodger. I recall first meeting him when I had a show at Millennium in 1973, where he was the projectionist. In later years I saw Lowell several times in New York and once in Los Angeles, when he had come to the Jet Propulsion Laboratory in Pasadena to be there when images were received from some early vehicle sent out into space. I always enjoyed his company. Later, he became interested in printing with hot metal type. He traveled to buy up fonts before they were melted down. He called himself a typographer and produced material printed by letterpress on a proofing press at his studio on Union Square. Once in a while he sent me examples, which I enjoyed very much and still have. He made films. His sensibility persuaded me that they should be of great interest—but I was never able to see any of them.

L. Bruce Holman lived some ways north of Binghamton. After my stay, he drove me to Bob Huot's farm in New Berlin. I had met Bob the year before at a film festival in London [the Festival of Independent Avant-Garde Film, held in London in 1973]. From there I went to Rochester to do research on the film about Muybridge that Thom Andersen was working on [*Eadweard Muybridge, Zoopraxographer*, 1975].

It was during that week (or perhaps during another of my visits to Binghamton in those years) that Larry Gottheim was doing a project with students on what he called para-cinema, titled "The Perils of Space." There were wooden constructions scattered around the campus that in various ways enacted references to film. The one I remember was made of what must have been two-by-fours. It looked like a free-standing vertical ladder; that is, parallel uprights between which were evenly spaced horizontal members—a diagram of a strip of film. It was maybe five feet across and the height was in proportion for a length of maybe five or six "frames." It was painted matte black. "The Perils of Space" was certainly an evocative title, but I can't say that I understood it.

I stayed at the Vestal Motel. At the time "Bennie and Jets" by Elton John was on the charts. It played incessantly at the bar across the parking lot from the motel, where I ate dinner. Cheeseburgers and fries and beer and "Bennie and the Jets" for a week. I despised the song then, and still do, not for any unhappy associations—there weren't any, although I was lonely—but because I find it a wretched song.

I remember the weather being gray and overcast. Puddles and mud. I think the snow had just melted.

Dan Barnett: A significant moment for me was finishing *White Heart* [1975] and realizing that *very* few people got it. I had had much higher expectations. Of the cultural mavens, I think Steve Anker was just about the only one who understood the film. Saul Levine also, definitely, but he was already in tune with what I was doing: Saul's aesthetic and mine were so complementary that I intuitively understood almost everything he did and vice versa. At the time, I was involved with the usual avant-garde issues: poetic and musical structures, surfaces, frames, ellipsis, plasticity, the musicality of motion . . . I was more curious about the ontology of the image and the psychology of perception than most people, I think, and I was actively exploring, particularly in *White Heart*, the concept of omnivalence that I talk about in my book.

One of the reasons I'd accepted the job at Binghamton was that they had a mixing studio and I'd finally be able to explore sound in a way that I couldn't afford to do before.

At Binghamton I taught the technical side of production really emphatically because I could tell that this was a weakness of the department. I had worked as a union editor and as a cameraman and as a sound recordist and sound editor. I started out at Education Development Center Film Studio in Waltham, Massachusetts. I left EDC to freelance—though I was still working intensely on my own films. I was really the only one there (besides Nick Ray) who had a "professional" filmmaking background. The bias in the department against craft often bothered me.

There was also Bruce Holman, the department's technical assistant. He was dedicated and very knowledgeable, also very friendly—the students liked him. I have a clear memory of Bruce's face and his spirit.

Alan Berliner: I think the best thing about Ken and Larry and the Binghamton experience was that the focus was always on what it meant to be an artist in the world. They weren't teaching filmmaking so much as they were sensitizing us—*inspiring us* might be a better way of saying it—to make connections with history, with culture, to art, to books, to music, to philosophy, always emphasizing the sacrifices and dedication required in a lifetime commitment to art-making. Of course, each of them approached that mission in a different way.

At Binghamton, production classes were never about the technical mastery of equipment. We learned what we needed to learn in order to do what we needed to do; what we *were* learning at Binghamton was how to think as artists.

I think the department's ownership of Lecture Hall 6, which had been transformed into a black-box theater was *very* important; it was *ours*; no one else had access to the space, even when we weren't using it. Lecture Hall 6 had an aura; the room's dark walls, the enclosed projection booth, and the focused intensity of what went on there—classes, visiting artist talks, student film shows, senior thesis screenings, conversations, debates, even filmmaking (I shot my first 16mm film, *Patent Pending* [1975], in that room)—always made it seem special.

My personal affinity was to Larry, but I strongly felt the impact of Ken as well. I bonded with Larry, and I suppose many people might say I also emulated him. When he showed me his methodology for making *Horizons*, with all those index cards,* I remember thinking to myself how Larry's extraordinary attention to subtlety and detail, combined with his incredible obsessive energy, was something I could totally relate to, something I aspired to. I always felt that I was an ideal audience for Larry's films, and I loved talking with him about them. In many ways, Larry taught me how to look at images, how to savor details and nuances, and how the ways in which we describe and notate images while we work with them play a critical role in what we end up doing with them.

Larry also introduced me to the idea of para-cinema, and I was part of a small group of students who presented a performance at the Collective in 1976, called "The Perils of Space." The idea that you could work with cinematic ideas and concepts without actually making films was something that excited me, and in many ways helped inspire the installation work I continue to produce to this day.

I remember hearing that Ken had been doing shadow-play performances in the early seventies, but I never had a chance to see them. Of course, later he began his "Nervous System" performances, which are not only breathtaking, but continue to push the boundaries of cinema.

Larry and I had a special relationship. I even babysat for his children. Though I don't see him very much these days, he has a permanent warm spot in my heart.

Larry Gottheim: The contributions of Saul and Dan cannot be overestimated. Dan and Saul had their own version of the twenty-four-hours-

*See Scott MacDonald, *The Garden in the Machine* (Berkeley: University of California Press, 2001), pp. 30–37 for a discussion of the process that resulted in *Horizons*.

a-day commitment to the department. They lived together and would have screenings practically every night, or at least very frequently, at their house. The students would be showing work, as would Dan and Saul, who were always working. This was a very strong thing. (See fig. 33.)

In addition each had a presence in the editing facilities in the Lecture Hall basement. Saul's students worked in 8mm, and we had a room with individual cubicles with 8mm editing stations. These would be busy all the time, and frequently Saul would be there.

I had worked hard to get information on the equipment that would be needed for a 16mm sound transfer and editing facility, though I didn't myself have experience in working with this equipment. Dan came and was not only familiar with that kind of facility, but was using it in his work on what became *White Heart*. So when you went down to the basement at night, you might find students at work on their 8mm projects, and Dan working on his film with some students around. It was only after this that I myself started to work seriously with 16mm sound. I didn't get a Steenbeck until shortly before I left Binghamton, so I too worked on my films, from *Mouches Volantes* [1976] on, in the basement of Lecture Hall. Later, I regularly taught the advanced filmmaking class that dealt with sound.

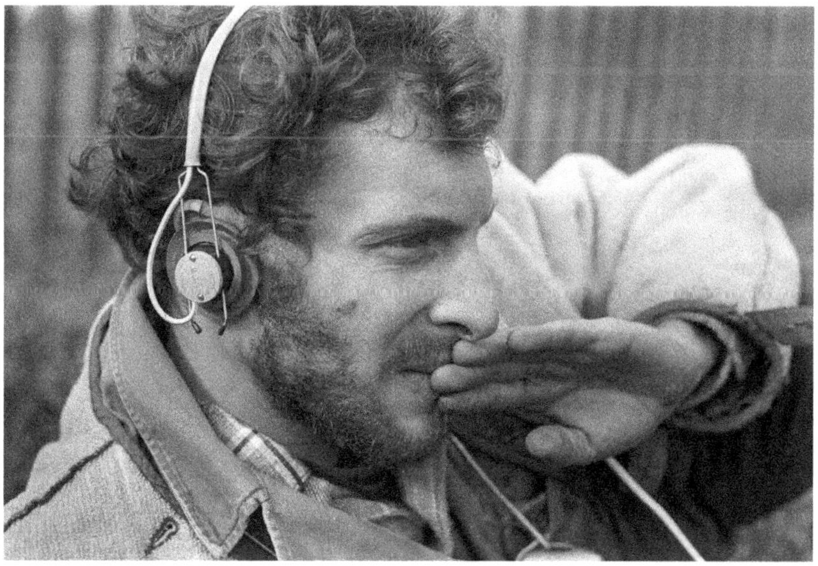

Figure 33. Dan Barnett, possibly in Binghamton. Photograph by David Vogt. Courtesy David Vogt.

7

Politics

Alan Berliner: Saul Levine and Dan Barnett were popular and inspiring presences, offering alternative approaches to the poetics and politics of filmmaking. Saul in particular often led with politics. He was a member of Looking Left, a radical collective at Binghamton that also published an occasional newsletter; I believe he was the only faculty member in the group. At that time Saul's 8mm films emphasized an intense, rhythmic, single-frame montage, sometimes containing hundreds of cement splices. In some of his films, the splice bar (and the implied act of making all of those hand-made cuts) is the dominant visual element.

Saul and Dan were a generation younger than Ken and Larry; they were, each in his own way, "hippies," closer in age to the students, and more comfortable hanging out with them outside of class. At some point, I think Ken became a bit wary of this, especially when he sensed that some students were also beginning to emulate Saul's single-frame montage aesthetic.

Dan Barnett had been a philosopher, or at least a serious student of philosophy, and brought a jaunty, high-minded cerebral energy to the department. He had a devilish smile and a mischievous demeanor, and he was also technically savvy with the tools of filmmaking. In many ways, Dan and Saul were like-minded comrades who offered an alternative poetics—and also a complementary countercultural politics—to the life and spirit of the department. For many students, they helped balance the prevailing influences and looming presences of both Larry and Ken. (See fig. 34.)

Also not to be forgotten is Ralph Hocking, who was a kind of gentle giant—a tall, Buddha-like figure with a long, thick white beard, who

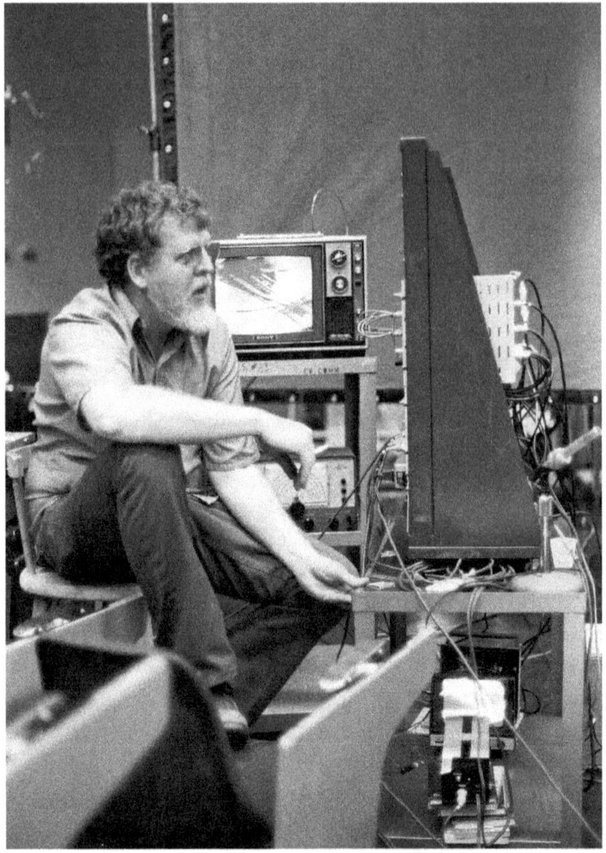

Figure 34. Ralph Hocking at the Experimental Television Center. Courtesy Mark Goldstein.

always wore the same blue denim jacket. In his own way, right in front of our eyes, Ralph was quietly (he was a man of few words) championing and pioneering the development of video art in his own kingdom, the Experimental Television Center in downtown Binghamton. Ralph was almost always above or beyond the fray of department politics, and managed to stay on good terms with everyone. Then again, you might say that behind the scenes he had the best seat in the house.

Of course, Ernie Gehr brought his mysteries and his magic. Alfons Schilling came from Switzerland and gave classes on art and visual perception. Visiting filmmakers and artists were passing through all the time. It was an incredibly dynamic place.

Ernie Gehr: At some point after the summer of 1972, Binghamton offered me a full-time, tenure-track position. I had just started teaching at Bard College on a one-year contract, so I said, "I would be interested, but I have a contract at Bard for this year and after that, I'll need a break before I start teaching full time." They agreed to this, so in 1974, I went to Binghamton as a regular full-time faculty hire—but didn't stay there for very long.

Initially I thought of commuting between New York and Binghamton (as Ken did), at least until Myrel [Myrel Glick, Gehr's wife] graduated from NYU. I thought the weekly bus commute would be easy, but that did not turn out to be the case for me. I found the bus rides stressful and exhausting. In time it also became clear to me that neither Myrel nor I were ready to move to Binghamton.

But also, the atmosphere in the department had changed. In the absence of Ken, who was on leave, and what seemed to be Larry's primary focus on his own work, Saul Levine and Dan Barnett were more or less running the department and determining its character. I was not comfortable with the changes. I stayed about a year, then resigned.

David Marc: I graduated in 1972, then came back in 1974 for an MA in English—after I'd worked at NBC, which Ken liked very much—I remember him saying, "That's a rigorous thing to do!" I became Ken's TA.

During my years as a graduate student, Dan Barnett and Saul Levine were teaching. In terms of background and conventional academic credentials, Dan, who I think had left the Art Institute of Chicago before finishing, fit right in with Ken. Saul was (and has remained) very political. I think for Saul, Ken and Larry's devotion to art, to aestheticism, was a bit much.

I had a sense that Ken expected Saul and Dan to model what they were doing on what he did, but their approaches were very different.

Dan Barnett has remained a friend of mine. We're on opposite coasts now, but when I was at Brandeis, he was living in Boston and we picked up again as friends. Whenever I go out to the San Francisco area I see Dan—his wife is very high up at Lucasfilm. In some ways Dan is a consummate intellectual, and a compliment from him is worth ten compliments from anybody else. When my book, *Bonfire of the Humanities*, was rejected by Hill and Wang after they had given me an advance,

I was very down. Dan read the manuscript from one end to the other and told me, "You've really achieved something here; don't let anybody tell you anything different." His response sustained me; I'll always owe Dan for that.

By 1974–75 the Cinema Department was already losing its mystique. When I was Ken's TA, students complained about his courses, even writing derogatory letters to the school newspaper. This new student generation couldn't see what Ken was delivering; they could only see what appeared to them to be egotism, pretension, and vanity. Of course, those things were *there*, and Ken's classes could become *only* that if you didn't understand what you were being offered in return.

Daniel Eisenberg: Binghamton was a very male environment and to be frank, a very abusive male environment. Many women had to suffer the sexual advances of their professors. I found it repellent. I would say that many of the professors had a predatory approach to the women in the classroom. I come from a generation that reacted very deeply to that; the ethical universe we live in is all about the relationship of professor to student being a kind of sacred space in which certain lines can't be crossed.

It was very clear that the *attractive* women in the class—or the women considered attractive—were dealt with very differently than the men; you could tell they were given favors, and you knew there was a subtext: something was going on, and though you didn't know exactly what it was, you *knew* what it was.

I ran the Harpur Film Society for one year, just after Ken Ross and Richard Levine; they handed it off to me with the coffers empty. Those guys were kind of crazy, and I think they used the Film Society money as their personal slush fund—so I had to start pretty much from scratch. I did a subscription series that was quite successful, and I was able put some money back into the Film Society. I remember handing the money off to Alan Berliner, saying, "You know what to do with this, right?"—which was to rent better films and bring interesting people to Binghamton. (See figs. 35 and 36.)

All in all, my Binghamton experience was leavened by my deep interests in literature and in history. I split my time pretty evenly between the Cinema Department and the English Department. I did a lot of independent research on the notebooks of James Joyce in the libraries at Cornell and Buffalo. I learned as much about producing time-based work from looking at those notebooks as I did from the visiting artists.

But Binghamton was a place where my initial interest in cinema was nurtured and expanded, and I learned from many teachers and visitors that cinema was still to be invented by all of us. In the end, that was an incredibly empowering force that has endured in my creative life.

Saul Levine: Wherever you go, there's some anti-Semitism, but SUNY-Binghamton was the most Jewish campus I've ever taught at. I remember once being in line in the cafeteria and somebody saying, "I want a bagel with cream cheese and lox" in this New York Jewish-inflected accent. I turned around and it was a black person! From my point of view—I was coming from Chicago and Boston—Binghamton was *not* the most anti-Semitic place I had experienced. There were a lot of Jews in the administration: Norman Cantor, the undergraduate dean, for example. It was Upstate New York, not the Lower East Side and some of the Binghamton natives saw SUNY-Binghamton as "Jew York," but I thought that was *great*. It was exciting to be in a place with so much Jewish culture.

I remember running into a more specific kind of prejudice. When Dan Barnett and I were looking for a house, we wanted to live out in the country and were about to rent a place when the owner said, "It's great that you're Binghamton professors! What department do you teach in?" We said the Cinema Department and that killed the deal—she had rented to Nick Ray, who had cut holes in the ceiling.

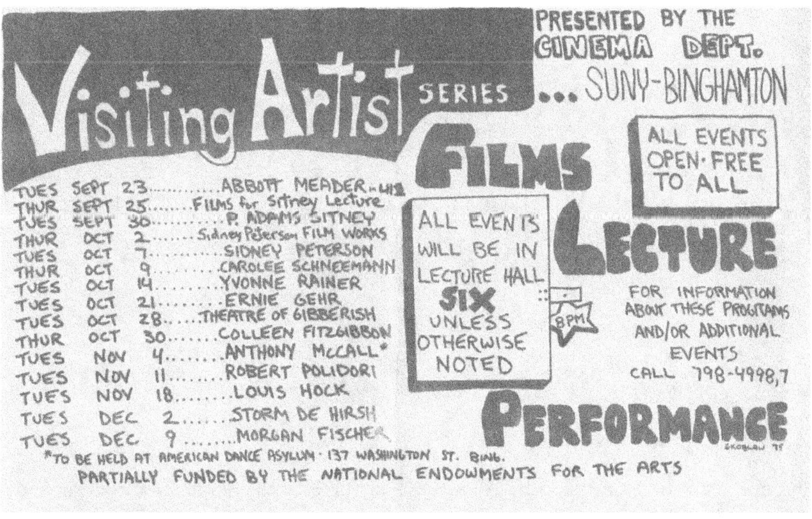

Figure 35. Cinema Department schedule of visiting artists, fall of 1975.

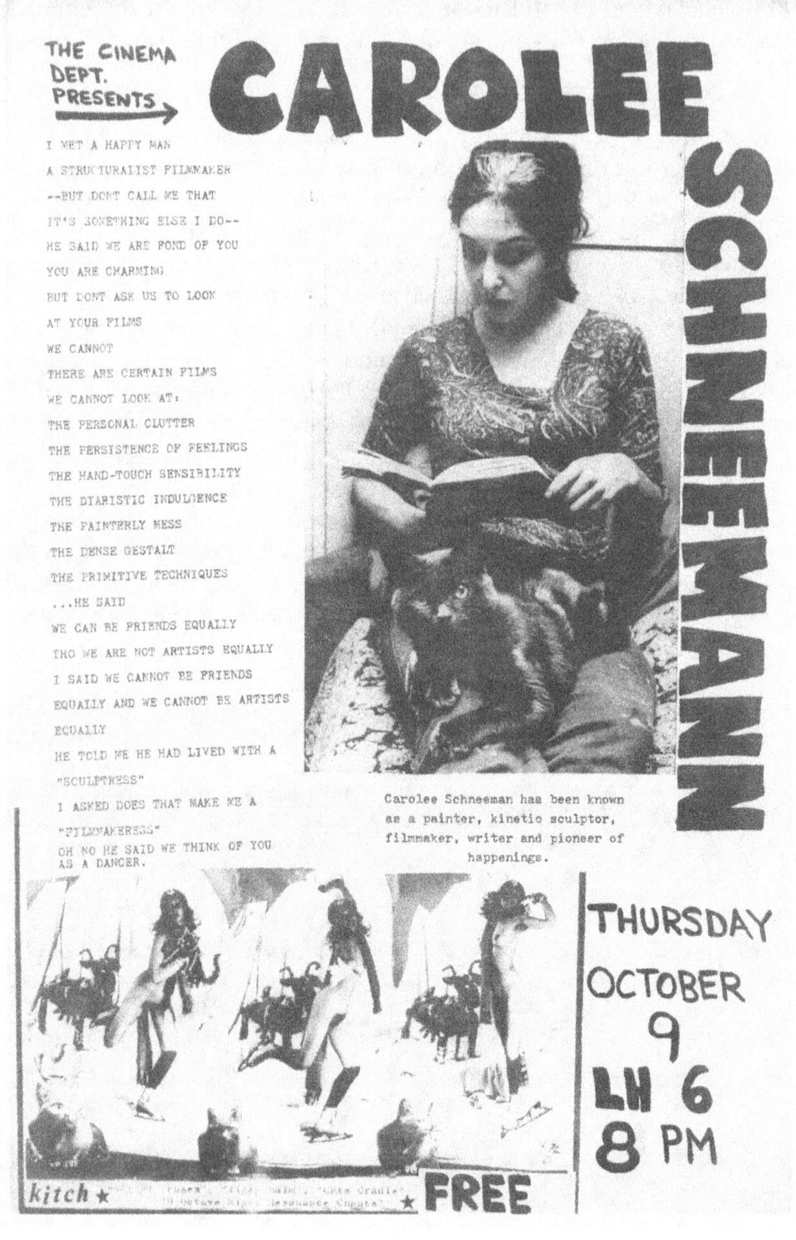

Figure 36. Poster designed by Alan Berliner for Carolee Schneemann appearance on October 9, 1975. Courtesy Alan Berliner.

Peter Kubelka was a very forceful presence at Binghamton. I remember him bringing Jack Smith up from New York—he was a big fan of Smith, who was selling moldy slices of Wonder Bread that he had signed.

At one point, I was put in charge of the visiting artists program. We would bring up people in the afternoon for a seminar, then do a public show at night—a format based on the programs P. Adams Sitney did at Yale that I had attended in the sixties. We brought people who weren't filmmakers, but who were thinking seriously about film, including P. Adams. I wanted Annette Michelson to come; I can't remember if she did. We hosted a wide range of people: Diego Cortez, Sidney Peterson, Carolee Schneemann, Morgan Fisher.

When we brought Carolee, we outed a big aesthetic division in the department. I had met Carolee early on, in New Haven in 1965–66, but this was the first time I'd ever gotten a chance to talk to her. I loved her work and was in awe of her. Dan and I picked her up at the airport; she got off the plane with Kitch the cat, which we didn't expect, so then we had to go buy kidneys for Kitch.

Larry and Ken were not Carolee fans—why would we bring *her*! Ken said, "She's great at parties, but not as a filmmaker." Maybe this was a generational difference, because Dan and I agreed about Carolee, and I'm sure Coleen [Fitzgibbon] and Margie [Marjorie Keller] would have agreed—but not P. Adams. There's no chapter about Carolee even in the new edition of *Visionary Film*.*

Sidney Peterson was a real eye-opener. I'd heard a lot about him from P. Adams and I'd known his daughter in San Francisco. I was thinking, "What am I gonna talk about with a seventy-year-old guy?"—now that I'm close to seventy myself, I realize how ageist I was! Sidney gets off the plane and *never* stops talking; he talked us into the ground—and *not* chit-chat, really interesting stuff.

*In *Visionary Film: The American Avant-Garde, 1943–2000* (New York: Oxford University Press, 2002), Sitney mentions Schneemann twice: once in connection with Brakhage's film *Loving* (1957), on p. 176; and in connection with his discussion of an exchange between Marjorie Keller and Abigail Child: "This exchange looks back to Carolee Schneemann's *Fuses* (1964–1968), an erotic lyric in Brakhage's manner—hand-held camera, superimpositions, enacted by the film-maker and her lover, James Tenney. Feminist film-makers of the seventies and eighties called attention to the remarkable candor and energy of *Fuses* and especially to its celebration of female desire. It also anticipates the explicit sexuality of Peggy Ahwesh's and Keith Sanborn's *The Deadman* (1989) . . ." (424).

Binghamton was like what you imagine Black Mountain College to have been. There were lots of arguments; people were passionate about their opinions, and often blinded by them. I was blind to things myself. When Ken insisted on bringing Storm de Hirsch, I was "*Storm de Hirsch?!*" But over the years I've come to appreciate her work, and I'm glad to have spent time with her.

Lloyd Bruce Holman: I grew tired of working with self-declared geniuses. And I felt that there was no appreciation for what I had accomplished, both in terms of my own teaching and filmmaking, and in my projects for the Cinema Department. I was still writing for *Filmmakers Newsletter*, and I had continued making films: John Tyo and I were completing a live-action and animated film for the Ministry of Educational Radio and Television of Iran. I traveled to England to make a film about an American ballroom dance team who were competing in an international dance competition. I also made more personal films, ranging from *Blue Lady*, an erotic animated film, to *Turn On Red*, half an hour watching a traffic light through a rain-spattered window. And I took leave from Binghamton to direct one of the first computer-animated films at Computer Image Corporation in Denver.

For the Cinema Department, I had reengineered the sound recording studio to make it functional, established a system of maintenance for the department's equipment, installed two film processing machines, obtained an Arriflex M camera at no cost to the department, designed and built what was probably the most advanced college film theater—with interlocked 16mm and 8mm projectors, and quadraphonic sound—in addition to attending to the everyday technical problems. When I returned to Binghamton from having directed the film at Computer Image Corporation, using the most advanced computer animation system in the world, *students* asked me about the experience, but not one faculty member asked a single question.

Sherry Miller Hocking: At one point Ken got into trouble showing a film of his that had nudity in it at a screening of *Shadows of Forgotten Ancestors* that had attracted a group of Eastern Orthodox Christians from the community.

Ralph Hocking: Ken had tried living up here, but, after that episode, he moved back to New York and commuted. The Dean never liked that; he would say, "You've got to get him back on campus; he's got to live up here." And I'd say, "I can't do anything with Ken, *you* talk to him."

There was also Ken's way of dealing with authority. At a meeting with the dean, he might get a bug up his ass about something, and he'd scream and dress people down, beat up people verbally—you don't treat colleagues that way.

Sherry Miller Hocking: We were at a big meeting at SUNY-Buffalo where Ken got angry at something and climbed onto a table and walked all the way around this table overturning the coffee cups. People were really upset about it. Ken left the room and Ralph followed him.

Ralph Hocking: Ken couldn't understand why everybody was so upset!

When it came time for the next five-year plan at the university, we got supported to the level that we were at, but after the mid-seventies we went twenty years without an additional line.

Larry Gottheim: Ken had moved back to New York and was commuting to Binghamton for a few days a week. This was terrible for the department—and the administration was angry about his being away from campus most of the time. (Years later, when a more recent administration understood Ken's growing reputation, this became less of an issue; but during a crucial time in the life of the department, the administration was set against us.)

Ken's moving back to New York also affected the office and his student assistants. He had students driving him back and forth to New York, or picking him up at the bus station. He would call the department office in the morning and ask for films to be ready, or things to be photocopied and handed out, or other details, and if his demands were not met he'd become furious.

When I had to devote myself to my duties as chair, I resented it, because it took me away from my creative role as artist and teacher. I remember Brakhage remarking to me, "So *you're* the glue holding this thing together." Well, whatever truth there might have been to that, there's no glory in being glue!

While Saul was a great teacher, he was also very politically committed, and with those early years behind us and the new administration in place, this also created a problem for the department. Saul was very involved in the organizing of the university's cafeteria workers into some kind of strike. I think he was involved in picketing the president's house. And there was the ongoing hatred of the Cinema Department by a lot of the more traditional art-oriented departments.

Suddenly we got cut back. Not only could we not hire new people, we found that when people would leave, we couldn't hire replacements. There were still great things happening, but it wasn't on the earlier level.

I think all the New York State universities suffered those cutbacks, except maybe for Buffalo, which was emerging, partly because that department had a full-time administrator, Gerry O'Grady, who was very aggressive, very plugged into the fortunes of his program, and didn't have to teach. Just when we were declining, their fortunes were rising.

Ken Jacobs: Flo had stopped living in Binghamton, and I was going back and forth on the bus. My classes would keep me alive and I had some friends, but it was lonely. I do not like sleeping alone, and there were young women from time to time that I'd be interested in. I'm not going to go into detail, but will say that I found it impossible to be around beautiful young women with vivid personalities and not fall in love. I was really good at falling in love. And I'm the kind of person who can't adapt to just having some nice times together, then moving on. I couldn't be with anybody without their whole person and my whole person coming into it. I always felt an inner obligation to develop everything to its fruition, which of course was impossible.

I was not interested in injuring my relationship with Flo, but I didn't keep things secret from her. I didn't go on about these relationships, but I didn't hide what happened.

After a while, I just stopped; it was too painful. I felt I was betraying the women I was meeting with, so I just slept alone, which was bad also. When Nisi and Azel were old enough to not need Flo's attention, she began driving back and forth to Binghamton. I'm still haunted by the feeling of betraying the women I got caught up in. I remember each one, and each relationship was beautiful and painful.

Saul Levine: I was a leader . . . *leader*?—a major activist on campus, part of a group called Looking Left. Mainly students; I was the only professor. An odd collection of people, we had all been in other groups in the Movement and even though our politics should have made some of us enemies, we found we agreed on many things.

When there started to be statewide cutbacks, beginning with the service people at the college, I was part of a group called "Students and Workers against Cut-Backs" that led the opposition. The administration had a very odd attitude toward us. They were liberals who believed in public education. The administrators and Dean Norman Cantor, one of the leading intellectual historians of the time, not only agreed with us, but helped educate us. We would pass out a leaflet, and Norman Cantor or one of the other administrators would tell us, "This leaflet is wrong; you don't realize that what's going on is worse than you think. The state is going back to the Dark Ages; they're gutting public education; this is an attack on working people."

Of course, what to do about this was the issue. Our group was confrontational, though we knew we were fighting a losing battle. We had come back from Albany, where, with students from all over the state, we'd stormed the legislature and actually talked to the legislators. Back at Binghamton, I remember giving a speech to a group of twenty or thirty people: "People say what happened in Albany was a symbolic action, but everything's *symbolic* until you actually seize state power. So we should do it!" We took over the administration offices. Fortunately a thousand people showed up to support us or we would have been screwed.

Eventually we reached a stalemate. Norman Cantor, the deans, all of those people who had agreed with us, who had *educated* us, were perfectly willing to have the State Police come and arrest us. I would have wound up in some god-awful place, but at that point the president of the union, who had been supporting us, said to me, "You guys should leave; you're not gonna win; we're worried about you; we're worried about the students. Somebody's going to get hurt. Please do it for us. Leave." They were right. That administration building was glass; people *were* going to get hurt. So we left, and went on strike.

Andrea Weiss: I arrived in January 1974, and graduated and left Binghamton in December 1976; I was there three years in all. Soon after I arrived I joined a political collective, Looking Left, where I met Saul Levine.

I must have gotten involved with the Cinema Department around September 1975 through my connection to Saul. Before that, I didn't know much about cinema, experimental or even mainstream. I started watching these weird films and they were strangely compelling and captivating.

It was a small and active department so I quickly knew all the faculty and students. That was one of the reasons I was drawn to it; I was an English major and the English Department was a huge factory with no sense of community among the students.

The Cinema Department was the place to be if you were drawn to creative thought in any domain. I might have considered becoming a cinema major, but for some reason I was in a hurry to graduate and didn't want to start all over again with a new major. I was able to cobble together my own major—English and women's studies—from courses taken in various departments.

Saul Levine: The funny part about my political involvement at Binghamton is that during the same year, I had the official title, Director of Undergraduate Studies—so I went from an occupation of the office where the budgets were overseen to having this normal academic discussion in the Cinema Department about what our budget should be. It was like taking off one mask and putting on another.

Oh boy, were there repercussions! There are things I don't want to say. I do think that the school pressured Larry and Ken into going along with my being laid off. This was done with both carrot and stick, promising them things for themselves and the department and simultaneously threatening them.

At the time, I had hard feelings about this. When I look back, a more reasonable attitude for me to have taken would have been that, even if I had not been a protester, I would have gotten laid off. I was probably the lowest-paid faculty member on campus—it was a very distinguished faculty and I hadn't been there long. Altogether I taught at Binghamton for two and a half years, though I stayed around for an extra year after I was no longer teaching.

Ken supported the strike, but he was away, and I think Larry was away too. I was really more pissed off at the Sociology Department, which was filled with famous leftists—James Petrus was there. *They* called what we were doing a petit bourgeois struggle. The sociologists were trying to hire Emmanuel Wallenstein, and they probably didn't want to screw around with the administration.

Later, there was a confrontational meeting among faculty and a small number of students—Danny Eisenberg was one of them—at which Ken (I have a tape recording) gave this long speech about how I was crazy, that I had an inferiority complex because I was short and that, unless I grew five inches, I would never be sane. But he came around at the end of this speech to say he wouldn't support my being fired.

It was a very Ken moment, especially for me, since his girlfriend—not Renée at this point, a different girlfriend—had come over and talked to me all night, then had gone and told Ken that I wasn't a bad guy, that I *wasn't* crazy.

Dan Barnett: In time I came to feel like I was just too young to spend the rest of my life being a college professor in a little college town. After a couple of years, I wasn't learning as much from the situation and felt that I needed a different environment—I was single and Binghamton was not a good circumstance for me. In those days, New York City was dirty and acoustically polluted, not to mention financially bankrupt, so I moved to Boston. Right away, I was kind of handed a job at Massachusetts College of Art. Even though I wasn't sure that I wanted to continue teaching, this turned out to be a great thing.

The transition from Binghamton back to Boston was wonderful; I have fond memories of MassArt—I still think of it as *the* most open-minded, adventurous student body and faculty of any place I've been. I got there at a really fortuitous moment; they had just decided to expand their filmmaking department, so I had the opportunity to hire a whole new faculty, to bring in new graduate students (Mark LaPore and Phil Solomon were the first), and to design the environment and its relationship to the burgeoning independent film scene in the city. It's *there* more than at Binghamton that I feel I had influence, not necessarily on individuals, but on an overall circumstance.

At MassArt I didn't feel like I needed to be an Artist. I could just be who I wanted to be. At Binghamton I came to associate the word *artist* with an attitude that had too much prance in it for me. Maybe I was afraid that I was being pressured to be something that didn't fit me, or that I too was becoming brittle and prickly in a way that isn't much tolerated in the ranks of documentary production workers. Several incidents brought this home to me.

One of the great things about Binghamton was that, at first, we had a very large budget for film rentals and visiting artists, so people came from all over the world to do guest stints. Nam June Paik had a performance work that he wanted to do while he was visiting. He claimed he needed a toy piano for the work and borrowed one from Ralph Hocking, claiming that it would be returned to Ralph undamaged after the performance. Paik destroyed the toy piano as part of the performance, and when I accosted him about it, he dismissed me, saying something like "I needed it for my *art*." This attitude manifested itself again and again in ways large and small. Being an artist at Binghamton seemed to condone the most egregious acts of irresponsibility.

Another incident: centerpieces of the department were the analytic projectors, very expensive machines that were invaluable in analyzing work frame-by-frame in classes. Larry, Ken, and I made extensive use of them. Video feedback was all the rage at the time and Tony Conrad decided to either emulate it or parody it in a film [*Film Feedback*, 1974]. He devised a system where a Bolex shooting high-speed black-and-white film was set up in a dark room, aimed at a candle outside of the dark room that was burning dimly in front of a movie screen. The film would run through the camera (with the side door off) and directly into a bucket full of developer, then into a bucket of acid fixer, through some sponges and then directly, *while still wet*, into an analytic projector that then projected the image, at slow speed, onto the screen behind the candle. When I saw this I went ballistic.

I don't think Tony was being malicious or willfully destructive, just oblivious—this kind of unconsciousness was fostered by a prevailing attitude at Binghamton: in the name of *art*, the destruction of property, even property used by teachers and students, was not an issue. The concept of Tony's piece might be interesting, but destroying a projector for this piece seemed to ignore all the ideas that could have been engendered by the pedagogical use of that projector.

Peer Bode: I remember a performance by Nam June Paik at the Watters, the Binghamton University Music Department theater, with its grand piano and antique harpsichord. Right before the performance began, Sherry Miller told me that Ralph had lent Nam June his toy piano for the performance and had told him, "Don't fuck it up!"

Nam June had a reputation for provocations in his Danger Music performances. He had unexpectedly cut off John Cage's tie, and Cage was apparently a bit afraid of him. At the Binghamton performance one of Nam June's first pieces involved his standing on the edge of the stage, holding a violin by the end of its neck, his arms extended. After holding it still for what seemed a long time, holding it, holding it, Nam June suddenly smashed the violin, which exploded in what seemed like slow motion. The symbolic violence of the gesture was clear; and the time-bending perceptual aspect was surprising, amazing, even shamanistic. After this, the audience—faculty from various university departments and students—was no longer relaxed. There was excitement, adrenaline, anger in the room. What a setup for what took place next!

Nam June proceeded to have the precious harpsichord placed on top of the grand piano. And on top of the harpsichord he placed the toy piano. He proceeded to play a single note on the grand piano, then the same note on the harpsichord, then on the toy piano. If I'm not mistaken, that was when members of the music faculty got up and left the theater.

The music Nam June played at this point in the performance was beautiful. One note at a time, one instrument at a time. But once some audience relaxation had set in, Nam June again broke the calm. He proceeded to methodically tear each key off the toy piano as he played it. This is when Ralph and Sherry left the theater. There was shock and concern in the air: Was Nam June going to break the Music Department's beloved harpsichord?

He did not. He did not. Nevertheless, the provocations at that performance were such that the Music Department faculty did not speak to the Cinema Department faculty for years—well, this may or may not have been true, but that was what we students told each other later.

At the end of the Nam June Paik performance, I remember Dan Barnett being quite agitated. He told me he felt this was very much an old-hat avant-garde performance. At the time I thought he might have been right; it surely was a different set of strategies than we were practicing. The performance was, however, powerful and memorable.

I wonder what Dan would have thought of the Hermann Nitsch performance that had happened two years earlier—during my second week of undergraduate studies at Binghamton!

Alan Berliner: By my senior year, I was a teaching assistant for both Larry and Ken. In fact, when Ken became ill early in the semester, the department asked me to teach the course. They even paid me! That's when I found out how much I enjoy teaching.

At some point along the way, Larry and Ken sent me to New York City to make arrangements with Harry Smith, who wanted to donate a print of one of his films to the department to fulfill a requirement of a recent CAPS (Creative Artists Public Service) grant he'd received. Harry asked me to bring a cassette tape recorder with me; his idea was to make a recording that would also be a gift to the students. And so on the Saturday night of Thanksgiving weekend in November of 1976, I visited Harry Smith in his disheveled room at the Chelsea Hotel. We spent hours talking and smoking pot (we bought the marijuana from a dealer in the Chelsea; Harry got me to pay for it). I remember being amazed by Harry's erudition, his scraggly beard, the intensity of his eyes inside the frames of his thick black glasses, his unforgettable voice, and what was for me at the time, his utterly unprecedented eccentricity.

In many ways Harry was intimidating, even quite frightening, but he also emanated kindness and vulnerability—the combination of which was both mesmerizing and endearing. Harry and I kept in touch for a while after that, and we even went out for lunch a few times (for which I also paid). Later, I visited him at the Breslin Hotel on Twenty-Ninth Street, where he moved after he was forced out of the Chelsea. Getting to know Harry Smith, even just a little, was one of the big thrills of my life, and I have Ken and Larry to thank for that.

I was also active in the Cinema Department on other fronts. Besides being a teaching assistant for Ken and Larry (Larry called us "docents"), I designed publicity posters for the visiting artists program, I was a projectionist for classes, and also a work-study student assigned to Bruce Holman, the technical wizard who repaired all of the camera and editing equipment for the department (and who stayed far, far away from any departmental politics or intrigue).

I was also president of the Film Co-op (we arranged to buy film stock and other supplies at a cut-rate to sell to students) and coprogrammer (with David Kasakove) of Harpur Film Society, where our programming was a clear extension of the department and its experimental mission. We used most of the profits from the Film Society to buy prints of 16mm films for the department library.

And of course, during my last years there, I was also feverishly making films and para-cinematically inspired photographs, collages, and sculptures. The department allowed me to convert a room in the basement of the lecture hall into my own private art gallery, where I had a one-person exhibition of this work as part of my senior thesis.

Andrea Weiss: I took film courses from Saul and Ken, although Ken got pneumonia early in the semester and the class was run in his absence by Alan Berliner and another student I don't remember. Saul Levine and Dan Barnett played an important role in the department. People always mention Ken and Larry, but I know that at least some students felt a stronger connection to either Dan or Saul or to both of them, partly because of their respective filmmaking practices, which offered additional points of entry into avant-garde film, and partly because they were the younger generation and very accessible.

Saul was on the faculty, but he seemed more like a graduate student. One never had the sense that Saul believed in or even tolerated a faculty/student hierarchy. He and Dan Barnett shared a house together in downtown Binghamton, and I must have gone in and out of that house dozens of times, probably without even knocking! I recall feeling that Saul was undervalued. Since I had graduated and left town a semester before he was fired, I don't know the whole story about that, but I wasn't surprised.

I never took a course with Larry, but I knew and respected him. He seemed to be kind and considerate to everyone, regardless of whatever tensions and alignments were going on in the department. I recall going to his beautiful house up the hill from the campus and thinking (in my eighteen-year-old mind) that he had a perfect life. And when he completed and showed part of his *Elective Affinities* series, he blew us all away. Of course, our access to the cultural references in those films must have been pretty limited—a lot of the allusions probably went over our heads—but in terms of sheer visual power we were held in thrall by Larry's films.

Dan Barnett: When Saul's contract wasn't renewed (hence his *Notes of an Early Fall*), he went to work at his dad's gas station in New Haven, and when I got the job at Mass College of Art, John Pennington, who I'd hired as the film technician (on Saul's recommendation) and who was an old SDS colleague of Saul's, started plotting how we could get Saul hired. Saul was not all that amenable to coming to MassArt. I think he'd kind of had it with the academic world, so John and I drove down to New Haven and twisted his arm.

I'm still working in imaging, recently having moved into digital imaging. Not exactly film, but related—and a pretty steep learning curve for me.

Andrea Weiss: I went to all the department's events and it was there that I first encountered Carolee Schneemann, Yvonne Rainer, and Marjorie Keller, who made a huge impression on me. Maybe this makes it sound as if Binghamton was a hub of feminist filmmaking activity but it certainly wasn't that—these filmmakers represented a small minority of the many who came during that time. Nonetheless, it was there that I first saw their films and heard them talk in person about their work. They weren't just women who were filmmakers; they were making films about female experience. It's hard to imagine today how eye-opening that was back then.

The faculty member I was most influenced by at the time was Saul, because he introduced me to avant-garde film in the first place, and his own films brought together art and politics in a very poetic and subtle way. Ernie Gehr's *Serene Velocity* was filmed in our department hallway and was considered a Very Important Film. Perhaps it was, and perhaps still is—I can't say. It was the decade of structuralist filmmaking and that kind of work usually left me cold. I was much more interested in the personal filmmaking Saul was doing because it was emotional and intuitive and messy, like life. Saul wasn't striving for perfection, the way the structuralist filmmakers seemed to be, but every now and then his work was somehow just achingly perfect.

What I learned most from the Binghamton experience was not how to make films but how to watch films, I mean *really* watch films, which informed my own filmmaking later on, and also my teaching. The other important factor to consider is how demanding and often inspiring the films we were exposed to, along with the discourse around them, actually were. Binghamton was a boot camp for what Hannah Arendt called "a life of the mind," and those of us who went through it have brought that training to bear on whatever endeavors in life we've subsequently pursued.

Alan Berliner: There's something else I got from Ken and Larry. A few years ago when I was presenting my work in Sheffield, England, my film came onto the screen *without sound* for about thirty seconds because of some technical problem. As soon as I saw what was happening, I shouted across the room, "No, no, no! We only do this once, so please, let's do it right!" I made them stop the projector, and we started the film over again, this time with sound.

The audience applauded me! After the show many people remarked that my having the audacity to actually stop the show and start over made them appreciate how the intensity and dedication involved in filmmaking doesn't end when the work is completed, but carries over into protecting the integrity of the film viewing experience—and also includes the responsibility for engaging in meaningful postscreening discussions with the audience. All of that is certainly a carryover from Binghamton.

Andrea Weiss: The *student* I was closest to was Alan Berliner, whom I had met my first week at SUNY-Binghamton. We were very close during my last year; we lived together for a while and have remained close friends to this day.

I don't know if Alan influenced me as a filmmaker—he was deeply committed to making very abstract films—definitely not my direction. I did make some films while I was in Binghamton. I don't list them in my filmography, and I think they're best left in the drawer—though I have one sweet 8mm film of a very young Alan Berliner (we must have been 18 or 19 at the time) focusing his Bolex on the white lines in a parking lot.

I was (and am) a very politically concerned person and I was strongly influenced by the social movements of the late sixties and early seventies. When I started making documentaries in the early eighties, Alan was still making abstract films, and only slowly moved toward documentary himself. But I guess in some ways I was influenced by him, because I work as my own editor and for me it is in the editing room that the magic of filmmaking really takes place. The importance, the necessity of craft—I'm sure Alan influenced me in that.

The Cinema Department was a very male environment at that time. There were no female professors on the faculty until Maureen Turim came, which was after I graduated, so I never met her—and she was a film theorist, not a filmmaker. There were no female role models on the faculty, and if you look for female students from the department back then who are still working filmmakers, you'll have a hard time finding many. That can't be a coincidence.

The strongest adult female presence was the wonderful department secretary, Marilyn Aigen, who was a kind of surrogate mother to the students. (See fig. 37.)

I recall several incidents that today we would term sexual harassment. But the line on sexual harassment back then was much more loosely drawn than it would be today. It was also a looser time around

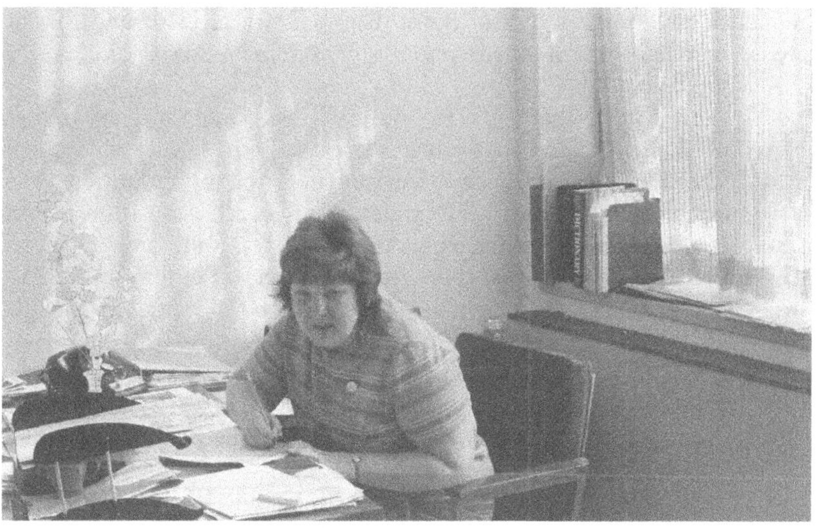

Figure 37. Marilyn Aigen, secretary of the Cinema Department during its early years. Courtesy Mark Goldstein.

sex generally, coming out of the "sexual revolution" of the sixties. No one thought much about students and professors having affairs.

But I knew students who put up with discomfort and anguish from things said to them by professors that would be "actionable" today. A roommate of mine almost dropped out of school after being repeatedly propositioned by a cinema professor; she had a work-study job projecting films for his class, so she didn't feel she could say anything.

Although it was the height of the women's movement, female students didn't necessarily think of such incidents as harassment, just very distressing encounters. And even if we *had* understood them as harassment, there was no one you could turn to back then. Maybe there were only a few such incidents, or maybe there were many, but they definitely had an effect on the overall social and intellectual climate.

Larry Gottheim: Looking back, one of the things I was never very comfortable with was Ken's idea that the students would continue with the same professor for two semesters in "Introduction to Cinema" and also take the subsequent film production class with that same teacher. This seemed likely to foster (and indeed it did) a system of disciples under the "master." Of course, many students would drop out before completing the full sequence, but those who remained would be under the influence of a single professor more than was typical in an undergraduate department. Of course, despite my discomfort I myself took part in this arrangement.

Another thing that came to bother me was how the presentations of senior theses evolved. It seemed a great idea to have each student, during the final year, produce a work or body of work that would be the pinnacle of his or her achievement. This could have been in film studies/appreciation or filmmaking, though it was only after Maureen Turim joined the faculty that there were some theses in film studies. My problem was Ken's idea that the work should be presented before the full faculty *and all the students*. For years there was this big painful show in Lecture Hall 1, in which each prospective graduate was put under the (often strutting) crossfire of the faculty. Any latent conflicts between the faculty could surface during these screenings, and the poor student could be subject to grueling and embarrassing attack.

These sessions were dominated by Ken; they became a forum in which he demonstrated before all the students that he was the arbiter of taste. Now I admit that I myself sometimes was frustrated with students who seemed to have failed to grasp even the basic concepts of all our teaching, but as these were undergraduates who had worked with individual faculty over a period of time, the senior thesis presentations should have been received in a more receptive manner, which could of course have included serious critique. I did finally succeed in having the senior theses presented to the faculty alone, but very subjective conflicts still emerged, and the students were the victims of these.

8

Denouement

Alan Berliner: I'm not sure what happened at Binghamton later on—at some point things seem to have drifted away from the intensity of the mid-seventies. I know there was talk about starting a graduate cinema program, which for a variety of reasons, including budget problems within the State University system, never came to be. That's a real shame. And by the late seventies the English Department had taken over the Harpur Film Society. When I heard this (I had graduated a year or two before), I recognized it as a clear sign that the university was no longer allowing the Cinema Department to operate with the unrestricted freedom and independence it had enjoyed for so long. It was as if the "adults" had taken over, and were going to keep a watchful eye on their wayward children. Harpur Film Society became a much more traditional film series, the kind you found at universities everywhere.

Another disappointment—and this isn't limited to Binghamton—is that the Cinema Department never turned out enough people who could write critically about cinema, in particular about the avant-garde. Of course, Jim Hoberman is a Binghamton graduate. We've needed more people like him who can articulate and champion radical cinema—and not only to the "true believers," but also to more mainstream audiences all over the country. That never happened on the scale everyone initially hoped for.

Daile Kaplan: In the years after I left Binghamton, photography was emerging as a legitimate art form, and through friends, I was exposed to a fledgling community of photographers. In the seventies I worked for

Jonas Mekas as an administrative assistant at Anthology Film Archives. With Shigeko Kubota, I codeveloped and curated Anthology's video program, and exhibited my own multichannel video installations at several venues. I continued to create photographs and, for a time, had shows in cutting edge alternative spaces in SoHo. But, by the late 1980s, I'd switched gears and was working as a curator and writer in the world of photography.

Before transitioning to my current job at Swann Auction Galleries, I had become an independent scholar, curator, and writer. At the outset of my scholarly projects in the 1980s, after discovering a lost cache of Lewis W. Hine's photographs at the Library of Congress, I became interested in how photography related to the vernacular (Alan Trachtenberg's books mentored me). In 1989, I was invited to curate an exhibition celebrating photography's 150th anniversary and I coined the term *pop photographica* to describe the materials I selected for the show: snapshots, commercial images, family photo albums, as well as household artifacts and objects highlighted with photographic images. At the time, I remembered a comment Ken Jacobs had made during one of his inspirational lectures: "If you coin a new word and contribute it to the lexicon, you've made a mark"—or something like that. I smiled at the memory of Ken's remark: here I was, a young curator, doing just what Ken had described.

During the past twenty years, there's been a seismic change in the field of photography and, of course, in the marketplace for photographs. Museum curators now embrace pop photographica, and actively collect and exhibit vernacular items (even if they don't employ my term), and I also have an active public life as a collector of photography. Over the years, I've lectured about my collection and written extensively about vernacular photography. It dawned on me only recently that the New American Cinema, which Binghamton introduced me to, inspired my passion for collecting! Just as the New American Cinema explored the convergence of art and everyday life, introducing a new genre and language of cinema, I like to think my collection is exploring the intersection of the art of photography and vernacular life—and hopefully influencing the course of photographic thinking and popular culture.

Alan Berliner: The founders of the Collective for Living Cinema had been graduates of the Cinema Department, and there was always a deep spirit of connection and continuity between the Cinema Department and the Collective. The idea of making films worthy of being shown there was a motivation for many students. It certainly was an important goal for me. Knowing the Collective was there gave a tangible "real-world" dimension to the highly aestheticized environment we were immersed in at Binghamton. Not only that, but it was also a compelling reason to move to New York City after graduation. In many ways, with all due respect to Anthology Film Archives and Millennium, the Collective became *the* center of the avant-garde film universe in New York—at least during the late seventies and early eighties.

Larry Gottheim: The new atmosphere of the university, once the administration had changed, was accompanied by a heavy theoretical approach to things. One result was a split in the Art Department, which became two departments: the Studio Art Department and the Art History Department, which became focused on theory. The administration decided that the Cinema Department also needed to become more "academic," meaning more *theoretical*. Early on, other departments had wanted to have cinema as part of their turf but I had been able to outmaneuver them. Now, these departments saw this theoretical turn as an opportunity to try again. It was mostly different people, but with the same agenda. In the end I was given a directive to hire an *academic* person.

Other departments were presenting people we thought were impossible. We asked Myrel Glick, Ernie Gehr's wife, to apply—she had taught a course in theory. And suddenly here was Maureen Turim: she would soon have her PhD and she was a woman—there was growing pressure from the administration about this: we'd had visiting filmmakers who were women, but not a faculty member. And Maureen was writing a dissertation on experimental cinema; in fact, my work was discussed in her dissertation.

Given the circumstances, it seemed like Maureen was our dream come true: we could actually hire somebody who was acceptable to the administration as an academic, but who was sympathetic to avant-garde cinema. Maureen was hired. I don't remember exactly who was involved in the hire—though I think both Ralph and Ken were opposed to it.

Ken Jacobs: Maureen Turim was hired because the administration wanted to get us in line, make cinema more of an academic discipline, and Maureen was the perfect Good Girl to come in for them. That was one of the times Larry and I had a big difference. I thought Maureen was absurd. Not unintelligent—but doctrinaire and screwball. And cheap in her personal ambition.

Larry Gottheim: Another thing that affected us was the development of the Women's Studies Department, which at one point later on hired

Barbara Hammer, who wanted to teach courses in filmmaking, limited to women, an idea we found problematic.*

Maureen continued her interest in avant-garde cinema, and her dissertation was ultimately published as *Abstraction in Avant-Garde Films* in 1985, but there was ferocious antagonism toward her from Ken. Some of it was personal, but there was also something hard to deal with that had to do with the strength of our original program.

We'd always paid a lot of attention to many different kinds of cinema in the sequence of courses that we had agreed on. When we first began offering Introduction to Cinema, it would attract 400 students. It was a very unconventional cinema course; it involved other arts, it involved other activities, and it fed not just into people wanting to become filmmakers but into people interested in understanding and appreciating the whole range of cinema. Now, a negative side of that, at least for somebody coming from a more academic program, at least at that point, was that we used no standard written texts.

In the new film academe, there was all this French theory and it was assumed that if students said they were cinema majors, there were certain periodicals and books they would read, certain theoretical ideas they could explain, certain touchstone films they would know, certain important conferences that they would attend. Maureen felt that it was her mission to bring this approach to the Cinema Department, and even though I could see that there was a way of doing this, I also felt that these two approaches were so radically different that you couldn't effectively mix them. Though some students might be able to bridge the difference, often the kind of people who would be attracted to one approach would not be attracted to the other.

So, once Maureen got here, the personal turf issue that had always been part of the department, now for the first time represented an ideological difference. We tried to patch it up and develop different kinds of classes that made sense together, but it was difficult.

---

*In her book, *Hammer: Making Movies Out of Sex and Life* (New York: Feminist Press, 2010), Barbara Hammer explains that, in the spring of 1983 she taught at SUNY-Binghamton, as a "cross-hire by the women's studies and film departments," and "proposed and taught a new course, 'Experimental Films Made By Women'" (168); "The second class I taught that semester was an artmaking class, 'Collaborative Filmmaking.' . . . On the first meeting day . . . I decided to divide the group [of 17 students] in half—all men and all women—thus creating two manageable groups suited to the production of a collaborative film. One young man challenged this decision. I explained that I wanted everyone to have an equal chance to use the equipment; that women are culturally trained to fear equipment, and men are just the opposite. I wanted to avoid the men taking the camera, watching the women float into actress roles. Everyone then agreed to the structure" (170).

For her own survival as a person as well as for her integrity in the profession as *she* understood it, Maureen began to make alliances with other departments, and the result was that the unity we had always had within the department when we faced opposition disappeared. When Maureen left, there wasn't enough support for the Cinema Department to hire a replacement. And from then on, the department functioned in an effective, but smaller—I think less visionary—way.

Maureen Turim: Already by the time I got to Binghamton—I arrived in 1977, left to go to the University of Florida in 1990—there was a feeling that I'd missed out on the good times. There was the sense that earlier on, there'd been the resources to be able to do things that were no longer possible.

Larry Gottheim, Ken Jacobs, and Ralph Hocking were the three other people in the department when I was hired, but part of the problem was that the administration of the university was putting a heavy hand on this hire: they wanted somebody who would be sympathetic to the department, but do something different from what had been going on. They wanted a theorist-historian who would also interact with the Comparative Literature, English, and Art History Departments. The goals of the dean were reflected in the hiring committee, which included people outside the Cinema Department.

I was happy to get the job, my first job. I was very young, ABD [All But Dissertation] when I was hired, and my story at Binghamton is a lot about finishing my dissertation on American and Canadian avant-garde film, written from a very specific theoretical perspective. I focused on the abstraction of images, images which were at the borders of representation in one way or another. Larry's films were important in that book.

I admired Ken and knew some of his work; in many ways he was probably the most famous and influential of the Cinema Department faculty at that point—and knew it. For him, here was a book on the avant-garde and he wasn't in it, and that remained a tension in our relationship. He never accepted that the premise of my book meant that his work wasn't central to it. *He* felt that I didn't appreciate his work as much as I *did*; I thought his work was fantastic—it just wasn't what I wrote about.

I hadn't known about Ralph Hocking before I got to Binghamton, because he didn't distribute his work back then. What he did with video, so early on, was incredible, and his bringing so many people into the Experimental Television Center was very exciting.

Those three gave me a hard time. I was a *girl*! I was *young*. But it wasn't all struggle. Sometimes I rode to New York with Ken and visited with him and Flo at their apartment, met their kids.

There were genuinely wonderful moments during my teaching. We did critiques of the students' work that I think were unparalleled in terms of the amount of time an undergraduate doing a senior thesis would get from a committee. We devoted to our undergraduates the kind of one-on-one attention that some universities barely give their graduate students. I'm proud of that work.

Of course, you can imagine what it must have felt like for an undergrad to present thesis work in front of *that* committee and get their responses. Sometimes it was glorious and sometimes devastating. I was very aware that these were only undergraduates, so the approach of "How *dare* you show me this film! You think I would like *this*?" as was sometimes the case, was troubling. But that was the art-school atmosphere that existed at Binghamton, which involved very high standards and very *particular* standards in terms of what students should be making.

Ralph Hocking: I think Maureen was the first person we hired (I was chair at the time) who had anything to do with video theory.

Sherry Miller Hocking: She tried to integrate both film and video into her classes, and organized a couple of video exhibitions of ETC work at the university art gallery . . .

Ralph Hocking: Yes, though in the end I grew tired of her constant belittling of anything that wasn't based in superfeminism.

Maureen Turim: Larry was very erudite, with a background in multiple languages and comparative literature. But Ken was very learned himself and had brilliant ideas. I remember some of the wonderful work that he did on Jewish stereotyping—I sat in on some of his classes.

Ken had certain qualities as a teacher that would get the kids involved as if class were a kind of workshop: small groups of students would act out little scenarios in relation to the films. Ken was imaginative as a teacher and while you might complain about some things he did, he was cutting edge in terms of what you can do in the classroom, and that was intriguing to me. It was very different from what I did in class, and the kinds of work that I wanted from my students were different from the kinds that he wanted from his—but that was okay.

Insofar as there were debates on how women artists could fit into that program, there are some things I should say. When it came down to who we should bring or even what we could show in classes, there was intense argumentation. For example, there was an incredible antagonism to Yvonne Rainer's work. I wanted to show her, and I wanted to bring her, but it was impossible. I remember an invitation extended to Henry Hills to show his films, which he wished to do as a duo event with his partner at the time, Abigail Child. I doubt that the department would have extended an invitation to Abby on her own, but I was extremely grateful for this introduction to her work, and would later write about her films repeatedly. Women students told me how much they appreciated this powerful example of a woman working in the experimental mode, especially with the intensity they saw in her work.

I didn't want to interfere with what Ken and Larry and Ralph were doing because I thought it was great; I just didn't want my own circumstances interfered with, and that came up a couple times. There was an attitude on the part of some of the faculty that the French New Wave, which of course I was and still am very involved with, was not worth teaching. And when I wanted to teach a course in Women in Film, there was heavy resistance. This was a course I'd team-taught at the University of Wisconsin with Sena Bathwick and Diane Waldman—the first TA-team-taught course in that department and maybe at the university. When I tried to offer the course at Binghamton, I was told that this was not a good way to approach film art.

So it was a challenge. Because my colleagues were also my tenure committee!

I did get tenure, and Ken and Larry and I did many more things together than people probably realize, and did them in some very intriguing ways. At a certain point I started writing about video and got quite close to Ralph and Sherry, and did a lot of work with the artists who were coming into the Experimental Television Center: Peer Bode and other brilliant talents that were around then.

I also started spending a fair amount of time in New York City, although I only tried commuting for one year: it was grueling, especially in winter, so I know what Ken was up against.

Binghamton and Buffalo were in a kind of competition when I was there. I ended up *marrying* Buffalo!* But even before my connection with Scott Nygren, I used to drive up there to visit friends, and occasionally I was invited to speak. For me Buffalo was wonderful; it was amazing what they were doing. I think part of the difference is that Buffalo was far enough from New York City that everybody living there—all the filmmakers and grad students—had to put all their energy into Buffalo;

*Turim married the late Scott Nygren, who earned a PhD at the Center for Media Study at the State University of New York at Buffalo in 1982. Both subsequently taught at the University of Florida, where Turim currently teaches.

they were trying so hard to make it work for them. And, of course, Buffalo had a grad program, which Binghamton never did.

David Marc: Everybody has a blow-up with Ken eventually. Helene Kaplan [Wright], who was my roommate senior year—we lived in Johnson City and Ken and Flo lived underneath us—might be the one exception. Anyway, I did a reading at the Collective of a short story I wrote where Ken and Flo were two of the characters (they were "Fred" and "Clo" in my story, which was meant to capture the way they spoke). The audience went berserk, but some of Ken's friends, like Richard Foreman, were aghast, and Ken never spoke to me again.

Jim Hoberman: After I visited Binghamton as part of the Theater of Gibberish, Ken and I were friends again until we had another big fight—because of something I wrote in the *Village Voice*. At the time I didn't fully realize the significance Jonas Mekas has for Ken's generation of filmmakers. Jonas had the power to make them famous, at least in a limited way, and to get their films distributed. The filmmakers always felt like they didn't get enough recognition, so when it became apparent in the mid-seventies that I was capable of writing—even though I *backed* into writing; I didn't set out to be a writer—it had an effect: these guys all wanted me to write about them.

Instead, I became a champion of the Super-8 filmmakers: Beth and Scott B, Eric Mitchell, and in particular, Vivienne Dick. Ken hated this stuff and I was shocked, because I thought that in her own way, Vivienne was expanding on Ken's early movies. I was angry at Ken's hostility and called him out: I thought it was a sexist thing. I mean, to this day, Jonas is still looking around to see what new is happening, and during the early eighties I felt that Ken was making less interesting work and was ignoring new work that *was* interesting. He would have had a major part in an 8mm/Super-8mm show I was involved in, but withdrew his films and wrote me a nasty letter that entirely ignored our long history.

The thing is, I was always supportive of Ken in my writing. I even wrote about him when we weren't talking to each other—something that amazed him. But I felt that no matter how much I wrote about Ken, it wouldn't be enough: if it had been up to him, it would have been the *Village Jacobs*, every week. At the time, I didn't allow myself to understand how powerful it is for people to see themselves in print.

I'm very grateful that Ken and I became friendly again. He and Flo were supersupportive when I was involved in the morass about the Jack Smith estate. When I see Ken, he looks great and has become terrifically prolific. He finally finished *Star Spangled to Death* [final version,

2004] and a lot of his new work is truly sensational. I think he's getting at least some of the recognition he deserves.

Ralph Hocking: Ken and I used to have humungous fights, but we always had an ability to pull things back together—that wasn't always true with Ken's other antagonists. After a certain point, fights seemed to happen at every faculty meeting. The classic battle was always about money. Who gets the raise? Larry and Ken would be making laundry lists of how they deserved more money. I was the lowest paid in the department (I was the lowest paid professor on campus for a long time) and I would finally say, "Fuck you guys; take the money; I don't want it!" and just walk out of the room.

When I became chair, I decided the best way to deal with Ken and Larry was to never have a meeting. I would meet separately with each of them on an issue. It worked beautifully. If you brought the two of them into a room and there was any practical or theoretical issue to deal with, they would take opposite sides. They'd go back and forth; they'd *scream* at each other.

Sherry Miller Hocking: It could go on for hours.

Ralph Hocking: We had a faculty meeting at the old ETC downtown, and they were screaming at each other until the middle of the night. It was a matter of one wearing the other down. They're both tough guys and real smart. But in the long run, they *were* worth the effort.

Danny Fingeroth: I'm on the board of the Institute for Comic Studies, which arranges the Comics Art Conference (CAC) academic panels that are part of San Diego's Comic-Con and other major comics conventions. Just a few years ago at the San Diego Con there was a discussion among the CAC people about how to mix theory with practice at their schools. Somebody mentioned that he had taken courses at SUNY-Binghamton where the filmmaking majors had to take theory courses and the theory majors had to take filmmaking courses. I jumped in to say, "I'm a graduate of that program; I can tell you about it!" It seemed strange to me that this was considered an unusual approach, but apparently, it is. When I teach comics writing, I always try to include some theory and analysis of comics stories, which is what Larry and Ken and Dan and Saul modeled for me.

Philip Sykas: Looking back, my experiences in Binghamton seem as if they happened in a different lifetime—except that the lessons of those days have remained with me. Arnie disclosed for me the magic of morning light; Linda Sokolowski showed me that the miniature can be monumental. The Cinema Department taught us the "musicianship" of film: its cadences, harmonies and dissonances, sustained by the persistence of vision operating at so many frames per second. But viewing film was also like viewing painting with its edge effects and figure-ground relationships, directionality and proportions. The ideal was a cinema made with a deep commitment to the physical and psychological aspects of the experience. Our attention span had been extended, our attentiveness was heightened. We had learned to watch film with the patient alertness of the hunter.

Susan Ray: In the years between Nick's death in 1979 and my making *Don't Expect Too Much* [2012], I was only peripherally involved in the film world, attempting to get *We Can't Go Home Again* off the shelf, serving on a couple of festival juries, and helping out on a little film about Tiny Tim. By necessity I was more focused on redeeming my soul to whatever extent possible and lived for periods at a Zen training center in California or wherever my teachers were teaching. I also continued to work as an editor and writer, as I had when I was with Nick, publishing some short pieces about pilgrimage and a book about Nick [*I Was Interrupted*], whom I considered my teacher as well as my mate. I studied indigenous healing ways, particularly with an African medicine woman, and helped to organize the International Council of the Thirteen Indigenous Grandmothers.

Nick was not at all comfortable with *We Can't Go Home Again* as it was when he left it. He was a central actor in it; it was being made as it was being lived, and he was in the grip of addiction throughout the process. He just didn't have the distance from it to see how to shape it; and once he did have both the sobriety and the distance, he still didn't have the money and he didn't get the time. This is not to say that he would have turned the film into a linear story with a tied-up-in-ribbon ending. Honestly I don't know what he would have done, and I don't believe he knew exactly either; but from conversations we had I'm guessing that at least he would have clarified the story *lines*—plural—and how they danced with each other, and cleared away the confusions that were the result of technical experiments still underway.

The Nicholas Ray Centenary Project has always been intended as three films, with *We Can't Go Home Again* as the centerpiece. I asked Bernard Eisenschitz to make the documentary intended to accompany *We Can't Go Home Again* at the Venice Film Festival, but his mother was dying and he had to withdraw at the last moment. No one else had sufficient background for the job and we had a deadline. Finally it seemed more efficient to do it myself than to try to get someone else up to speed. Given my near-complete state of ignorance about film craft, it was a crazy decision. Still, I knew what I wanted to do. I began what became *Don't Expect Too Much* in late February 2011.

Given that *We Can't Go Home Again* was never finished, I wanted to provide its background—how Nick worked with his student crew and what he'd intended for both the film's content and its form, multiple image in particular. And I was curious about how the experience of working on *We Can't Go Home Again* was sitting with his students forty years later, now that they'd reached the age that Nick was when he knew them. I was curious about who we were as a generation and what the era of our youth really had been about. I was curious about Nick's description of his own generation as a generation of betrayers. And I also wondered what exactly he meant when he described *We Can't Go Home Again* as a film about the search for self-image.

Although I made *Don't Expect Too Much* only by default, I fell in love with the process: it's so impossibly demanding, but it pushes me to the borders of known abilities and beyond, where I can surprise myself. The pressure is intense; there's just no time to think everything through, and so at a certain point all I can do is trust my instincts. It's important that the instincts be supported by knowledge and discipline, and I could use a lot more of both; but finally it's the instincts—or *something* beyond the cognitive mind—that run the show. As Nick would say, the film takes on a life of its own. I find that joyous and inspiring.

I'm hoping I'll be lucky enough to get to explore further while making *ACTION!*, the third and final film of the triptych. *ACTION!* will be about a life in art, what it demands, why one would choose it. Specifically it's about filmmaking as a way of life, as taught by Nick Ray. We will hear Nick discussing the craft of the director, the actor, the cameraman, hear him analyzing what works and doesn't work in his own films and the films of others as we watch the scenes he's citing, and also trace his own education, acquired by living and doing and apprenticing to the masters before him.

Harvey L. Silver: I wasn't there for Nicholas Ray, who arrived just after I left. I've always regretted that (a few years later, I was in a master's program at Indiana University and left just before *Breaking Away* [1979] was shot, so I missed crewing on that one too—I have lousy timing!).

What now feels poetic, at least to me, is that in a recent piece, film critic Richard Brody writes, "The freely expressive and symbolically dense realism of such Hollywood heroes as Howard Hawks, Vincente Minnelli,

Nicholas Ray, Otto Preminger, Douglas Sirk, and Ernst Lubitsch finds its current-day counterpart in films by such directors as Josephine Decker, Joe Swanberg, Alex Ross Perry, Nathan Silver, Eliza Hittman, and Tim Sutton . . ." [Brody: "The Best Movies of 2014," *New Yorker*, December 11, 2014]—here's my son Nathan Silver being compared to Nicholas Ray! I may not have become a filmmaker but I passed what I learned at Binghamton down to Nathan, helping to shape his concept of cinema, and I'm fortunate to work as executive producer on his films.

Nathan was at a film festival recently and ran into Alan Berliner, and when Alan heard I'd gone to Binghamton, he sent me pictures—Mark Goldstein's I think—of Nicholas Ray, Dennis Hopper, and other visitors.

Phil Solomon: Binghamton was a cornerstone for the avant-garde as it exists today. What Larry and Ken started all those years ago still lives on in cinemas, classrooms, books, films, and in our students' students. I'm grateful to have been part of it.

Bill T. Jones: There was something very romantic about being in Binghamton in those days—I'm very proud to have been there, to have been just a small part of that moment. At first, I remember feeling that Binghamton was a little bit off the beaten track, but obviously it was *not*!

Heinz Emigholz: In Binghamton, I saw a free and interdisciplinary way of teaching, and I tried to maintain that tradition when I taught at the University of the Arts in Berlin from 1993 until 2013.

Klaus Wyborny: My experiences in Binghamton have resonated again and again through the years. The Cinema Department was something like the Bauhaus in Dessau. It produced a lot of students who went on to have interesting careers: Jim Hoberman, Ken Ross, Steve Anker, Dan Eisenberg . . . And, perhaps most important: the Binghamton students founded the Collective for Living Cinema in New York, the best place to attend screenings ever!

The winter landscapes: the snow, the ice, the river, the wind, the long, long weekly bus rides from New York to Binghamton and back—strong memories.

Daile Kaplan: Those were halcyon days. As a young adult, I had no real sense of how lucky I was to be introduced to the extraordinary people I met at Binghamton. My most vivid memories were of Ken's intensive six- and eight-hour classes—and the visiting filmmakers. Of course, I also took classes with Larry, who taught differently, asking philosophical questions and sharing his process in an unusually transparent manner. Interestingly, today Larry is also part of the photo world. He's a collector who sometimes conducts private auctions online—I see him from time to time.*

Looking back, I wish we had also heard Storm De Hirsch and some of the other women associated with the New American Cinema articulate *their* perspectives. We *were* taught how pictures—moving and still—now dominated popular culture. Remember: although it may seem ridiculous today, for a long time photography was dismissed as a fine art because the photographer relied on a mechanical instrument! And the academy, including Binghamton, did not offer courses in photographic history. But in the Cinema Department, we were primed to think visually and trained to be very sophisticated about what we saw. We came to understand that photography, film, and video were unprecedented fine art practices, worthy of our best attention and our commitment.

Peer Bode: I'm still amazed by what happened in Binghamton and am nourished by it to this day, as a teacher and as an artist.

In the introduction to *Buffalo Heads*,** the catalog for "Mindframes: Media Study at Buffalo 1973–1990," Peter Weibel makes it sound as if Buffalo was the only place where anything was happening during that period—he ignores Binghamton completely. A lot of what's in that book came out of Woody Vasulka's archive, and when Ralph Hocking saw the book, he freaked out. I think this caught Woody by surprise because Ralph's and Binghamton's not being included wasn't *his* choice: Peter was probably trying to find a focus that wouldn't be confusing. I was in Karlsruhe, Germany for the opening of the "Buffalo Heads" show, when Gerry O'Grady stepped into the fray to say, "Ralph is totally right! Peter's writing is ridiculous; it makes no sense at all; it's an exaggeration; it's not historically correct. The *Binghamton* story *has to be written*!"

Gerry has told me this on more than one occasion.

---

*Early on, Gottheim's photography business, Be-hold, specialized in daguerreotypes and stereopticon images, but in recent years has broadened its reach to include both nineteenth-century photographers (Eugene Atget, William Henry Jackson, Carleton Watkins, etc.) and major twentieth-century photographers (Margaret Bourke-White, Imogen Cunningham, Andreas Feininger, Robert Frank, William Klein, John Pfahl, Annie Leibovitz, Jerry Uelsman, Weegee, etc.). See www.be-hold.com.

**Woody Vasulka and Peter Weibel, *Buffalo Heads: Media Study, Media Practices, Media Pioneers, 1973–1990*, catalog for a show at ZKM, the Center for Art and Media Karlsruhe, Germany, December 16, 2006–March 19, 2007, published by ZKM and MIT Press, 2006.

Ralph Hocking: You can't have invention without having crap flying around all the time. That's part of what art *is*. It's constant irritation, constant denial of the present time, or at least of the present thinking. New ideas are bubbling up and they create volcanoes. Looking back, I think it was all worth the effort, worth the energy. I know Larry gets blue once in a while about the whole thing: Was it worth it? And I say, "Hell yes, it was worth it! It was great; it was a wonderful time."

Appendix 1

A Pedagogical Cinema

Looking back from nearly half a century later, one of the exciting aspects of teaching cinema during the late 1960s and early 1970s should have been the fact that there seemed to be no recognized pedagogical rules for the new field. Those of us who were able to convince administrators that we should be allowed to offer film courses (or who answered administrative calls to offer courses in film) were, to an unusual degree, free to define both the content of such courses and the methods for teaching them. I say "should have been," because I expect that many, perhaps most novice cinema pedagogues tended (as I did) to fall back on their academic training and offer film history courses similar to the literature courses we were familiar with: that is, we presented a series of what we saw as masterworks of film history (or at least masterworks of feature narrative filmmaking) and discussed them with our students—perhaps a bit of filmmaking (in Super-8mm or 16mm) was included in the course, on the assumption that the hands-on process of shooting, seeing the results processed, then editing the rushes into a continuity was an efficient way to create more awareness of what the filmmakers whose work we discussed had done, or had directed others to do.

At Binghamton, Gottheim and Jacobs devised a quite different, more theoretical approach. While both men had developed their own senses of what film history was, they were less interested in accepting even the particular films they admired simply as models worthy of analysis and perhaps of imitation, than in considering what, fundamentally, cinema *was*—not only what it had been, even at its best, but what its ways of representing experience might be capable of revealing: that is, what was possible for cinema and for the study of cinema, whether there were cinematic precedents or not. For Gottheim and for all those who joined him in the Cinema Department during its early years, film study and filmmaking were essentially the same thing: one studied film history and made films in order to learn more about the medium. Ideally, this learning about the medium would enable both faculty and students to more fully understand not just cinema, but the world in which cinema had developed, and, in at least some circumstances, to make noteworthy cinematic contributions to this history. Cinema was a new academic discipline, but it was distinctive in its ability to be a nexus of many traditional art forms (literary fiction, drama, poetry, music, painting, photography . . .) and of the many dimensions of history and contemporary life it could represent and speak to. Those who were establishing cinema studies in academe could imagine that the new field might invigorate American academe itself.

Since virtually all the faculty who taught in the Cinema Department until the hiring of Maureen Turim in 1977 were active moving-image artists, it was inevitable that their creative activities would be an implicit (and sometimes explicit) part of their pedagogy. And not surprisingly, in many instances, the creativity of the faculty resulted in films, videos, and other forms of moving-image art that should be considered important contributions to the history of modern cinema—contributions that, in some cases, continue to offer a variety of valuable pedagogical opportunities for those teaching cinema.

Gottheim decided on Jacobs as his first full-time hire, in part because Jacobs had already produced a substantial body of film, but also because Jacobs had been, in his own way, using filmmaking as a way of thinking about the nature of cinema, and by the late 1960s, as a form of teaching. The often pedagogical nature of Jacobs's work of this period was evident, for example, in his decision in *Soft Rain* [1968] to show the same 3-minute long-shot of a Lower Manhattan street through the space between two buildings, three times. This was his way of suggesting that this cinematic space and the visual events occurring within it (the film is silent) needed to be reseen to be fully perceived and recognized as an investigation not just of the outer world of New York street life, but of the ways in which this particular space evokes the inside of a camera, and the distant street, a movie screen—that is, the ways in which cinema can be understood as endemic to urban life. Of course, Jacobs's pedagogical urge was most obvious in the epic *Tom, Tom, the Piper's Son* [1969, revised 1971], which was begun during Jacobs's first university teaching job, at St. John's University, and completed (and revised) simultaneously with Jacobs establishing himself at SUNY-Binghamton as Gottheim's colleague.

Tom, Tom, the Piper's Son is a landmark of what might be called pedagogical cinema, and, by all accounts, it encapsulates Jacobs's highly theoretical, but also resolutely personal approach to teaching film in the classroom. Jacobs's *Tom, Tom, the Piper's Son* begins by presenting in-full, the original *Tom, Tom, the Piper's Son* (1905), produced by the Biograph Company and probably directed and shot by G. W. "Billy" Bitzer (Jacobs worked with a print made by Kemp Niver from the Library of Congress's paper print collection, which became available to cineastes and filmmakers during the late 1960s). Within the body of his *Tom, Tom*, Jacobs provides an extensive exploration of the original film, more or less sequence-by-sequence, concluding with the original film, again seen in-full—as if to say to the viewer, "See what you can perceive in that early film *this time*, now that we've explored it in detail. Have you learned anything?"

The nature of Jacobs's exploration of the original *Tom, Tom* deserves attention, both since it characterizes Jacobs's pedagogy and also since it defies not only what, a decade or so later, would come to be understood as cinematic analysis—Jacobs's "analysis" is visual, not verbal, and it employs no identifiable theoretical framework as a way of coming to grips with the "cinematic text"—but also the approach of "structural film," which, beginning in the 1960s, represented a major attempt by independent filmmakers to explore the essential nature of cinema.[1] As P. Adams Sitney suggested long ago, and reconfirmed in the 2002 edition of his *Visionary Film*, while Jacobs's *Tom, Tom* uses strategies consonant with structural film (rephotography, most obviously and the flicker effect), and while a description of the film can make its structure seem relatively simple, *Tom, Tom* does not fit within a "cinema of structure," in which "the shape of the whole film is predetermined and simplified"; and in which "it is that shape which is the primal impression of the film."[2] The experience of Jacobs's *Tom, Tom* is anything but simplified and its overall structure is violated—in each of the versions of *Tom, Tom* that has existed—in a variety of ways.[3]

1. Bart Testa provides a useful overview of Jacobs's method of analysis in *Tom, Tom*, in his *Back and Forth: Early Cinema and the Avant-Garde* (Toronto: Art Gallery of Ontario, 1992): 7–14

2. See P. Adams Sitney, *Visionary Film: The American Avant-Garde, 1943–2000* (New York: Oxford University Press, 2002): 348, 344.

Sitney defines four "characteristics of the structural film": "its fixed camera position (fixed frame from the viewer's perspective), the flicker effect, loop printing, and rephotography off the screen"—rarely "will one find all four characteristics in a single film" (348).

3. Sitney explains that in "the three versions of the film I have seen, there is a marked difference of architecture. They each violate symmetry by appending a series of slow-motion details after the second presentation of the original film. The second version, however, introduces color inserts of a shadow play (another mixed form which Jacobs practices, especially in three-dimensional stereoscope) which violently interrupt the continuity of the black-and-white film" (344).

Jacobs's analysis of the original *Tom, Tom* is resolutely personal and perceptually and conceptually exploratory: during the body of his *Tom, Tom*, one can sense that Jacobs's method of rephotography—his use of an analytic projector to slow the original film down, the ability to provide close-up looks at spaces within the graphic space of the original film detached from their larger context—allowed him to discover elements of form and chiaroscuro, as well as conceptual implications, that wouldn't be evident in even the best experience of the original film.[4] Eivind Røssaak mentions how Jacobs reveals within the rather chaotic opening tableaux of the original *Tom, Tom* moments when the "spectator may momentarily forget the filmic diegesis and see, instead, real people working on a stage in downtown New York in 1905."[5] Jacobs himself has said that looking at the original *Tom, Tom* "popped my eyes out! But it was the longest time before I could grasp *any* narrative order to it—I mean dozens of viewings before there was even a *pig* there. It was the welter of commotion that fascinated me, and then the hide-and-seek thing of picking out people, objects, events. And it was so beautiful, so beautiful."[6]

What makes Jacobs's exploration of the original *Tom, Tom* distinct from more usual forms of film analysis, however, is his interest in not simply seeing into (and seeing through) what happens during the "seven infinitely complex cinetapestries" (from Jacobs's description of the film on the Film-Makers' Cooperative website), but his determination to engage with this material, to transform it into something quite his own, often into a series of perceptual/conceptual experiences that reflect his personal history and his then-current fascinations.

One of the more obvious dimensions of what is essentially a redirection of the original material is the long passage early in *Tom, Tom* during which the filmstrip is moved past the projector gate so quickly that none of the original imagery can be seen, but so that the fast-moving filmstrip itself creates the illusion of simultaneous vertical motion both

4. In "Acts of Delay: The Play Between Stillness and Motion in *Tom, Tom, The Piper's Son*," Røssaak Eivind describes Jacobs's method as Jacobs described it to him: "Two people actively took part in the production of the film: a person operating a projector behind the [translucent] screen (Jacobs), and a camera operator (Jacobs and his friend Jordan Meyers) in front of it. Jacobs used an RCA home sound-projector with a hand-controllable clutch that allowed for showing and even stopping the film. Jacobs directed the activities and edited the material in postproduction." See Paul Arthur, David E. James, and Michele Pierson, *Optic Antics: The Cinema of Ken Jacobs* (New York: Oxford University Press, 2011): 99.

5. Ibid., 103.

6. Ken Jacobs in interview in Scott MacDonald, *A Critical Cinema 3* (Berkeley: University of California Press, 1998): 380–81.

down and up. Another is Jacobs's frequent reframing of the original imagery so that portions of the imagery become resonant of the history of abstract painting that Jacobs was familiar with from studying with Hans Hoffmann and from seeing work by such painters as Jackson Pollock, Franz Kline, and Robert Motherwell.

In his comments on the original *Tom, Tom*, Jacobs has always been deeply respectful of the film, and this respect is evident in his extensive and painstaking exploration (the original film's 10 minutes is expanded into approximately 90 minutes of visual analysis). Jacobs has always been an autodidact, and his recognition that early cinema was worthy of serious attention predates the work of pioneering scholars like Charles Musser and Tom Gunning—indeed, the seriousness with which *Tom, Tom, the Piper's Son* takes an early film may have helped energize their work.

But for Jacobs, respect for an early work means more than detached admiration, even more than an opportunity for retraining perception and sensitizing our ability to fully see a film. For Jacobs respect means creating an ongoing, two-way relationship with a work: on the one hand, making his insights part of any subsequent engagement with the respected original (could anyone now discuss the Biograph *Tom, Tom* without discussing Jacobs's "reading" of it?),[7] and on the other, incorporating the original film into his own, quite different work—an approach which would some years later come to dominate Jacobs's "Nervous System" performances.

7. In *The Emergence of Cinema: The American Screen to 1907* (Berkeley: University of California Press, 1990), Charles Musser defends the Biograph *Tom, Tom, the Piper's Son* from this comment by Noël Burch: "It is, of course, with the future course of film history that Ken Jacobs' work on this film engages directly, through his refilming procedures. The opening shot of the film, so typically primitive in that its narrative substance is totally unreadable for the modern eye at first viewing, is analyzed in a way evocative—though only evocative—of the linearizing editing procedures of the institution [presumably the "institution" of narrative cinema as it evolved], so that it becomes readable on second viewing. Here, I feel, is a wonderful example of a combination of work and play on the materials of a crucial historical process"—see Burch, "Primitivism and the Avant-Gardes: A Dialectical Approach," in Philip Rosen, ed., *Narrative, Apparatus, Ideology* (New York: Columbia University Press, 1986): 502. Musser sees Burch, "inspired by experimental filmmaker Ken Jacobs' *Tom, Tom, the Piper's Son*," as overestimating the difficulty of reading the Biograph *Tom, Tom*. For Musser, the original nursery rhyme and the reference to Hogarth's *Southwark Fair* (1734) make the film's opening tableau "a sophisticated, if not totally successful principle of organization, whereby references to the poem and engraving provided some spectators with a basis for deciphering the film's complex, busy opening scene" (and "the other shots in this film have clearly 'readable' compositions"): 383. That Jacobs's film would be seen as a support for the idea that the original *Tom, Tom* is a "primitive" film seems ironic—indeed, Jacobs confirms Musser's take on the film at the beginning of his digital work, *Return to the Scene of the Crime* (2008), which revisits both the original *Tom, Tom* and his own—the digital piece begins with Hogarth's *Southwark Fair*.

During the early years of his tenure at SUNY-Binghamton, Jacobs channeled his creative energies into his teaching—he understood his lectures as pedagogical performance art—and into what he called "shadow play," performances made collaboratively with Binghamton students that explored, among other aspects of moving-image art, 3-D, which in time would become a crucial dimension of Jacobs's filmmaking. The one film Jacobs began and completed during the years documented in this study is *Urban Peasants* (1975), like *Tom, Tom, the Piper's Son* an exercise in the recycling of earlier film, but in this instance of home movies shot, according to Jacobs's description on the Film-makers' Cooperative website, by "My wife Flo's family as recorded by her Aunt Stella" and "chance assembled by Ken Jacobs from uncut 100-foot lengths." *Urban Peasants* is an early honoring of home movies as a record not merely of a particular family's special occasions, but of a moment in American cultural history—it seems a premonition of SUNY-Binghamton veteran Alan Berliner's *The Family Album* (1986).

During the fall of 1970, his and Flo's first months in Binghamton, Jacobs shot material for a film that was never completed, but which has become something of a legend because of its provocative title: "Binghamton, My India." The title (which is not on the lone print of this film, nor are there end credits) suggests that for Jacobs, living in Binghamton was—after a lifetime in New York City—exotic. It is tempting to imagine that he saw the Binghamton area as destitute of what is necessary for the sustaining of a full life (in the 1970s India was, for most Americans, emblematic of Third World poverty), but at this early moment in his time at SUNY-Binghamton, cynicism seems unlikely. The 35 minutes of *Binghamton, My India* offer a series of rolls of 16mm film in which Jacobs explores the mundane life around him in something like the way he explores the original *Tom, Tom, the Piper's Son*—often, for example, he discovers abstract compositional moments within the panorama of normal reality. The early rolls of the film focus on Binghamton; the final rolls are a portrait of Flo Jacobs as a young mother. As for not completing the film, Jacobs has said, "I didn't reject it. I care for it very much, it just got away from me"; he seems to have despaired that "anyone would acknowledge it. It's so quiet."[8]

By the time Gottheim established the Cinema Department, he had made several films (occasional films useful within the university, and a variety of experiments), but just as the Cinema Department was coming into being in 1969–71, he was rebooting his fledgling filmmaking career by making a series of films that were not simply individual works of film

8. E-mail to the author, May 10, 2014.

art, but an attempt at using film—as Jacobs used film in *Tom, Tom, the Piper's Son*—"as a way of teaching people how to see," and to raise a question "about what 'to see a film' means"[9]—though Gottheim's sense of what it was important to look at was rather different from Jacobs's.

Gottheim's new exploration of the nature of cinema was closely related, at least conceptually, to a slightly previous "rebooting" that had occupied Ernie Gehr, who had agreed to teach filmmaking at Binghamton the summer before Jacobs arrived and the department was formally in operation. Like Gottheim, Gehr had experimented early on with more conventional kinds of film before committing himself to an exploration of the fundamental conditions of cinema, first in his *Morning* (1967) and *Still* (1967) and subsequently in other films, including those he shot in Binghamton during the summer of 1970: *Field*, which exists in a long version (19 minutes at 16 frames per second; 1970) and in a shorter version (9½ minutes, 1970), and *Serene Velocity* (1970), which is discussed in more detail at the conclusion of this essay.

In *Field*, Gehr was coming to terms with the cinematic "field" defined by the frame, as well as the fields he was seeing around him during this summer in rural New York State:

> All the films that I made before *Field* and *Serene Velocity* were made in New York City and were urban pieces. *Field*, on the other hand, might be called a "country" piece. Interesting what I came up with working in nature! The title is a reference to the "field" that brings us cinematic works, the screen rectangle, as well as to a "field" in nature. However, because of the speed at which I was filming, you never see that place depicted realistically, only in terms of what that resulting field of gray might evoke in your imagination.
>
> I could have chosen color, but I was interested in working with a field of grays.[10]

Gehr recorded "a little field that included some grass, a small lake, and a row of trees in the background" by swish-panning back and forth across the scene. In the resulting imagery all that is clear is that there *is* motion.[11] As P. Adams Sitney has described it, "The speed [of Gehr's camera movements] is so great and the optical highlights so homogeneous

9. See interview with Larry Gottheim, in Scott MacDonald, *A Critical Cinema* (Berkeley: University of California Press, 1988): 84, 83.

10. Interview with Ernie Gehr, in Scott MacDonald, *A Critical Cinema 5* (Berkeley: University of California Press, 2006): 373.

11. Ibid.: 372.

that it is very difficult to determine whether the movement is downward from the upper left corner of the screen or upward from the opposite corner."[12] On one level, *Field* functions as a metaphor for the idea that cinema *is* movement and for a recognition that cinema tends to distort, to refashion into mystery, whatever it records. Basically, as he would do later in *Serene Velocity* (with particular relevance to the achievement of the Binghamton Cinema Department), in *Field* Gehr demonstrates the power of cinema to transform the mundane into the ineffable.

Several of Gottheim's films from the early 1970s—in particular, *Fog Line* (1970), *Barn Rushes* (1971), and *Horizons* (1973)—can be understood as premonitions of the now burgeoning cinema of Place as well as important contributions to what has come to be called "ecocinema."[13] What was fascinating to Gottheim during the early 1970s—though in an entirely different way from what fascinated Gehr in *Field*—were the subtle intersections between the natural world surrounding his home in the pastoral landscape outside of Binghamton and the mechanical/chemical medium of film, that is, between natural process and the technology that recorded it.

Gottheim's films from this period can be read as a conscious set of pedagogical exercises, made to help Gottheim himself, and whoever else saw these films, explore the nature of cinema and its theoretical and historical underpinnings, cumulatively, one element at a time. Gottheim's first focus was the single, continuous shot. A series of single-shot films—*Blues* (1969), *Corn* (1970), *Fog Line* (1970), *Doorway* (1971), and *Harmonica* (1971)—offered a panorama of single-shot possibilities for representing everyday realities: for *Blues*, *Corn*, and *Fog Line*, the viewer is asked to contemplate carefully framed moments recorded by an unmoving camera in close-up, medium shot, and long shot, respectively. In *Doorway* and *Harmonica*, Gottheim moves the camera, in a continuous pan (in *Doorway*) and in a kind of tracking shot (in *Harmonica*).

While all of these films can be understood as explorations of basic cinematic elements and a form of cine-training in patient presence when viewing the world and cinematic images of it, two of the films seem to be more directly *about* pedagogy, one of them metaphorically, the other quite directly. In *Fog Line* the foggy landscape gradually clears so that the particulars of an expansive pasture become increasingly visible

12. P. Adams Sitney, in *Gehr*, a monograph published by the Walker Art Center and Film in the Cities in 1980: 10.

13. See, for example, Dean Cubitt, Salma Monani, and Stephen Rust, eds., *Ecocinema Theory and Practice* (New York: Routledge, 2013).

(and so that midway through the film, viewers can, just barely, see two horses graze across the lower part of the image from right to left—an implicit, wry reference perhaps to Eadweard Muybridge's motion study photographs). As simple as *Fog Line* can seem, it is rich with subtlety and implication—and can easily be read as a cine-metaphor for the process of coming to understand: at first we are literally "in a fog," but gradually, if we are patient and see the film through, we recognize where we are (if my memory serves, Gottheim himself suggested this reading to me).

Harmonica is the only one of the early single-shot Gottheim films that includes a human character: Shelley Berde, a student at the time, who sits in the back seat of a car, playing his harmonica, as the car is driven around an autumnal landscape for 10½ minutes. The side window of the car is open and gradually Berde realizes that not only can *he* play the harmonica, but the air blowing past the window can also play it, and once he has discovered this, Berde explores a range of ways of collaborating with the wind to make music. His inventiveness with his "mouth harp" is a veritable demonstration of the creative process, of learning by doing (Berde's persistence in exploring what the wind can do was presumably instigated by Gottheim's decision to use an extended shot, and is a reflection of it), as well as an allusion to the Aeolian harp, the stringed instrument played by the wind, so dear to the Romantic poets as an emblem of the natural world as the source of creative inspiration. Of course, here, as in the Aeolian harp metaphor, the music is made by a combination of natural forces and human inventiveness, including, in the case of *Harmonica*, the inventiveness embedded in the modern technologies of the camera and the automobile.

Having explored some of the possibilities of the single shot, Gottheim (like film history itself) turned his attention to editing, beginning, in *Barn Rushes* (1971), by simply editing rushes together: *Barn Rushes* is composed of eight, silent, one-hundred-foot-long tracking shots filmed from car moving past an old barn at different times of the day and during different moments in the year. Like his earlier films (and like *Tom, Tom, the Piper's Son* and Jacobs's other work of this period), *Barn Rushes* is, on the most obvious level, a perceptual teaching process. Evocative of Monet's haystack series, each "rush" by the barn reveals different dimensions of cinema's capacity for representing space and chiaroscuro, revealing and emphasizing different visual relationships between the barn and its foreground and background. As in so many of the films of Warhol, who seems to have been a crucial influence on Gottheim, each shot in *Barn Rushes* begins and ends with flare-outs and perforations, emphasizing the medium of film in the way that Monet's brushwork emphasizes the act of painting.

Gottheim's process of teaching himself (and his students and those public audiences that saw his films) about the nature and possibilities of cinema reached an apogee in the two feature films that would follow: *Horizons* (1973) and *Mouches Volantes* (1976). Gottheim would come to understand these two films, along with *Four Shadows* (1978) and *Tree of Knowledge* (1980) as parts of a four-part epic, called—after Goethe—*Elective Affinities*.

In *Horizons* (the "Overture" of *Elective Affinities*) the cinematic "horizon" was the splice, the line that in film separates one space from another, as well as editing in a more general sense, which Gottheim approached in a thoroughly distinctive manner. Having spent many months collecting imagery mostly in and around the pastoral landscape near Binghamton, Gottheim chose 596 individual images and then studied them, making detailed notes of every nuance of each image on three-by-five note cards. Having decided to arrange his first feature (*Horizons* is 75 minutes) as a seasonal cycle, Gottheim organized the images into the four seasons in a manner that reflected the seasonal realities around Binghamton (summer is the shortest season; winter, the longest), using a visual "rhyme scheme."

A different "rhyme" was devised for each season, beginning with summer, in which pairs of shots are separated by one-second moments of monochrome green. Within each pair of images, one or more particular visual incidents are repeated—"rhyme." The simple rhyming structure of the summer section prepares those viewers who tune into the rhyming (it is possible to enjoy *Horizons*, or not enjoy it, without becoming aware of the rhyme scheme) for the more complex rhyming in fall and winter: in fall, "stanzas" of four images, each stanza separated from the previous by one second of red, rhyme a, b, b, a; in winter, the four-image stanzas, separated from one another by one second of blue, are arranged a, b, a, b. And for spring, Gottheim chose a variation of Dante's terza rima, within which each stanza is made up of three images separated from the next stanza by one-second moments of yellow. Classic terza rima involves a complex relationship both within and between stanzas: the organization of the rhymes in successive stanzas is a, b, a, then b, c, b, then c, d, c; Gottheim's terza rima is a variation: b, a, b is followed by c, b, c, then by d, c, d—allowing viewers to recognize a rhyme in the first triad of shots, then carry this recognition over to the following triad and find the rhyme in the second image (had Gottheim used the classic terza rima, viewers wouldn't know what to look for as they transitioned from one stanza to the next).

The pedagogical function of this complex, and unprecedented, organization of images is to challenge viewers to examine each film image thoroughly, to become aware of every sector and every implication of each composition. In one sense this is not so different from Jacobs's quest in *Tom, Tom, the Piper's Son* to reveal a panoply of visual events within a recycled film, but whereas Jacobs shows us what *he* has noticed, Gottheim challenges us to discover the specifics of individual images and the various relationships between images for ourselves, just as he discovered them during the process of deciding what was in the images and how they should be organized within *Horizons*.

The concluding minutes of *Horizons* include an extended homage to the Cinema Department. A few moments after the arrival of spring is announced by shots of Peter Kubelka playing a flute (a nod to Pan), we see imagery recorded on the Sunday afternoon following the conclusion of the first university-wide film symposium in April 1972. Here, Gottheim's referencing of classic mythology and works of literature (particularly, Virgil's *Georgics*) and music (Vivaldi's *The Four Seasons*) reaches an apogee. Within the pastoral landscape at Gottheim's home in the countryside above the city of Binghamton and the SUNY-Binghamton campus, Ken Jacobs and a group of students are sitting in a circle with Jacobs apparently speaking about some aspect of cinema (Nick Ray walks nearby). The scene seems meant to evoke Plato's Academy, located near a sacred grove of olive trees outside of Athens—an apt reference for Gottheim and his vision of the Cinema Department as the potential fountainhead of a new school of (cinematic) philosophy, cinema-as-theory in direct engagement with the real world.

Whatever tensions were developing among Ray, Jacobs, and Gottheim, among their students, and between the Cinema Department and the university seem unimportant in this idyllic scene, subsumed within the living (if momentary) ideal of a new form of cinematic education. Gottheim's excitement at having transformed his life and successfully brought the department into being seems encapsulated by his participation within this moment as filmmaker, and it is confirmed by the film's concluding imagery of his wife Deborah Chess and their children walking through a glowing Edenic landscape—a golden moment evocative of a golden age.

Gottheim's next challenge was to bring sound into play in his work, in a manner more complex and challenging than was evident in his sync-sound recording of Shelley Berde in *Harmonica*. The result was *Mouches Volantes* ("mouches volantes" refers to the "flying gnats" described by H. Von Helmholtz in *Physiological Optics* [1866], which float within the vitreous humor of the eye, visible just at the edge of perception). During the film Gottheim presents a series of seven separate sequences filmed in and around his home and during a family vacation in Florida, organized within a highly formalized structure: the seven sequences are arranged so they are seen as 1, 2, 3, 4, 5, 6, 7, 7, 6, 5, 4, 3, 2, 1. Each sequence lasts 4 minutes and 51 seconds; a glue splice can be seen and heard dividing each sequence from the next—*Mouches Volantes* is 69 minutes long.

The soundtrack is composed of seven repetitions of a set of reminiscences about blues singer Blind Willie Johnson by his widow, Angelina Johnson, edited from a Folkways record. Johnson's reminiscences are intercut with passages of near silence (the film running through the projector creates auditory mouches volantes: crackles from dust, the sounds of the glue splices); that is, each sequence of imagery is heard both "silent" and accompanied by Angelina Johnson's reminiscences, which are heard with the first presentation of sequences 2, 4, 6, and the second presentations of sequences 7, 5, 3, and 1.

Here, Gottheim's approach echoes Jacobs's in *Tom, Tom* to the extent that our opportunity to see sequences of imagery twice, in different contexts, and to hear a sound sequence seven times, each time opposite different visuals, continually alters our sense of what we are seeing and hearing. Experiencing the visual sequences in different contexts foregrounds different details, and the sevenfold repetition of Angelina Johnson's comments allows for an evolution in the audience's comprehension of her dialectical particularities and thus of the story she tells.

The idea of mouches volantes is evident throughout *Mouches Volantes*, in that we become conscious of qualities of image and sound that at first lie so close to our perceptual thresholds that we tend to ignore them. For example, the first sequence of imagery, the most abstract in the film, begins with black-and-white strobe-like flashes of what we come to realize are images a child in the surf (the imagery is at first out-of-focus, then in focus), followed by shots of the moon within barely visible images of palm trees. This Florida imagery is intercut with gestural, handheld images of snow, scintillant against a pitch-black background. The opening sequence is first seen in silence, but when it is repeated as the conclusion of *Mouches Volantes*, accompanied by the recording of Angelina Johnson's reminiscences, the strobe-like flashing that opens the sequence matches a tapping sound, barely audible within Johnson's comments, bringing that tapping into the foreground of consciousness. By 1976 Gottheim had come to understand that his job as film professor was about using the movie theater to expand his students' ability to see *and hear*.

Though the experimental arrangement of image and sound is the primary area of exploration in *Mouches Volantes*, the film can also be seen as Gottheim's engagement with a variety of dimensions of cinema beyond the kinds of composition, camera movement, and editing explored in his earlier films. While *Horizons* is shot entirely with handheld camera,

Mouches Volantes was shot with both handheld camera (often more gesturally than in *Horizons*) and tripod-mounted shots in which Gottheim explores the possibilities of adjusting the lens to create a variety of in- and out-of-focus events and manipulating the aperture to explore chiaroscuro, as well as (in sequences 6 and 7) combinations of black and white and color.[14] Ultimately, the film's combination of widely diverse subject matters—silent home movies of a middle-class European-American family at play during a Binghamton winter and on vacation in Florida (and in sequence 3, Deborah Chess beekeeping) and recycled audio material focusing on moments in the lives of two African Americans from the Deep South—seems a ground against which to figure conceptual mouches volantes: the film seems to challenge us to find ways of bringing these two very different social worlds and two quite different forms of representation together, to discover relationships between them.

Four Shadows builds on Gottheim's attempt in *Mouches Volantes* to combine imagery and sound in conceptually inventive ways. Here four, 4-minute sequences of imagery—surveyors working in a field, pages in an art history book about Cézanne, a series of winterscapes filmed in Binghamton, and a family of siamang gibbons filmed at the National Zoo in Washington—are juxtaposed with four, 4-minute passages of sound: outdoor country sounds, including a babbling brook; readings of a passage from Wordsworth's *Prelude*; a portion of Debussy's *Pélleas et Mélisande*; and the shrieks and hootings of the gibbons. The eight passages of image and sound are arranged so that during the 64 minutes of the film, each passage of visuals is seen in juxtaposition with each passage of sound. Within the four sections, imagery and sound are "synced" in a range of ways, though the only sync-sound passage is the concluding one, when the sounds and images of the gibbons come together.

As an implicit nod, perhaps, to the final section of Frampton's *Zorns Lemma* (1970), where six women read a Robert Grosseteste text, in *Four Shadows*, the lines from *The Prelude* are read, in each instance, by four different voices: the readers include, in order, Vincent Grenier, Heinz Emigholz, Jonas Mekas, Rosalie Berdé; then, Reza Bassiry, Flora Moscatelli, Peter Kubelka, Taka Iimura; then, Giovanni Gullace, Miñuca Villaverde, Alfons Schilling, Babette Mangolte; and finally Oyebanjo

14. The arrival of color, once we've become accustomed to Gottheim's elegant, high-contrast black and white, is reminiscent of Jacobs's use of bits of color footage of shadow play in *Tom, Tom, the Piper's Son*, once viewers have become accustomed to his consistent use of black and white. The opening strobe-like imagery in *Mouches Volantes* also seems reminiscent of some of Jacobs's abstractions in *Tom, Tom*.

Olakunle, Akiko Iimura, Maja Frenkler, and Klaus Wyborny.[15] I read this implicit auditory gathering of Cinema Department faculty and visitors, as quite different from the one near the end of *Horizons*. This gathering seems to me a form of reminiscence on Gottheim's part about the excitement of earlier years, at a moment when he could feel the nature of the Cinema Department changing and his original enthusiasm fading.

During the time when Gottheim was using his filmmaking to explore the fundamentals of cinema, Ralph Hocking was finding his way into video. Bruce Dearing, then-president of SUNY-Binghamton, had hired Hocking before it was clear exactly how he might function as a faculty member. In the wake of seeing Nam June Paik's early work with television monitors in New York City, Hocking became interested in how television might be used in formal education; in time he explored the possibilities of the Portapak and made the new recording device available to his students. And he did a series of pioneering experiments exploring the nature and possibilities of what would come to be called video art.

While the series of videos Hocking produced between 1969 and 1977 seem to have functioned for Hocking as Gottheim's films after *Blues* functioned for him, there was a significant difference. By the time Gottheim began to systematically rethink filmmaking, there was not only a considerable history of commercial film, but a set of countercinemas—documentary, avant-garde film, experimental animation—each of which had its own history. As Hocking began to work in video, there was only the relatively brief history of commercial television and the most tentative experiments in video art. Gottheim was interested in rethinking film history by going back to fundamentals; Hocking was struggling to understand what the fundamentals of video *were*. *The Experiment* (1969, Hocking has said it was "the first tape I remember saving"), dramatizes his situation.[16]

From its opening moment, *The Experiment* declares itself a work about equipment and process: we see Hocking walk from the foreground (in fact, from behind the video camera making the image we're seeing)

15. According to Gottheim (in an e-mail to the author, July 7, 2013), Rosalie Berdé was the mother of Shelley Berde, the harmonica player in *Harmonica*; Reza Bassiry was a "Persian poet" (his term for himself, according to Gottheim) who took classes with Gottheim; Flora Moscatelli, was a friend of Gottheim's wife Deborah Chess; Giovanni Gullace, professor of Italian at Binghamton; Miñuca Vallaverde, a filmmaker "from someplace in Latin America" ("I befriended her when we were on an arts panel"); Oyebanjo Olakunle, one of Gottheim's students, from Africa ("Nigeria, I think"); and Maja Fenkler, a graduate student in comparative literature at Binghamton.

16. In 2004 Hocking released a DVD, "Work 1969 to 1986," with a sampling of his video work, accompanied by a brochure with comments on his history as a video artist and on the specific videos. His comments on his biography seem to have been recorded in 1986.

into a makeshift studio where a dolly, more or less center screen, holds a television and, below it, a reel-to-reel videotape deck. Hocking turns on a radio just outside the frame at the left and tunes it to classical music (a piece by Vivaldi), after which he steps to the dolly, begins to thread a tape onto the deck, and turns on the television, which broadcasts a skit from the *Carol Burnett Show*: a man and a woman have apparently met on a park bench and seem to be seducing one another. As the couple, now in close-up, comically kiss, Hocking walks behind the dolly where he picks up a speaker that he places on top of the television. The man in the skit realizes he is late for an appointment and leaves, and the television show cuts to a second skit in which a woman describes the problems with her broken watch and asks a watchmaker, "What do you think?" The watchmaker responds, "I think I am falling in love with you." At this point, Hocking comes around to the front of the television, turns on the tape deck and, for a moment, we see a close-up of a woman. Hocking stops the tape and replaces it with another.

Now we see the makeshift studio *on* the television screen as well as surrounding it, Hocking walks into the space-within-the-space, echoing his entrance at the beginning of *The Experiment*. When his TV-screen double bends down to thread a tape, Hocking, who has been watching himself on TV, turns from the TV and walks into our foreground and out of the frame. The position of the camera that is recording what we're seeing is then adjusted so that the screen of the television becomes a full-frame image. Within this image-within-the image, Hocking is again seen walking out of the frame and again the framing is readjusted so that the television within the image-within-the-image is seen full frame. Hocking walks out of the image once more, and repositions the camera so that the television image (within the image within the image) is, once again, roughly full frame—this time when we see him entering the studio, he is moving the dolly into the position where it has been from the beginning. Hocking turns on the television and lights a cigarette; the music fades out and the tape ends.[17]

---

17. In his program notes for the DVD *Work 1969 to 1986*, Hocking explains that the original tape was 20 minutes long and that the 8 minutes on the DVD is "an unedited portion from the beginning of the tape." To make *The Experiment* Hocking used a camera/recorder and a tape deck and monitor for playback (the camera had no playback option). He recorded the activities in front of the camera, then played that tape on the playback setup and recorded it on a second tape; the second tape was then placed in the playback unit, and, using the first tape (recording over that first tape), Hocking then recorded the second tape as it played on the monitor. In other words, in watching *The Experiment* we are moving back through the process that produced the tape: what we see at the beginning is the last tape Hocking recorded for the project; what we see at the end is the beginning of the process.

The two fundamental elements of video that Hocking seems fascinated with in *The Experiment* are its ability to play with time and space and the way in which, when the television image is recorded by the video camera, the image becomes less clear, the raster lines more obvious. It is also obvious that Hocking sees the enterprise of exploring video as a turning away from what had become the conventions of cinema. This is clear in the way he ignores the excerpt from the *Carol Burnett Show* (which viewers tend to become involved in), going about his work as it plays; and it is evident in the "plumber's crack" that is visible every time Hocking crouches to put a tape on or take a tape off the VCR (it's as if he's mooning our conventional assumptions of what we might see on a television screen), and in the fact that immediately after the man in the second skit says, "I think I'm falling in love with you," Hocking replaces that image first with a taped image of a woman, then for the remainder of the video with a tape of himself "falling in love with" the possibilities of video that are made evident as Hocking proceeds to create/discover a mind-bending layering of time and an Escher-esque collapsing of space within a single, continuous recording.

What is enacted in the "present" of the video (as it is excerpted on Hocking's retrospective DVD) is a defiant everydayness, a choreography of the everyday à la Yvonne Rainer's early performances. *The Experiment* is a demonstration of some of the capacities of a new art medium—Hocking essentially demonstrates to us how he taught himself. The Vivaldi music, which plays throughout the piece, suggests that Hocking sees video not just as a potential challenge to commercial television, but as heralding a new era in the evolution of culture, an electronic art that has the capacity to produce work that someday will be as fully accepted as classical music.

In the years that followed his production of *The Experiment*, Hocking demonstrated other capacities of video. In *Fishing* (1971) he "goes fishing" with his video camera at Sag Harbor: he records Dom Annacone cleaning fish at the edge of an inlet, then increasingly focuses on the surface of the water, first as the wake of a boat affects it, then in a 7-plus-minute shot (there may be an invisible cut during this passage) as the surface of the water is disturbed by fish jumping (they were eating the guts of the fish Annacone was cleaning), then becomes increasingly calm. While cineastes in 1971 would, no doubt, have complained about the quality of the imagery in *Fishing*, seen on their own terms the opening shots evoke Whistler and Ralph Albert Blakelock, and Hocking's subsequent meditation on the water allows the complexity of the soundscape within and around the frame to become the foreground of our attention: the ease with which video could record sound and the quality of that sound, especially in comparison with the sound on 16mm optical tracks, would soon lure others to the new medium.

In *Second Bach Dance* (1973), *Sitting by the Window* (1977), and *Scrambled Legs* (1977), Hocking continued to explore and demonstrate the manifold potentials of his new medium. In *Second Bach Dance*, Hocking combines imagery abstracted from Sherry Miller (now, Sherry Miller Hocking) performing various movements (in response to seeing herself on a monitor) and a television broadcast of a basketball game. When, halfway through the excerpt included on the *Work* DVD, the basketball game fades in to become the background for the colors and textures of/around Sherry Miller's mirrored and doubled movements, Hocking is not only revealing that video allows for on-the-spot combinations of very different kinds of imagery, but is demonstrating how far from its earlier history as a simple broadcasting and recording medium video has come. Again, the use of classical music (Bach, here) signals Hocking's continuing commitment to the idea of video as a new art form.[18]

Sitting by the Window and *Scrambled Legs* demonstrate the capacity of what was by 1977 a new video option: switching between multiple cameras simultaneously recording the same activity. In *Sitting by the Window* Sherry Miller sits on a futon by a window as several video cameras (Hocking thinks it was probably six), record her from varied angles and distances. The cameras are arranged so that we see a sequence of bits of the scene. The piece begins in the dark with the electronic sound of the switching—rhythmic bips that function as a kind of music. Gradually, the scene is revealed as various images of Sherry Miller's movements dance in time to this music. A mirror placed to the right of the space creates a further doubling of her movements. It is the immediacy of this process that was revolutionary: a physical action is transformed into a visual phantasmagoria as it is happening, and without the necessity of editing. Though the imagery itself—a nude woman relaxing by window—recalls the reclining nude tradition in painting, the video itself is at least as close to music, to the *performance of music*, as it is to filmmaking.

In *Scrambled Legs* Sherry Miller crosses and recrosses her legs, over and over, as oscillators switch from one to another camera (again, Hocking remembers six). More central to this video than to *Sitting by*

18. In his notes on *Second Bach Dance*, Hocking suggests that in retrospect he came to feel that his use of Bach "was troublesome. Stealing the music was not honorable. Stealing the ball game didn't matter," and that after this, he "gave up stealing and used only my inventions." The distinction he makes between Bach and the ballgame confirms his respect for a classic composer and the implication that what he is doing might become the new classicism.

the Window (though it is also evident there) is the introduction of a then-new palette of video color and texture. As in *Sitting by the Window*, the tapping created by the switching becomes a rhythmic background for Sherry Miller's movements and the transformations created by the switching cameras—though here the effect is less that of flickering views of a space than a flowing overlay of continuous in-close movement on the part of the subject.

Hocking's consistent use of the nude in these early videos has a number of implications. It not only recalls the centuries-old tradition of the female nude in painting and sculpture—Hocking's way of positioning his work within a fine art context; it reflects his fascination with the new sensuality he was discovering with his partner and lover Sherry Miller (in a sense they perform for each other in these videos); it evokes Eadweard Muybridge's motion studies, which helped to open the way for cinema, video's elder sibling—and, in time, it brought Hocking into collision with the sometimes puritanical feminism that was arriving in academe during the late 1970s. This generation of academic feminists questioned, and often rejected, the very historical antecedents to which Hocking's videos refer, and especially the nudity of women in film (and video) and what Laura Mulvey called "the male gaze."

A number of filmmakers who visited the Cinema Department made work during their visits. Hollis Frampton's visits were particularly important, both because of the films he shot during 1971, and also because his not being hired by the Cinema Department (in part because of these films) seems to have represented an early fissure in the department's collegial solidarity. Gottheim and Frampton had met when Gottheim attended Oberlin College as an undergraduate, and they were back in touch during the formative years of the Cinema Department.[19] In February of 1971, Frampton visited Binghamton to screen films and to work with some of the Cinema Department faculty and students in making *Critical Mass* (1971) and *Travelling Matte* (1971)—what turned out to be the third and fourth sections of *Hapax Legomena*. For *Critical Mass* Frampton enlisted two students, Barbara DiBenedetto and Frank Albetta, as actors in a lovers' quarrel (see Frampton's memory of this process on pages 92–93, 95). Gottheim served as a sound recordist. Frampton made

19. The relationships between the work of the two filmmakers have not been explored—despite the considerable scholarly work done on Frampton in recent years. Both used what, in retrospect, seem game-like structures to engage viewers in thinking about the nature of cinema and to engage themselves in the realities of living in central New York State. *Horizons* bears comparison with *Zorns Lemma*; and the four-part *Elective Affinities* series, with Frampton's seven-part *Hapax Legomena*.

three copies of the image and sound he had recorded, and, during the following months, edited *Critical Mass* so that the resulting film provides an implicit conceptual riff on the commercial cinema's dependence on sync sound, particularly in films focusing on romantic relationships.

In commercial films, sync sound has always been most important for spoken dialogue, and traditionally this required a double system: that is, sound and image were worked on separately and "married" during the final stage of production (in celluloid cinema a "married print" cannot be edited—since the sound that accompanies a particular image is located several frames away from the gate of the projector). Frampton seems to have understood the pun implicit in "marrying" image and sound: so many Hollywood films made during the 1930s to 1950s, when Frampton was growing up, end in marriage or assume that marriage is the culmination of whatever romantic action and dialogue fuels the narrative. As a filmmaker committed to working independently ("independent," specifically, of the film industry), Frampton used his first sync-sound film as a way of critiquing the assumption that marrying is the endgame of both narrative romance and film production.

As is true in Jacobs's *Tom, Tom, the Piper's Son* and in the films Gottheim made during the early years of the Cinema Department (and in Frampton's earlier work—most notably *Zorns Lemma* [1970]), *Critical Mass* is, as Frampton once put it, "a process of training the spectator to watch the film. The work teaches the spectator how to read the work."[20] At the beginning of the film, we are literally in the dark, but as *Critical Mass* continues, we not only discover the film's methods and structure, we experience one of film history's most realistic and memorable arguments between two lovers.

The overall four-part organization of *Critical Mass* alternates between passages where we hear but do not see DiBenedetto and Albetta and passages when we hear *and* see them, dressed in black against a white wall. Of course, this structure reflects the implicit narrative of the film, since one partner in the "marriage" of image and sound, as well as in the relationship enacted in the film, is sometimes "away," sometimes present.

Throughout *Critical Mass* the lovers argue about where the man has been for two days and why he won't confide in the woman. Early in the film, Frampton edits their dialogue so that it is continually interrupted and proceeds through a process of partial repetition: each statement by each speaker does take the dialogue a bit further, but only after much of what has been already said is heard in repeated sync-sound bits. For example, at one point the woman says,

20. Frampton, in *A Critical Cinema*: 65.

. . . days, when we're suppose
when we're supposedly living to . . .
when we're supposedly living together
. . . living together.[21]

In this auditory strategy, one can hear the influence of Gertrude Stein, especially the dialogue in her great story "Melanctha" (the second section of *Three Lives*, 1909), whom Frampton admired and was fond of quoting.

This first, sync-sound, regularly interrupted rendition of the argument is followed by a 6-minute passage during which the sound continues, but the image of the couple is absent (during this passage they appear to make up, even—judging from some sound bits—to make love, then they resume the argument). This sound-only passage is followed by a second sound-image version of the original argument, framed and lit in the same way and using the same interruptive strategy, but no longer in sync: from here until the image flares out near the conclusion of the film, the distance between our hearing a comment and seeing the man or the woman uttering it grows increasingly large.[22] At the beginning of this section, we hear what is being said approximately a second before we see it—though because of Frampton's interruptive-overlapping strategy a repetition of sound and image can seem nearly in sync.[23]

Just after the 21-minute mark in the 25¼-minute film, Frampton drops his repetitive strategy and, for the first time, we hear and see DiBenedetto and Albetta in real time, though they remain about a second out of sync. At 22¾ minutes, *Critical Mass* becomes more freeform: we rehear statements we've heard before, but now entirely out-of-sync with

21. As Melissa Ragona has suggested, "Frampton achieves through analog editing techniques what would come to be known as digital delay." See Ragona, "Hidden Noise: Strategies of Sound Montage in the Films of Hollis Frampton," *October*, no. 109 (Summer 2004): 110.

22. At times, a different sort of unraveling occurs within *Critical Mass*: at one point during the second image/sound section of the film, DiBenedetto and Albetta seem to laugh at "a little slip" in their exchange. Of course, this could be part of the argument they are enacting, but it seems just as likely that Albetta and DiBenedetto are amused at a misstep in their enacting of the situation of the lovers.

23. To shoot *Critical Mass* Frampton was using an Arriflex camera, which accomplishes the syncing of image and sound without a clapboard, by creating a mark on the film and within the sound recording as the camera begins to run—an auditory screech is heard if the mark is not eliminated during the editing. Frampton includes these screeches as both emblem of the production process and as implicit metaphor. The only other film I'm aware of that uses the screeches is Alfred Guzzetti's *Family Portrait Sittings* (1975).

the now-familiar imagery.[24] At 24-minutes, the image flares out, again dissolving the "marriage" of image and sound, and presumably the lovers' relationship, once and for all. We hear the couple for a few seconds more before their voices fade out.

The performances of Albetta and DiBenedetto are so convincing in *Critical Mass*, and the lovers' quarrel they enact is so effectively communicated by Frampton's unusual editing strategy, that it is easy to forget that the film functions also on a more metalevel. *Critical Mass* was not only Frampton's first foray into sync sound, but his earliest directed scene involving multiple characters. But having flirted with conventionality in his filming a dialogue between lovers, Frampton used what he had shot as raw material for a series of manipulations that would be, to say the least, unlikely to occur in a Hollywood feature. As he filmed Albetta and DiBenedetto, Frampton had to have been quite conscious that he was working with a film department that didn't ignore commercial film history, but was committed to a more individualized artists' cinema that would both defy and reflect on the film industry and its products. His decision to make *Critical Mass* at Binghamton, with Cinema Department students, suggests that he saw the making of this film not only as a collaborative experiment and an artistic creation, but as a pedagogical demonstration.

There is also a biographical dimension to *Critical Mass*. As Frampton explained during a recorded Q&A that is included on the Criterion DVD of his films, he filmed and edited *Critical Mass* during a moment when his five-year marriage with Marcia Steinbrecher was unraveling (they separated during the summer of 1971, were divorced in 1974). Whatever his relationship with Steinbrecher had been, it seems likely that their struggles leading to the separation and divorce are reflected in the failure of the lovers in *Critical Mass* to find a way to be "in sync."

---

24. In his remarks on *Critical Mass* in *A Critical Cinema* (65–66) Frampton oversimplifies the changes in the relationship between image and sound in the second image/sound section of the film, focusing instead on the repetition of Albetta's saying "bullshit" in that section. Generally speaking, the image and sound are increasingly out of sync as the section proceeds. During the first 3½ minutes, interruptive auditory statements seem to slightly precede their visual counterparts; then the interruptions stop and the sound is more clearly about a second ahead of the visuals. As the section continues, this one-second gap is at best only roughly consistent; and during the final moments of the section the sync is not simply delayed, it is nonexistent.

Critical Mass remains among the most remarkable of Frampton's films. That his return to Binghamton to present the finished film to the Cinema Department ended in fiasco must have seemed, at least to Frampton, a kind of metairony—Frampton had forged a working relationship with the Cinema Department and his joining the department as a full-time hire had seemed imminent—until his return and presentation of *Critical Mass* (and other portions of *Hapax Legomena*) resulted in a "divorce" between Frampton and the department.

Travelling Matte is something of a conundrum, and in a sense the perfect "hapax legomena," since there is nothing quite like it in Frampton's oeuvre, or, for that matter, within the history of cinema. The original imagery for *Travelling Matte* was recorded on videotape during the same visit to Binghamton when Frampton filmed DiBenedetto and Albetta. Frampton has explained the instigation of the project:

> I had never touched a piece of video gear, and two students there absolutely pressed the portapak upon me. They had both worked with Ralph Hocking, who was teaching in the film department. . . . The two of them absolutely insisted that I had to do something with video, so I thought for a time about what that might be. They checked me out on the machine, which, of course, was simple to use, and I went and made that tape.[25]

For the duration of *Travelling Matte* (the finished film lasts 33½ minutes, when shown at 16 frames per second), Frampton walks around the SUNY-Binghamton campus, "thirty typical state university specimens of immaculate penal modern, rising from a sea of mud," recording his walk in a single continuous shot.[26]

As he was recording, Frampton covered the lens of the Portapak with his hand so that only a small portion of the late winter landscape is visible. Frampton's hand is used as an extension of the tube of the lens, and in effect, creates the inverse of a conventional traveling matte. In industrial filmmaking a traveling matte is a means for combining disparate imagery filmed at different times and in different places—most usually it is used to create an environmental background for dialogue shot on a soundstage. One part of an image becomes a matte that allows another part of the negative to be exposed so that the matted section, filmed in a different location, can be exposed later ("traveling" refers

25. Frampton, in *A Critical Cinema*: 67.

26. Ibid., 66.

to the fact that when imagery that is moving is combined with other imagery filmed elsewhere, the precise shape of the matte is changing frame by frame).

In *Travelling Matte* Frampton's hand becomes the *foreground* of the image and continually reshapes the portion of the landscape visible through the hand and the Portapak lens. Here, as in many films that use traveling matte technology, a close-up is combined with a long shot, but in this instance both the close-up and the long shot are filmed simultaneously and within the same location—though it is quite clear throughout the walk that the close-up of part of Frampton's hand and the shots, mostly long shots, of the campus represent different registers of reality. Further, while the function of traveling mattes is to make the combination of imagery shot in disparate places as invisible as possible, Frampton's combination of close-up and long shot is the most visible dimension of the imagery; here, the traveling matte technology is not a means to the end of a realistic image and smooth continuity, but the end itself—and a metaphor for artisanal, as opposed to industrial, filmmaking. The filmmaker's hand literally shapes this image as *he* "travels" through the Binghamton campus, not creating an illusion of reality distinct from the filmmaking process, but an experience in which an experimental process is what we see.

Later, as he worked with the material he had shot on his walk, Frampton combined disparate forms of imagery in still another manner, also distinct from the conventions of traveling mattes during the 1970s. The imagery recorded by the Portapak was subsequently refilmed from a television monitor in 16mm. Obviously, the video imagery of the hand and landscape became filmed imagery, but since the filmed Portapak imagery includes video scan lines and at times other video distortions (or "distortions") apparently created by moving the Portapak in an awkward way, *and* since the low light conditions created by Frampton's "hand-matte" resulted in very grainy film imagery, the result is an unusual, imbricated texture that is made even more complex by the fact that the imagery reveals specks of something on either the Portapak or film camera lens, as well as by the slight flicker effect that occurs when the film is shown at sixteen frames per second. That is, *Critical Mass* is neither video nor film; it might be called *vilm*, a term suggested more recently in another context by sound artist Ernst Karel.[27]

27. See my interview with Lucien Castaing-Taylor in Scott MacDonald, *Avant-Doc: Intersections of Documentary and Avant-Garde Cinema* (New York: Oxford University Press, 2014): 383. Karel is a sound artist at Harvard who often works with filmmakers connected to Harvard's Sensory Ethnography Lab.

That the experience of seeing the Binghamton campus from inside what seems like a darkened passageway (and that the webbing between Frampton's thumb and index finger, seen in close-up, looks sensual, even vaguely labial), suggests, at least to me, that he might have understood his visit to the new Cinema Department as his becoming involved in the birth of a new kind of academic entity, one that combined both film-making and the new video art.[28] This birthing metaphor is obviously a stretch, perhaps too much of a stretch. Nevertheless it *is* clear that *Travelling Matte*, like *Critical Mass*, is a comment on the film industry and its procedures and that Frampton was clearly interested in combining film and video experimentation, both during his visit to Binghamton in 1971, and later during the process of creating the finished vilm—precisely at the extended moment when he knew the Cinema Department was in the process of bringing film and video together and Gottheim and Jacobs were considering Frampton as a possible new hire. Some years later, when he had become a member of the faculty at SUNY-Buffalo (now the University at Buffalo), Frampton would disavow this early foray into video,[29] but in 1971, the allure of the burgeoning new department could very well have been strong enough to instigate a vilm about it.

Frampton once said that *Travelling Matte* was his adaptation of Tolstoy's short story, "How Much Land Does a Man Need?" in which the central character, the peasant Pahom, is never satisfied with the amount and quality of land under his control—if he had enough land, he claims during an argument, he wouldn't need to fear the Devil Himself. The Devil hears the claim and decides to respond.[30] At the conclusion of the story, after traveling to various locations where he accesses more land, Pahom arrives in the country of the Bashkirs where he is told he can call his own as much land as he can walk around between sunrise and sunset, as long as he returns to his starting point by the time the sun goes down. Excited by the prospect, Pahom leaves early, but being greedy, walks too far and must struggle so hard to return to the starting point that he falls dead just as he reaches it, and is buried in a grave—as it turns out, all the land he ultimately needs.

---

28. During March of 1972, Frampton spent some time working with a version of the Paik-Abe video synthesizer that had been developed at Binghamton under the auspices of Ralph Hocking, and made *Memoranda for a Dream of Magellan* (1972).

29. In the transcript of his introduction to a screening of the video work that he had made at Binghamton, recorded in 1974 and published in *Film Culture* 77 (Fall 1992), Frampton would say, "the closer I have got, which is not very, to having anything to do with video, the more I have felt that what I most want to do is dig my heels in" (7).

30. I am grateful to Kenneth Eisenstein, who pointed out this reference to me.

In the months before coming to Binghamton to shoot *Critical Mass* and *Travelling Matte*, Frampton had moved out of New York City and had bought a home in the pastoral landscape of central New York, about an hour north of Binghamton. Excited at the expansion of his new country domain, he may have been thinking about the story of Pahom (the Tolstoy story opens with an argument about the virtues of city life versus country living). The obvious connection between *Travelling Matte* and the short story is that *Travelling Matte* is as long as the walk Frampton takes around the Binghamton campus, from a point seemingly near the Lecture Hall building to a sidewalk made out of hexagonal steppingstones and back to the beginning point. The Portapak could make longer continuous shots than were possible for 16mm filmmaking—but the quality of the resulting video imagery was inferior to what was possible with 16mm film. Did Frampton see the Portapak as potentially dangerous to his "aesthetic life"?

The most notorious and controversial film produced at SUNY-Binghamton during the period explored in this study is *We Can't Go Home Again*, which was directed by Nicholas Ray during the two years he was employed by the Cinema Department (September 1971 through August 1973). Then, unfinished, it became the stuff of legend for nearly forty years, until it was restored and reconstructed (from the version that was shown at Cannes in 1973), and released in 2011 through the efforts of Susan Ray and a number of SUNY-Binghamton alumnae who had been involved in the original shooting. The legendary status of *We Can't Go Home Again* was established and maintained by the memories of Cinema Department students and faculty, and by two documentaries: *I'm a Stranger Here Myself: A Portrait of Nicholas Ray* (1975), directed by David Helpern Jr. and written and edited by Helpern and James C. Gutman; and *Lightning over Water* (1980), codirected by Ray and Wim Wenders. In both documentaries, *We Can't Go Home Again* plays a significant role, representing for Helpern and Wenders a final, major experiment in the career of a canonical American film auteur.

Particularly distinctive, at least within the body of cinema and video produced at Binghamton during Ray's brief tenure there, is Ray's foregrounding of the larger political context of the time. While the films I've discussed so far are certainly formally "political" in the sense that they were involved in a larger movement to rethink cinema and how motion pictures functioned within culture, they seem resolutely apolitical with regard to specific political events occurring nationally and internationally, even locally. In *We Can't Go Home Again*, Ray's decision to accept a position in the Cinema Department is framed by his experiences at the 1968 Democratic convention in Chicago (Ray explains that immediately after his arrival in Chicago to attend the "Festival of Life" sponsored by the Yippies, he was maced and his camera smashed) and at the trial of the Chicago Seven in the aftermath of the convention—both events are visually documented in multiple images during the opening of the film.

Further, having decided, as he explains in the film, "to buy a crooked cane, grow a goatee, wear a crooked smile and impress them with my rhetoric, rebellion and ponderosity"—that is, to become a Binghamton professor—Ray's first assignment for those taking his course was to document the demonstrations at the maximum security prison at Attica, then under siege not far from the Binghamton Campus. This emphasis on a larger political context remains important throughout the film and especially within the film's most powerful sequence: Tom Farrell's shaving of his beard near the end of *We Can't Go Home Again* in the wake of his trip to Miami to attend the 1972 Democratic and Republican conventions.

Despite its political consciousness, *We Can't Go Home Again* remains a formal conundrum. As Susan Ray has said, the film "is messy, flawed, and unfinished, at times infuriatingly so. But the mess, like the dirt of this earth, is fertile, teeming with life and potential."[31] Ray aficionados are quick to point out that the film's resolute use of multiple images within the frame was not a product of Ray's experiences at Binghamton, but evolved from earlier Ray work; and of course, multiple-image presentations were prominent at the 1964 New York World's Fair and Expo '67 in Montreal, as well as in Stan Vanderbeek's Movie Drome, in much performance art, and at rock concerts—though Ray's particular approach to using multiple imagery remains distinctive and worthy of exploration.

For the latest version of *We Can't Go Home Again*—the one reconstructed from the version shown at Cannes—Ray rear-projected the several channels of moving imagery (16mm, 8mm, synthesized video) on a screen so that a 35mm camera could record them within a single frame. This complex frame is always seen within a series of four still photographs of Binghamton and environs that function as mattes: a panoramic shot of the SUNY-Binghamton campus; a barn in the country outside of the city; what appears to be a snowscape; and a traffic intersection somewhere within the city. Only the edges of these photographic mattes are visible at the top and on the right and left sides of an inner (35mm) frame within which one, two, three, four, and sometimes five moving images are arranged (the photographs may signal the location of particular bits of action referenced by the moving imagery and the sound). This

31. From Susan Ray, "To the Viewer," an essay written for the 2012 DVD/BluRay release of the film.

complex visual arrangement of imagery is confirmed by the soundtrack, which is often layered with sync sound (and sometimes music) from the various film and video images.

Clearly Ray's understanding of what cinema *is* remained quite different from the understandings of Jacobs, Gottheim, Gehr, and most other Binghamton colleagues and visitors, throughout his two-year tenure. And this different understanding implied both a different kind of teaching and different formal assumptions. Ray makes this explicit in *I'm a Stranger Here Myself*, in an interview recorded near the end of his time in Binghamton:

> Most film courses or film classes concentrate on getting rid of the responsibilities of the students as quickly as possible by putting them off in corners and shooting 8mm films, which they can do all by themselves and present for a senior thesis. And therefore, the emphasis is on kind of static camera with cute ideas, or masturbatory ideas, or date-making ideas . . . anything except the relationship with other human beings. And film is a collective art, it's an eclectic art . . . and it's by its own nature become the most communicative art that we have in the world. . . .

For Ray cinema requires emotionally engaged, interpersonal relationships at every level: between director and actors and crew, and among crew members, as well as between the finished film and the audience. Making film was for Ray a group experience, virtually the inverse of the kinds of films Ray's Binghamton colleagues were making.

Nevertheless, as distinctive as it is within the Binghamton context, *We Can't Go Home Again* shares a number of elements with other work being produced in and around the Cinema Department during these years—beyond Ray's determination to rethink how cinema, and especially Hollywood cinema, has functioned within culture and beyond his commitment (like Jacobs's, Gottheim's, and Gehr's) to remake cinema from the ground up. Like Jacobs in *Tom, Tom, the Piper's Son*, Ray used rear projection and rephotography in order to create a version of *We Can't Go Home Again* for the Cannes screening. Like Gottheim, Ray used the mundane world around him—the campus production rooms, his own apartment and those of his students, the pastoral landscape outside of Binghamton—for his locations. Indeed the photographic matte of the barn evokes Gottheim's *Barn Rushes* and *Horizons*, as does a sequence recorded on a farm near the end of *We Can't Go Home Again*. Both Gottheim and Ray use mythic references involving Ray himself: Ray undercuts his own Hollywood past, mythic for the faculty and students at SUNY-Binghamton, by playing a character based on himself, and in *Horizons*, Gottheim images Ray as part of a cinematic pantheon.

Like Frampton making *Critical Mass*, Ray films improvised emotional interactions between Binghamton students, and both Frampton and Ray were intrigued with the potential of video, and accessed Ralph Hocking's Experimental Television Center and the synthesizer Nam June Paik and Shuya Abe developed there. Frampton has indicated that while at Binghamton in 1971, he shot two hours of synthesized video imagery as raw material for use in "one of six prenatal dreams of a fictitious person I have invented named Ferdinand Magellan";[32] and synthesized video imagery plays an important role throughout *We Can't Go Home Again*. Indeed, the change from film to video during the opening title credit may be Ray's suggestion that video is replacing film—a suggestion confirmed in Susan Ray's *Don't Expect Too Much* (2012) in interviews with Tom Farrell ("When Nick saw that Nam June Paik could electronically colorize images, he was completely freaked out by it; he said, 'This is the most revolutionary innovation in cinema since the close-up'") and Peer Bode ("Nick said, 'This is going to be a way of filmmaking in the future and we're . . . trying to learn how to do it and what the vocabulary is and how to be articulate . . .'").

Given their fundamentally opposed definitions of cinema—personal cinema versus collaborative cinema, cinema as a fine art versus cinema as a theatrical art—and the limited resources of the Cinema Department, the academic collaboration of Ray and his colleagues was probably doomed from the start. Nevertheless, for both faculty and students, Ray's presence and his unusual project was, and has remained, a crucial element of that period; and Susan Ray's completion of *Don't Expect Too Much* as a way of providing a context for Ray's unfinished project at presentations of the restored feature and on the DVD/BluRay release of the film seems sure to revive interest in both what Ray accomplished and failed to accomplish in *We Can't Go Home Again*. Whatever Ray's long-term plans for the Binghamton film were, his decision to format multiple images within the film frame for the Cannes festival had the effect of (literally) minimizing the human interaction he was intent on instigating and capturing during the shooting. *Don't Expect Too Much* includes much of the original footage, full-screen—revealing, more clearly than *We Can't Go Home Again*, the quality of the imagery Ray and his student colleagues shot and the humanity and complexity of the actors.

32. Frampton in *Film Culture* 77: 7. Frampton's joke that his fictitious character is named Ferdinand Magellan is similar to Ray using himself as a fictitious character in *We Can't Go Home Again* (this character hangs himself at the end of the film).

From 1973 to 1976, when they were Binghamton faculty, both Dan Barnett and Saul Levine remained busy as filmmakers. Barnett completed several films during his tenure at Binghamton, including *White Heart* (1975).[33] *White Heart* is an elaborate, 54-minute montage made up of a wide variety of visual and sound elements (found footage and imagery shot by Barnett, various film leaders, phrases of classical music, assorted noises) that become motifs or cinematic gestures appearing in continually different contexts—every gesture, as Barnett has explained,

> having to do with my aspiration for omnivalence. There's so much ambiguity around every gesture, hopefully you could lean this way in one instance, or view that way in another. The film is constructed with enough depth and coherence that each time you go through you should have on one level a feeling about the color, on another level the feeling about the relationship between the quality of the texture of a sound and a hit on a cut, so the ground is shifting always. . . .[34]

Barnett's "aspiration for omnivalence" seems related to Nathaniel Dorsky's exploration of what he calls "polyvalence," a form of montage in which successive images "are disparate *and* connected . . . and link back to earlier shots." The sound track of *White Heart* is as complex as the visual track: indeed, Dorsky himself has singled out *White Heart* as a particularly remarkable sound film.[35]

White Heart is embedded in the materiality of cinema, in its many audio and visual dimensions, including the place of its making and the others working there: Larry Gottheim is seen typing and making notes, presumably for a film; Saul Levine is filmed swimming in a pond and is heard saying "a rose" over and over. There's a shot of the forested hills around Binghamton. Viewers must find their way in to the dense reticulation of perception and conception in *White Heart*; and if one imagines the film within a pedagogical context, it seems as if Barnett's production

33. Barnett's oeuvre is ripe for rediscovery. His book, *Movement as Meaning in Experimental Film*, includes an incomplete filmography (p. 200). The films that seem to have been finished during Barnett's years at Binghamton include (the precise dates are unclear) *Pull Out/Fallout* (c. 1974), *Renée Is Wonderful* (c. 1974), *Dead End, Dead End* (c. 1974), *A Note in a Bottle* (c. 1974), *Popular Songs* (c. 1974), and *White Heart* (1975).

34. Ibid., p. 31.

35. Dorsky, in interview in Scott MacDonald, *A Critical Cinema 5* (Berkeley: University of California Press, 2006): 95, 97.

process is reflected in the viewing experience of discovering the nature of *White Heart*: "The entire five years that I was making the film I had my camera in a gas mask bag that I slung over my shoulder. And I would shoot very little. I would just look for what I was looking for and I didn't know what I was looking for . . . that approach demands a certain faith in the power of the method in order for the method to work."[36] Teaching film for Barnett seems to have been a process of demonstrating how a film artist functions, over time, with the material elements of cinema to create a distinctive and evocative form of cinematic experience.

As this essay is written (2013–2015), Barnett's films are not in distribution and are not generally available, even from Barnett. Therefore, further discussion of *White Heart* is impossible for me at this point (I have seen the film only once, this thanks to Saul Levine—a good 16mm print of *White Heart* is in the film library at Massachusetts College of Art), though one can hope that before long, these films will find their way to viewers, both in theaters and in a form that allows for their careful study. Barnett's *Movement as Meaning in Experimental Film* includes extensive reflections on Barnett's time in Binghamton and the many films he worked on and saw there.

During the period when Barnett and Saul Levine shared apartments, Levine was working on a variety of 8mm and Super-8mm films, including *New Left Note* (1968–1982), a frenetic, materialist, constructivist document that records Levine's life within an extended moment of political activism; *Note to Colleen* (1974), an homage to his friendship with Colleen Fitzgibbon (who also visited Binghamton), *Rambling Notes* (1977), *Resume* (1977), and *Portrayal: Memorial Day Weekend* (1978). Although these films were made in Binghamton, there is little in them that relates to the Cinema Department itself or to its pedagogical mission—the films are expressive of their maker in various ways, but not so much of the Binghamton experience per se.

Notable exceptions include *On the Spot* (1973), *Before the Fact* (1974), which was made as a class exercise with Bill Brand, who was coteaching with Levine during the summer of 1974; *Notes of an Early Fall* (1976), and *Departure*, which was shot in 1976–1977, but not completed until fifteen years later.[37] *On the Spot* documents the farm in Friendsville,

36. Barnett in Eersole and Jalbuena interview: 35.

37. On the box for the VHS version of *Departure*, produced in 1991, Levine explains, "Departure is a film that was shot in 1976–77 during a year when I lost my job due to both cutbacks at the campus at which I taught and my involvement in the movement against them. I collected footage and imagined I would edit the film together the night I left [Binghamton]. I was unable to do that and it took several years to finish it."

Pennsylvania, where Levine and Barnett lived during the first months of their Binghamton years (Levine remembers moving into the trailer seen in the film in August of 1973, and living there through October of that year). The 29½-minute, Regular-8mm, silent film records the farm—the barns, farmhouse and yard, surrounding fields—day and night, during the seasonal change from late summer to fall. For those familiar with Larry Gottheim's early work, especially *Fog Line*, *Barn Rushes* and *Horizons*, *On the Spot* provides a demonstration (one that for Levine probably had pedagogical implications) that two filmmakers coming from urban backgrounds to the same pastoral landscape might respond cinematically to their new surroundings in radically different ways.

In the films of Levine and Gottheim, the pastoral landscape around Binghamton becomes the ground against which are figured two distinct approaches to making independent film, approaches that in retrospect can be understood to represent a changing emphasis in the Cinema Department's pedagogy. Levine was an admirer of Gottheim's work, especially *Barn Rushes* and *Fog Line* (*Horizons* was completed as Levine was shooting *On the Spot*), but his method of engaging the rural scene around him was virtually the inverse of Gottheim's patient formalism and carefully articulated way of moving through the landscape. While Gottheim's work evokes nineteenth-century landscape painting (both the Hudson River School and the French Impressionists), Levine is a child of abstract expressionism and of Brakhage's gestural camerawork. While Gottheim tends to foreground the landscape itself, Levine explores how camera movements and in-camera editing can transform the landscape into visual experiences that reveal the potential of the 8mm camera. Gottheim's films are serene, meditative; Levine's, relentlessly energetic and idiosyncratic. Gottheim provides a graphic and temporal space in which viewers can explore the subtleties of each composition; Levine shows viewers what he is exploring and discovering as he is filming. If *Horizons* evokes classicism, *On the Spot* evokes cubism's fascination with multiple simultaneous views.

Before the Fact, which is available on Bill Brand's website (www.bboptics.com/cartoons.html), shows Levine in class with two students, being directed from off-screen by Brand, as the three listen to Levine say, "But there's a lot of stuff; that film touches on a lot of stuff." One of the students works with a tape recorder, recording the original statement, then replaying it over and over, as the students and Levine attempt to mimic Levine's original delivery of the statement (early on, another student, barely visible behind the three seated participants, seems to be writing something on a blackboard—whether other students are in the room is not clear). While the purpose of the documented exercise is not explained, what is evident is, on the one hand, the charming informality of this teaching moment; and on the other, the fact that this particular class session *is* the production of a film: Brand has explained,

> The idea for the class was mine. SUNY-Binghamton not only had an Éclair and a Nagra (i.e., a "sync rig"—a rare thing at the time), but also had a Mag film dubber (Magnasync), a flatbed editor, a double-system projector for projecting picture and magnetic sound together, and a film processor. In other words, the school had all the equipment necessary to shoot, develop, record, transfer, sync, and playback double-system, sync-sound film. So I had the bravado idea that we could make our way through the entire process in a single class![38]

Brand was using "the same equipment Hollis [Frampton] used for *Critical Mass* a few years earlier and I was quite aware I was making reference to his film."[39]

Notes of an Early Fall evokes Levine's disappointment and frustration during the months after his Cinema Department contract was not renewed. The film begins in the apartment to which Levine and Barnett moved after their brief time in the countryside (at the time Levine was shooting *Notes* Barnett had already left Binghamton), and ends with Levine returning to his family home in New Haven. The "fall" in the title is a pun, referring not only to the season but also, as P. Adams Sitney put it in a program note for the film, both "the aesthetic fall from the grace of pure vision into the worldly cacophony of synchronous sound . . . and the fall from a prestigious position in what was at the time the strongest academic program in avant-garde filmmaking in America." *Notes of an Early Fall* is full of metaphors for Levine's frustration and psychic struggle: an old, warped blues record endlessly repeating the same phrases as the warping causes the arm and needle to jump, a bird that seems trapped . . .

Departure is a more direct exploration of the idea of departing, a twenty-five-minute, Super-8mm sound diary of places and people

38. Bill Brand in an e-mail to the author, February 22, 2014. He continues, "Though I had some ideas to start—that I would record Saul on the cassette recorder operated by the student on the left and then have Saul and others repeat and mimic the recording all while recording both on the Nagra (off screen) and the Eclair . . .—the details of my direction were improvised on the spot."

39. Ibid.

Before the Fact is also reminiscent of Morgan Fisher's films, particularly *Production Stills* (1970) and *Documentary Footage* (1968); Fisher had visited Binghamton the previous spring.

in and around Binghamton. The film begins with a visual montage of the Susquehanna River, just down the street from Levine's apartment, with much emphasis on sunset (an emblem perhaps for struggling to find a positive in the negative of the loss of his teaching position), and includes a series of portraits of friends and filmmakers, including Marjorie Keller, seen in silhouette in her New York apartment (the only section of *Departure* not filmed in Binghamton), Cinema Department secretary Marilyn Aigen and Dan Barnett in the Cinema Department Office (Barnett is saying good-bye for the summer at the conclusion of his final year at SUNY-Binghamton); Elaine Johnson, a literature student who talks about a speech she has recently given and about the experience of living in Binghamton; and cinema student David Marc, who talks about his struggles with finding an active role for himself in the world. Levine also includes footage filmed off a television monitor of a campus broadcast of Levine himself talking with the then-head of the SUNY-Binghamton Board of Trustees during the student takeover of the administration building in 1975—the event that, more than any other, ultimately resulted in Levine's departure from Binghamton. The gap between the shooting and the completion of the film suggests that Levine was forced to "depart" from the footage until he could gain some perspective.

Morgan Fisher visited the Cinema Department for a week in 1974 and was able to shoot *240x* (1974), a film he had clearly in mind before his visit. *240x* focuses on the Maltese cross, a device that, within motion picture film projectors, allows each frame on the filmstrip to be seen at precisely the same place on the screen. In *240x* Fisher explores a new image-making technology—the copying machine—in somewhat the same way that Ralph Hocking was exploring the video camera and playback device in *The Experiment*, "an exploration of the machines as defined by their capabilities."[40] *240x* includes five scenes, beginning with a ten-second shot of an image of a Maltese cross. Fisher has explained: "A Maltese cross has the shape of an x, so the first scene is 240 frames of an x. In instructions for animation photography an x means a frame. 240x means 24 frames of whatever is in front of the camera, so the first scene, lasting 240 frames, or 240x, is the title of the film in a concealed form."[41] In the following four scenes, Fisher makes 240 copies of the image of the Maltese cross that was filmed in the first scene; then, using

40. Ralph Hocking, e-mail to the author, August 15, 2013.

41. Morgan Fisher, in *Morgan Fisher, Writings*, edited by Sabine Folie and Susanne Titz (Cologne: Verlag der Buchhandlung Walther König, 2012): 42.

a cel punch, punches holes in the 240 copies; then shoots the 240 sheets of paper, one by one, on an animation stand; and finally, presents the filmed copies as a ten-second, reanimated shot.

What is revealed by the this process are two limitations (and perhaps opportunities) of the copying machine: first, the reanimated cross is no longer black, but gray, because of limitations in the copy machine's inking; and second, the reanimated cross is not stable on the screen, revealing that, unlike the motion picture camera, which uses a Maltese cross, the copying machine—a new kind of combined camera and animation stand—does not include a device that allows each copied image to be precisely the same as all the others.

Fisher has suggested that *240x* "reproduces in displaced terms the form of drama. . . . At the beginning a situation is presented, and all is normal. Then something happens to disturb the situation's equilibrium. Efforts are made to deal with the disturbance. . . . In the end things are again in equilibrium, but it is a new one, different from the one at the beginning."[42] The film can also be understood as having implicit pedagogical functions: it demonstrates the importance of a generally little-known, but entirely crucial element of the mechanics of motion picture film cameras and projectors.[43]

One last film by a visiting filmmaker deserves mention. Klaus Wyborny taught classes at Binghamton during 1975 and completed a 50-minute film, *Pictures of the Lost Word* (*Bilder vom verlorenen Wort*, 1975), while at Binghamton. For *Pictures* Wyborny had filmed pastoral landscapes, industrial spaces, city scenes, and mountain vistas, with a handheld camera—though it was not filmed in the United States, at times the imagery has particular elements in common with Gottheim's and Levine's work; and in general, Wyborny shares their determination to defy industrial (and particularly Hollywood) cinema. *Pictures of the Lost Word* opens with a hand-printed text that explains, "GOBSEK-FILM is a film production company devoted to the production of films of the highest possible quality & lowest possible profit. This devotion projects it into opposition to 'classical' film-production companies which try to produce films of lowest possible quality at highest possible profit."

42. Ibid., 44.

43. Of course, since "Maltese cross" is not mentioned in *240x*, this pedagogical dimension is suppressed. Fisher's understanding of the importance of the Maltese cross seems to have been one of the instigations for the film, but his decision not to clarify what exactly the image is in that first 10-second shot probably created for most viewers a conundrum that the filmmaker refused to solve. Now, in the age of Google, this is no longer an issue.

For Wyborny "highest possible quality" seems to mean most fully engaged in experimentation with the materiality of film image and sound—and most challenging to conventional audience expectations. Wyborny presents the same visual imagery in various ways: in color and black and white, color negative and black-and-white negative—and with various levels of focus and film grain. The soundtrack is made up of two piano pieces, both apparently composed and performed in Binghamton by Wyborny, plus a passage from an opera, moments of silence, and several seemingly quasi-autobiographical voice-overs.

One of the courses Wyborny taught at Binghamton was editing theory and it is in its editing that *Pictures* is most demanding. Imagery is generally presented in brief clusters, intercut with moments of dark (or in negative, white) leader; the sound is often interruptive as well: much of the soundtrack seems to have been edited so as to transform Wyborny's piano performance into an audio montage. Various forms of interplay between image and sound are used, and as is true with the imagery, the sound is repetitive: the same music is heard, again and again, often with visual imagery seen anew in negative or positive. There is also interplay between various kinds of sound and silence; at times, Wyborny's interplay between his two piano pieces recalls *The Unanswered Question* by Charles Ives. Like other Cinema Department faculty, Wyborny understood that the film instructor's job was to model new ways of thinking about filmmaking, new experimental ways of working with the materials of cinema, and new understandings of the relationship between film and audience.

Presumably, much of the work produced by Cinema Department students did not exceed the category of "student work": that is, the production of films/videos as a means of learning the process of working in film and video. Nevertheless, there are student films and videos made during the extended Binghamton moment that remain noteworthy. They include J. Hoberman's *Customs & Immigration* (1971); Phil Solomon's *Nitelite* (1975); Alan Berliner's *Patent Pending* (1975); *Trail of Dreams* (1974) by Cheryl Gorman (Ficarra); and several videos by Peer Bode.

Customs & Immigration seems to have been important more for the fact that Hoberman *made* it than for its particular accomplishments—it is one of the earlier student films to come out of the Cinema Department and other students seem to have taken notice of it—though making the film also caused a rift in Hoberman's relationship with Ken Jacobs (see p. 89). In his note on the film in the *Filmmakers' Cooperative Catalogue* (no. 7, 1989), Hoberman calls *Customs & Immigration* a "sci-fi cheapster, thematically akin to *Forbidden Planet*," but basically the 34-minute film seems a collage of various experiments.[44] It opens with an extended sequence of a parking lot at SUNY-Binghamton pixilated in different lights—according to Hoberman the entire film was shot "on and around campus except for the last scene which was shot in an apartment on Main Street in Johnson City."[45]The most engaging sequence involves a beautiful young woman (Karen Robbins) nude (except for red panties) sitting next to a monitor showing excerpts from the *Flash Gordon* television series;[46] the most elaborate, a tableau in an apartment room involving four students (Helene Kaplan, Mike Lovell, Michael Gersten, and Alvin Ventura). At some point after Hoberman left Binghamton, Renée Shafransky would supply a program note, presumably for a SUNY-Binghamton screening:

> CUSTOMS & IMMIGRATION started as an adaptation of Kafka's "Amerika" but apparently Hoberman just got into shooting what interested him. A combination of non-access to equipment & other production problems caused the film to be ended arbitrarily but, according to Hoberman, "it worked out good." The film was finished in Endicott, N.Y. over the Unique Beauty Salon with the soundtrack mixed in his parents' N.Y.C. living room. But Hoberman feels "tacky" is a positive element.[47]

Nitelite was Phil Solomon's thesis and a premonition of what would become a major contribution to the cine-nocturne.[48] The 8-minute, silent film posits darkness—the darkness of night, the darkness of unexposed celluloid film, the darkness of the theater—as the ground of cinema.

44. The relationship of *Customs & Immigration* to commercial cinema and sci-fi seems roughly comparable to *Vinyl* (1965), Andy Warhol's strange, anticommercial adaptation of Anthony Burgess's novel *A Clockwork Orange*. For a discussion of *Vinyl*, see J. J. Murphy, *The Black Hole of the Camera* (Berkeley: University of California Press, 2012): 73–75.

45. E-mail to the author, October 7, 2013.

46. Hoberman: "Ralph Hocking helped me transfer the 16mm film [the *Flash Gordon* material] to videotape so that I could shoot it off the monitor. I remember that he was pissed I didn't film Karen totally nude: 'My wife has those red panties!' I showed the rushes to his friend Nam June Paik who was visiting (and whose only remark was 'it's a statement' which I took for approval)"—e-mail to author, October 7, 2013.

47. *Filmmakers' Cooperative Catalogue* (no. 7, 1989): 249.

48. I discuss the history and a number of instances of the cine-nocturne in "Gardens of the Moon: The Modern Cine-Nocturne," chapter 10 in *Technology and the Garden*, Michael G. Lee and Kenneth I. Helphand, eds. (Washington. DC: Dumbarton Oaks Research Library and Collection, 2014): 201–229.

Since so much of the film reveals only tiny bits of light within the larger frame (most frequently, the moon obscured by clouds), or more substantial full-frame images (cars, trees, houses, a pedestrian tunnel . . .) presented in tiny frame clusters, the theater remains unusually dark, except when illuminated by flashes of light. Solomon had made a number of films during his time at Binghamton, but *Nitelite* is the earliest film listed in his current filmography, a gesture that implies that by 1975 Solomon sensed that he had found his métier and, like Gottheim in *Fog Line*, saw this film not simply as a culmination of his Binghamton experience, but as a new beginning, one that would result in a series of more elaborate nocturnes, indeed the most distinguished contribution to the genre.

During the years following my personal "conversion experience" at Binghamton in April of 1972, I threw myself into an exploration of the wide world of avant-garde cinema, and in several instances made use of the Cinema Department's collection of 16mm prints. Alan Berliner was my projectionist for these research trips—I remember his seriousness and dedication to the task. In those days, avant-garde film was entirely a celluloid- and emulsion-based medium and required competent projection, and not surprisingly, Cinema Department students learned to be skillful with 16mm (and 8mm and Super-8mm) projectors. Of course, any capable projectionist understands that the projector must be watched, no matter how tempting it is to become engrossed in the projected film—it is always possible for something to go wrong that, worst case scenario, damages a print. *Patent Pending* can be understood as a report on some of what Berliner had learned from watching projectors during projection.

Patent Pending is a single, continuous, 11-minute (the length of a 400-foot role of 16mm film), sync-sound shot (Berliner's first foray into sync sound), during which the 16mm camera films a projector showing an 11-minute film (actually, 11 minutes of black leader), from the side—the projector framed so that only a portion of the feed reel, the arm supporting it, and the strip of 16mm film being projected are visible. At first, the image is still; then the projector is switched on and the projected film begins to unwind from the reel. For a while, the experience seems to evoke the inevitable boredom of watching a projector do its work, but as the film unwinds, the feed reel begins to revolve more and more quickly and, for a patient viewer, this produces a number of optical effects, including that reverse-motion effect familiar from stagecoach wheels in classic Westerns; at times something close to 3-D. And, near the end, when the feed reel is moving most quickly, the circular openings in the feed reel are imprinted on the retinas so quickly that they become animated. When the film runs out and the feed reel stops, we can read on the reel, "Pat. Pend." *Patent Pending* makes watching a 16mm projector an "adventure of perception," to use Brakhage's phrase, and a report on what a dedicated projectionist and aspiring film artist has discovered about the visual effects of his tools.

Cheryl Gorman's *Trail of Dreams* is a student film in the best sense: it not only reveals her dexterity with a variety of ways of working with 16mm, it is inventive in its recycling of the film history she must have been exposed to in her film studies classes. There are allusions to and evocations of George Méliès and *Ballet mécanique* (1924, by Fernand Léger, Dudley Murphy, Man Ray), the use of generations-old pop music by Jack Smith, the interrupted sound in Frampton's *Critical Mass*, and even Len Lye's patterned painting on celluloid. In some instances *Trail of Dreams* predicts developments that would occur later, both within a feminist context and in terms of Gorman's manipulations of the materiality of the filmstrip: a motif of a female figure whose face is a mask punctuates a visual and audio panorama that seems meant to evoke the history of the representation of women in cinema; and her many uses of hand-painted color and other manipulations of the filmstrip seem prescient of Lawrence Brose's exploration of the layers of film emulsion as masks that reveal the complexity of identity in *De Profundis* (1997). *Trail of Dreams* is poignant in its struggle to decide what a feminist film might be.

While graduates of the Cinema Department program sometimes visited after they graduated (Hoberman, for example, to perform with the Theater of Gibberish), these were not filmmaking visits. However, those students who had worked with Ralph Hocking at SUNY-Binghamton and at the Experimental Television Center sometimes returned to Binghamton to work on projects at ETC. For example, Peer Bode, who graduated in 1974, was employed by the university (as a night-time guard at a campus gate) for a year after his graduation while he was also working at ETC and also, together with Meryl Blackman, with the American Dance Asylum. Bode then studied at what was then the new program at SUNY-Buffalo, but continued to visit ETC, where he made a series of videos, several of them in homage to his Cinema Department professors.

Blue (1976)[49] is a video homage to Larry Gottheim's first single-shot film, *Blues* (1969): the subject, a close-up of a bowl of blueberries being eaten, is the same, but while Gottheim's film focus on elements of cinema—a certain palette of 16mm color, film grain, flicker (*Blues* was designed to be shown at 16 frames per second)—Bode's single-shot video

49. The date at the conclusion of *Blue* is 1979, though on the compilation DVDs Bode distributes and on the Video Data Bank website the video is listed as 1976.

(5 minutes) celebrates the newer medium's particular look: its way of flattening space, the texture of rasters, the somewhat over-the-top pastel palette—while alluding to the Gottheim film with affectionate humor: a pause just before the final blueberries are "eaten" (i.e., removed from the bowl with the spoon) in *Blues* is repeated in *Blue*.

In other early videos, Bode builds on what he had learned from Ralph Hocking. *1-87* (1976), for example, was "inspired by Ralph Hocking's fish biting video" [*Fishing*]: "Eighty-seven stones thrown, volumes shifting of water sound, a real time performance event. Holding the camera and throwing 87 stones into the frame. ½" reel to reel Sony portapack" (from Bode's Video Data Bank website). *100 Sec. Lumination* (1976) builds on Hocking's explorations of synthesized color; *Cup Mix (2 channels)* (1977) recalls Hocking's overlay of two very different kinds of image; and *Ring Modulation* (1978) evokes Hocking's early switching work—though it is also clear that Bode was interacting with other video artists at ETC, in Buffalo and elsewhere, and finding his own way.

Of all the films that were produced at SUNY-Binghamton during the period explored in this study, the most widely seen may be Ernie Gehr's *Serene Velocity* (1970), which was produced the summer before the Cinema Department's first full academic year, when Gottheim hired Gehr to teach two summer courses. Gehr arrived in Binghamton with an idea for a film:

> By late 1969 or early 1970, I became increasingly interested in an exploration of the intervals between frames, in activating the screen plane from frame to frame more dynamically than I had done previously, as well as in the idea of a composition taking place in time. I looked around for an appropriate space to film. Although I didn't know precisely what I wanted, nothing seemed right. Then as the summer approached, I went to Binghamton. The film department editing rooms were in the basement of the lecture hall, where there were a couple of long corridors.
>
> Toward the latter part of the six weeks I was there, maybe the fourth week, I was on my way to one of the editing rooms one evening. As I entered that basement hallway, the idea of *Serene Velocity* taking place in that space suddenly flashed across my mind: I took a good look and said to myself, "This is it! This is the space!" It was perfect.[50]

50. Gehr, in Scott MacDonald, *A Critical Cinema 5* (Berkeley: University of California Press, 2006): 374.

Having made sure he would have the space to himself for the entire night, Gehr set up his camera so that he could film the hallway by exposing four frames at a time—first, from a position on the focal length of his zoom lens just beyond its midpoint, then, from a position on the zoom lens the same distance behind the midpoint. Moving back and forth along the focal length of the lens, each time a bit further in one direction, then in the other, Gehr filmed continuously until morning (at the conclusion of *Serene Velocity*, what is apparently morning light is visible in the window of the door at the far end of the corridor).[51]

Serene Velocity has been understood in a range of ways over the years. The experience it creates remains unusual and challenging for many viewers. On the most obvious level, *Serene Velocity* can be seen as a cinematic form of op art; like the work of Richard Anuszkiewicz, Bridget Riley, and Victor Vasarely, Gehr's silent film works with static elements (during each of the four-frame bits, the camera's position is stationary), which in combination create unusual, even mystifying optical effects that evolve over time. A screening of *Serene Velocity* is far longer than most anyone would spend looking at an op art painting, and this extended duration allows for more dynamic effects: the film can seem, as its title suggests, serene one moment and violent the next. As Gehr has often said, the experience of *Serene Velocity* varies considerably, depending on the sector of the film frame one focuses on. During some moments, especially if one is focusing on the edges of the frame, the film seems to blink on and off, something like a neon sign, but if one focuses on the red exit signs above the door at the far end of the hallway and the door just in front of the camera, the signs become animated into a thrusting, piston-like movement. Indeed, in his program note for the April 29, 1972 screening of *Serene Velocity*, Ken Jacobs saw the film "as sexual metaphor, or sex-become-cinema."

Gehr's early films, like Gottheim's, were often explorations of fundamental elements of cinema, and this seems especially true of *Serene Velocity*, both on the level of the film's engagement with the way in which cinema functions in between the reality of a flat, 2-D screen and the illusion of deep space depicted by the imagery on the screen and in Gehr's focus on the zoom lens. The zoom lens can be understood as at least a metaphor for, and more precisely a miniaturization of, the hallway it is used to film. Just as Binghamton students needed to pass through that hallway to work on their own films, the light from outside the camera

51. The 23-minute film was designed to be shown at 16 frames per second, but since the silent speed option is usually not available even when 16mm projection is, *Serene Velocity* is usually shown at 24 frames per second.

must pass through the lens, the "hallway" into the camera, to get to the camera obscura—the "room" inside the camera—to do its work on the emulsion. Of course, the extended focal length of the zoom lens Gehr used reflects both the length of the hallway and the film's slow, steady journey "through" it.

Serene Velocity has been widely admired and influential. One of the more surprising influences of the film can be seen in Laura Poitras's Academy Award–winning documentary about Edward Snowden, *Citizenfour* (2014). When I first saw *Citizenfour*, I was struck by a motif in the film of institutional hallways (hotel hallways in this instance), filmed in a manner that evokes *Serene Velocity*. Like the hallway in *Serene Velocity*, the empty, nondescript hallways in *Citizenfour* can be seen as Kafkaesque evocations of institutional power and a demand for conformity—something that, in different ways, Gehr and Poitras (and Edward Snowden) mean to defy.[52] Gehr was Poitras's first teacher at the San Francisco Art Institute, as she has explained:

> I was working at a French restaurant in San Francisco (Masa's), and I started taking filmmaking classes at the San Francisco Art Institute on the side. My first teacher was Ernie Gehr, an avant-garde filmmaker. The first film he showed was his brilliant 1970 film *Serene Velocity*, a 23-minute structuralist meditation on a hallway. I started making Super-8mm and 16mm silent films while still cooking, but the filmmaking took over. Although my documentary work is more accessible than the avant-garde filmmaking I studied, I am still influenced by what I learned.[53]

When I asked Poitras about the similarity of the hallway shots in *Citizenfour* and *Serene Velocity*, she told me that this was not a conscious reference: "Ernie's films continue to influence my work in many, many

52. Filmmaker/installation artist Amie Siegel uses hallways in a similar manner, also evoking *Serene Velocity*, in her 5-channel installation *Deathstar/Todesstern* (2006). Siegel's description of the piece is relevant in the present context: "Five slow traveling shots down the hallways of early German modernist buildings built or appropriated by the Third Reich and their subsidiary companies (or later the GDR). These iconic or obscure buildings—including Berlin's Tempelhof Airport, IG Farben Bau, SFB Haus des Rundfunk and KDF-bad Prora—share the uniform, 'never-ending' hallways indicative of both national socialist architecture and a modernist program of hygienic building-machines free of the past." From Siegel's website: http://amiesiegel.net/project/deathstar_todesstern.

53. Poitras in an interview available at *Indiewire*, July 31, 2006: http://www.indiewire.com/article/indiewire_interview_laura_poitras_director_of_my_country_my_country.

ways, but not literally in this instance." Nevertheless, she added, "If you want to make the connection, I have no objections."[54]

❧

Whatever were Gehr's original goals for *Serene Velocity*, and whatever interpretations of the film one might want to suggest, the most obvious reading of the film in this current context has to do with what the experience of the film does to the original "subject." *Serene Velocity* transforms one of the quintessential modern spaces, endemic to modern academic architecture and to office architecture everywhere, into a visual phantasmagoria. A space one must move through in order to get to, or to escape from, an office or workroom, has been transformed into an end in itself—just as, for a period of a bit less than a decade, the Cinema Department transformed the process of learning what cinema is and can be into something quite new in the annals of American academe—into a collaboration between faculty and students that continues to inform and invigorate American media culture. As fully as any film produced by teachers and/or students involved with the SUNY-Binghamton Cinema Department, *Serene Velocity*, completed at the very dawn of this enterprise, can be understood as an emblem of what Gottheim and his colleagues wanted to accomplish, and at least for a time, did accomplish.

54. E-mail to the author, March 16, 2015.

Appendix 2

Ken Jacobs by Art Spiegelman

Art Spiegelman's cartoon *Ken Jacobs* was originally published (in color as a single page) in *Breakdowns: Portrait of the Artist as a Young %@&*!* (New York: Pantheon, 2008). Thanks to Benjamin Salzmann for black-and-white redesign and to Spiegelman for allowing it to be used here.

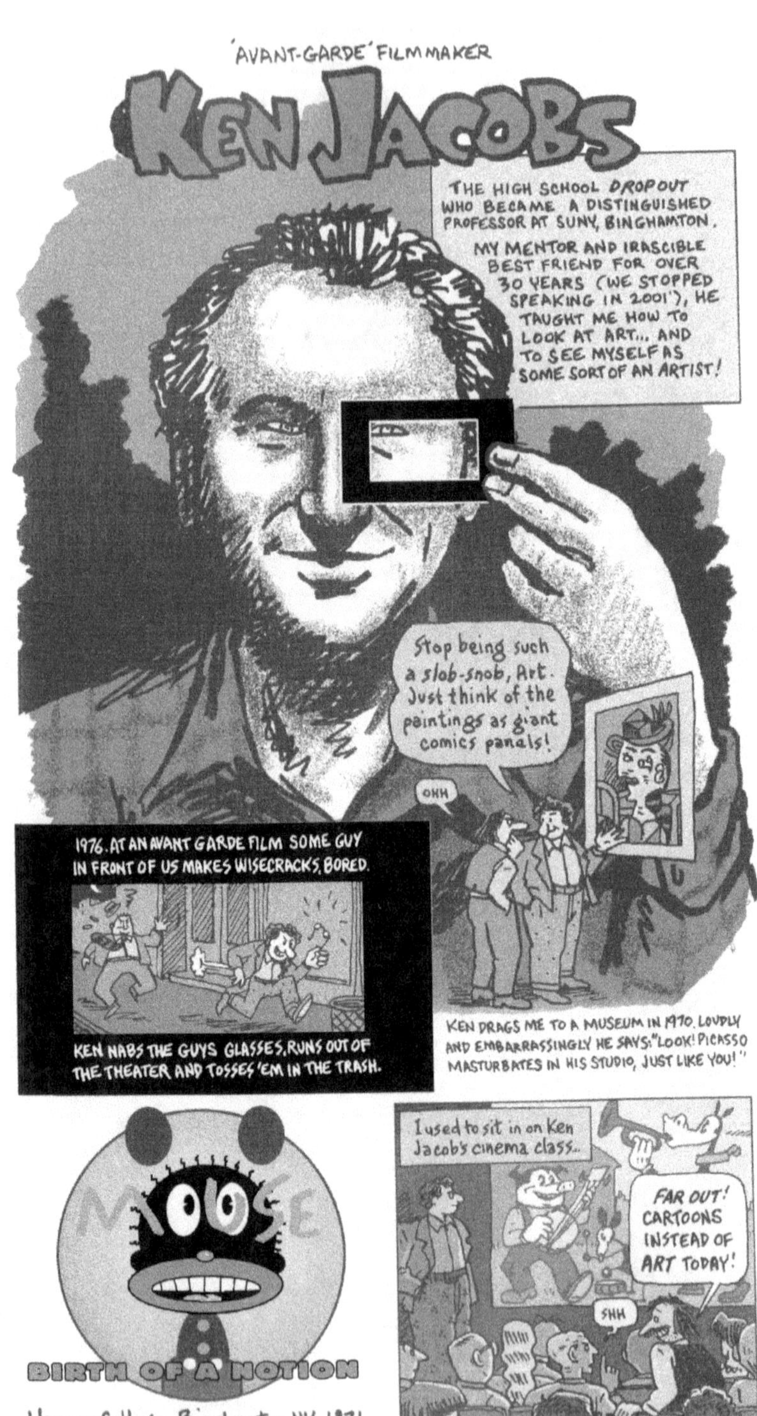
'AVANT-GARDE' FILMMAKER
KEN JACOBS
THE HIGH SCHOOL DROPOUT WHO BECAME A DISTINGUISHED PROFESSOR AT SUNY, BINGHAMTON.
MY MENTOR AND IRASCIBLE BEST FRIEND FOR OVER 30 YEARS (WE STOPPED SPEAKING IN 2001'), HE TAUGHT ME HOW TO LOOK AT ART... AND TO SEE MYSELF AS SOME SORT OF AN ARTIST!
Stop being such a slob-snob, Art. Just think of the paintings as giant comics panels!
OHH
KEN DRAGS ME TO A MUSEUM IN 1970. LOUDLY AND EMBARRASSINGLY HE SAYS: "LOOK! PICASSO MASTURBATES IN HIS STUDIO, JUST LIKE YOU!"
1976. AT AN AVANT GARDE FILM SOME GUY IN FRONT OF US MAKES WISECRACKS, BORED.
KEN NABS THE GUYS GLASSES, RUNS OUT OF THE THEATER AND TOSSES 'EM IN THE TRASH.
MOOSE
BIRTH OF A NOTION
Harpur College. Binghamton, NY. 1971
I used to sit in on Ken Jacob's cinema class..
FAR OUT! CARTOONS INSTEAD OF ART TODAY!
SHH

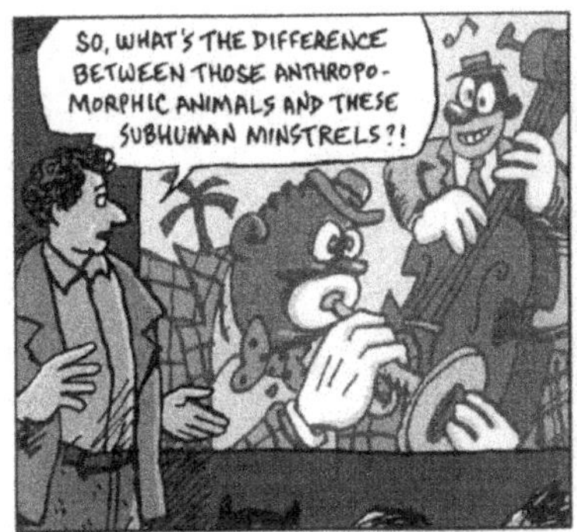

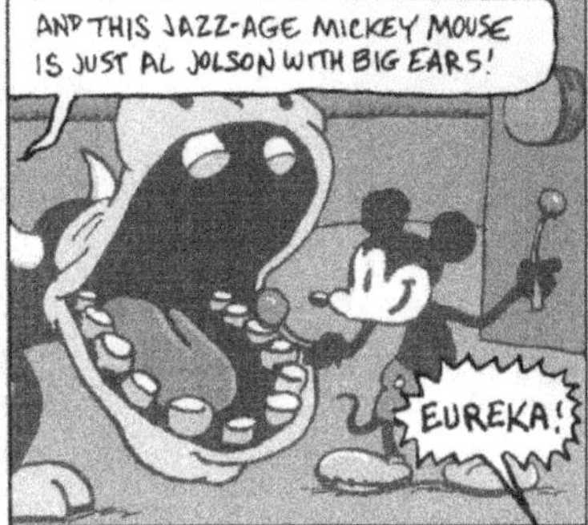

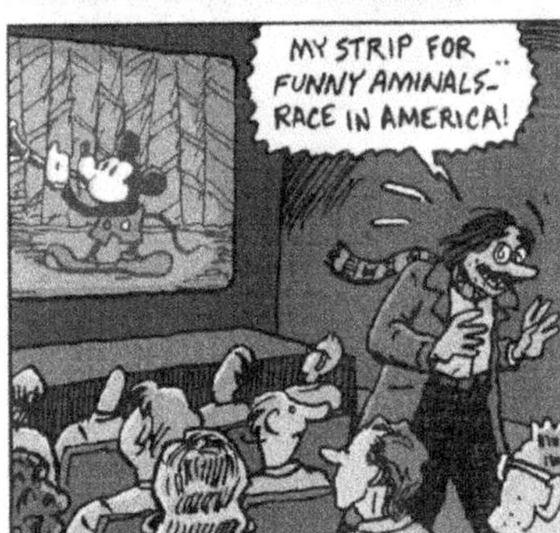

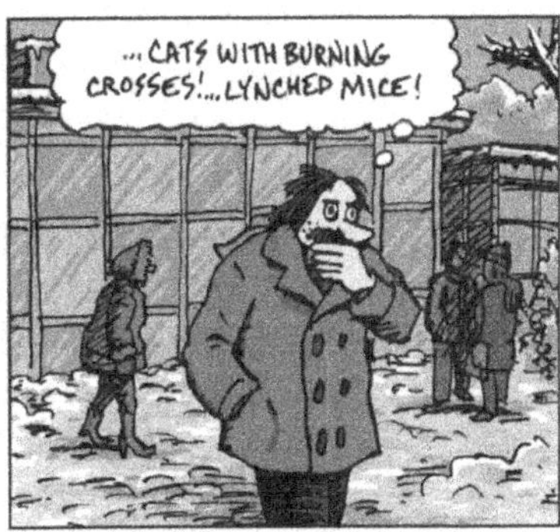

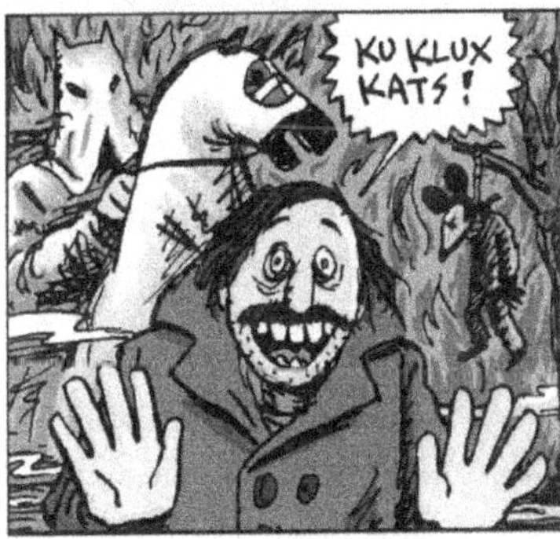

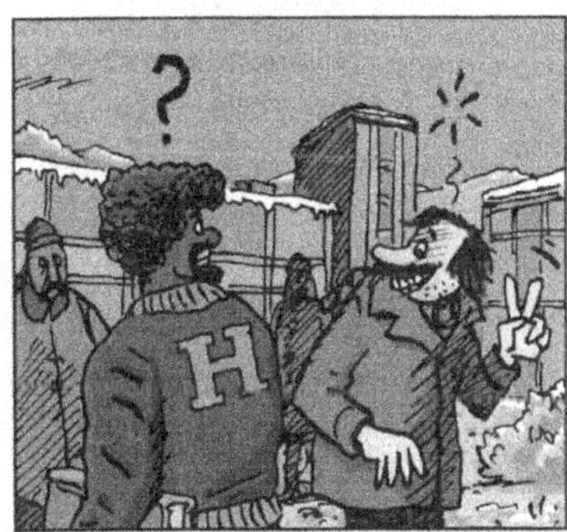

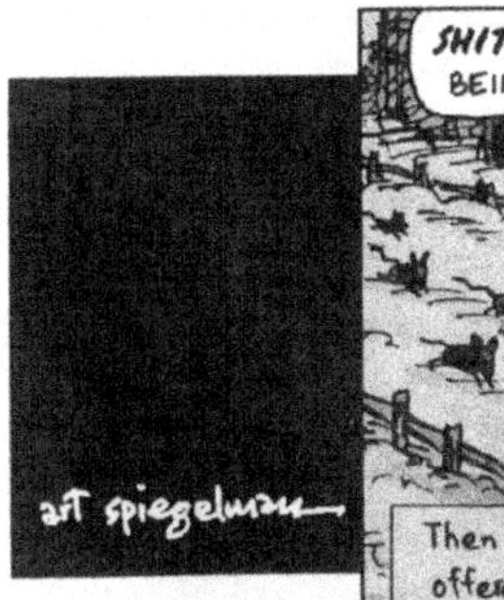

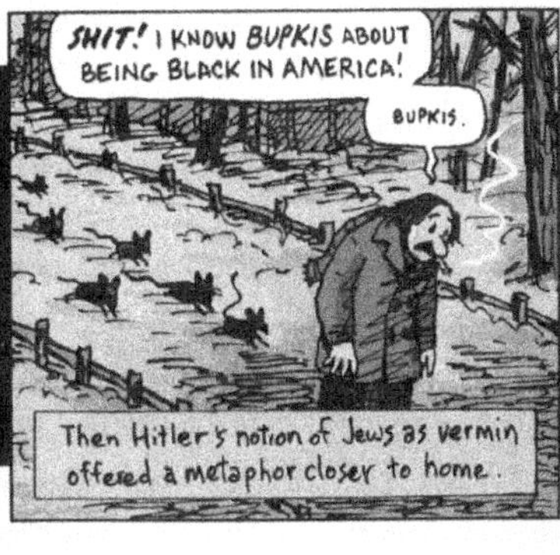

FOOTNOTES:

* speaking regularly again since 2008

** A 3 page version of MAUS appeared in FUNNY AMINALS #1 published by Apex Novelties in 1972.

Acknowledgments

As will be obvious, this book has been a collaborative enterprise. The men and women whose voices are included in "The Weave" have spent considerable time and effort speaking with me or writing to me, and helping me to revise and correct their comments. Many of them have suggested avenues for me to explore that I wouldn't have known about otherwise. Without their participation, patience, goodwill, trust—and their belief that their experiences at SUNY-Binghamton have been significant to them and might be to others—*Binghamton Babylon* wouldn't exist. I am deeply grateful for their honesty and, in many instances, their courage in being candid about a volatile time.

Several colleagues read the manuscript when it was moving toward its final form and offered thoughtful and detailed feedback. Ken Eisenstein was generous beyond the call of duty in providing not only a careful reading, but in finding and passing on to me various kinds of information that have enriched the manuscript (some particular instances are indicated in the text). Eisenstein devoted many hours to talking with me about the project as it neared completion.

Christopher Hanson read the manuscript and provided valuable moral support, as well as a good many helpful suggestions. I am grateful and humbled that Hanson and Eisenstein were willing to take time out of their busy schedules and their own work to help me with mine.

David Gatten made helpful suggestions about how to position *Binghamton Babylon* as a nonfiction novel. J. J. Murphy and Steve Anker helped me think more carefully about the process of compiling and presenting the weave of voices.

Discovering Mark Goldstein's photographs of Cinema Department personalities and activities helped this project come alive for me; Mark's generosity in sharing these photographs with me is deeply appreciated.

At Binghamton University I had the assistance of Nancy Wlostowski, then secretary in the Cinema Department, who guided me to various caches of information about the period this volume explores; and Ariana T. Gerstein, who helped me find people I needed to find to do my research. Thanks also to Tamara Richard, Vincent Grenier, Brian Wall, and Carl M. Schrecongost.

At Hamilton College, my home institution, Benjamin Salzman used his digital wizardry and his patience with me to help ready the imagery for the book; and Bret Olsen assisted me with readying the manuscript for presentation to publishers; research librarian Kristin Strohmeyer helped me track down leads to useful information; student Joseph Michaels helped me think through Hollis Frampton's *Travelling Matte*; and Art Department office assistant Heather Johnsen improved my efficiency.

Any number of colleagues not particularly connected with SUNY-Binghamton have directly and indirectly offered moral support. They include P. Adams Sitney, Abigail Child, and Gerald O'Grady.

At home, I had the continuing support of my wife, Patricia Reichgott O'Connor, who was enthusiastic about this project from the beginning and never lost faith in it—and who kindly suggested the title. The book is dedicated to her.

Index

Note: This is a limited index. It does not include the majority of those listed as "Voices" in "The Weave." The Weave has been constructed so that the reader can get a sense of the life of the Cinema Department as it evolved during a volatile decade. Throughout, the stories told by faculty and students intersect in a variety of complex ways for which an index is inadequate. Please check the listing of Voices and the individual speaker identifications to track what the various faculty members, students, and visitors remember about their experiences. Several filmmakers (Tony Conrad, Heinz Emigholz, Morgan Fisher, Hollis Frampton) whose direct involvement with the Cinema Department was of relatively short duration are indexed.

23rd Psalm Branch (Brakhage, 1966), 55
55 Days at Peking (Ray, 1963), 99, 115
240x (Fisher, 1974), 13, 157–58, 229–30
2001: A Space Odyssey (Kubrick, 1968), xiv

Abe, Shuya, 30
Abramowitz, Richard, 130
Abstraction in Avant-Garde Films (book; Turim), 186, 187
The Act of Seeing with One's Own Eyes (Brakhage, 1972), 3, 5, 6, 8
Aigen, Marilyn, 49, 62, 180, *181*, 229
Airshaft (Jacobs, 1967), 31
Albetta, Frank, 91–92, 95, 214–17, 218
American Dance Asylum, 16, 131, 133, 134, 135
American Falls (Solomon, 2010–12), 18
analytic projectors, 38–39, 54–55, 66, 89
Andrew, Dudley, xvi
Animal House (Landis, 1978), 54
Anker, Steve, *see* introductory note on this page
Anthology Film Archives, 29, 56–57, 72, 82, 127–28, 153, 184, 185
Apparition Theater of New York (Ken Jacobs), 67, 85, 98, 129
Arnulf Rainer (Kubelka, 1960), 62
Art Institute of Chicago, school of, 12, 140, 144–45
The Art of Vision (Brakhage, 1961–65), 60
Aspen School of the Arts, 38
L'Avventura (Antonioni, 1960), 22

B, Beth and Scott, 190

Back Where I Came from (radio show; Ray, 1930s), 103
Barn Rushes (Gottheim, 1971), 3, 5, 6, 7, 8, 51, 71, 98, 141, 204, 205, 221, 227
Before the Fact (Brand and Levine, 1974), *155*, 226, 227–28
Begin the Beguine (performance; Jones and Zane, 1973), 133–35
Baillie, Bruce, 22, 34
Barnett, Dan, *see* introductory note on p. 245
Berde, Shelley, 91, 205, 207
Berkeley in the Sixties (Kitchell, 1990), 12
Berliner, Alan, *see* introductory note on p. 245
The Bicycle Thief (De Sica, 1949), 52
Bigger Than Life (Ray, 1956), 115
The Big Sleep (Lang, 1946), 91
Big Stick (Levine, 1973), 146
Binghamton, My India (Jacobs; shot 1970, unfinished), 202
The Birth of a Nation (Griffith, 1915), 65–66
The Birth of a Nation (Wyborny, 1973), 151
Bitter Victory (Ray, 1957), 17
Blackman, Meryl, 111, 130, 131, 234
Blonde Cobra (Jacobs, 1963), 31, 35, 148
Blood of the Beasts (*Le Sang des bêtes*, Franju, 1949), 24
Blow-Up (Antonioni, 1967), 52
Blue (Bode, 1976), 234–35
Blue Lady (Holman, c. 1974), 170
Blue Moses (Brakhage, 1962), 127
Blue Velvet (Lynch, 1986), 28
Blues (Gottheim, 1969), 51, 52, 98, 204
Bock, Richard, *see* introductory note on p. 245
Bode, Harald, 112
Bode, Peer, *see* introductory note on p. 245
Bode, Ralf, 111
Bodger, Lowell, 157, 158
Bold, Alf, 128
Bornstein, Charlie, 110
Brakhage, Jane, 60
Brakhage, Stan, 6, 50, 55, 59–60, 61, 62, 75, 83, 85, 94, 96, 112, 113, 124, 146, 154
Brand, Bill, 135, 155, 226, 227–28
Braudel, Fernand, 153
Breaking Away (Yates, 1979), 193
Breathless (Godard, 1959), 52
Breer, Robert, 56–57
Breindel, Hali, 49, 56, 112, 119
Bridge Theater, 23
The Brig (Mekas, 1964), 23
Bronstein, Marsha, 89, 151
Buffalo Heads: Media Study, Media Practices, Media Pioneers (book, Vasulka and Weibel), 195
Bunting, Basil, 50

California Institute of the Arts (CalArts), 11, 50
Camper, Fred, 122
Cantor, Norman, 167, 172–73
Chafed Elbows (Downey, 1967), 32
Chelsea Girls (Warhol, 1966), 26, 137
Child, Abigail, 189, 244
Citizenfour (Poitras, 2014), 237–38
Clarke, Shirley, 33–34, 43
Coal Miner's Daughter (Apted, 1980), 111
Cobra Woman (Siodmak, 1944), 153
The Collective for Living Cinema, xi, 18, 19, 90, 127–28, *129*–30, 134, 138, 149, 151, 155–56, 184–85, 190, 194
Color Adjustment (Riggs, 1991), 12
Computer Image Corporation (Denver), 170
Conner, Bruce, 22, 146
Conrad, Tony, 126, 137, 138, 140, 156–57, 175–76
Cooper, Karen, 128

Corn (Gottheim, 1970), 204
Cortez, Diego, 169
Coutts, Julie, 74
Cracking the Maya Code (Lebrun and Halpern-Lebrun, 2008), 14
Critical Mass (Frampton, 1971), x, xvii, xviii, 92–96, 214–18, 220, 224, 228
Crouch, Robert, 51
Cup Mix (2 channels) (Bode, 1977), 235
Currey, Gail, 11, 140
Customs & Immigration (Hoberman, 1971), 49n, 89, 231–32
Cyclopean 3D: Life with a Beautiful Woman (Jacobs, 2011), 15

Dance of the Maize God (Lebrun and Halpern-Lebrun, 2014), 14
Dauler, Karen, 74
Dead End, Dead End (Barnett, c. 1974), 225
Dearing, Bruce, 29, 45, 210
Deathstar/Todesstern (Siegel, 2006), 237n
The Decay of Fiction (O'Neill, 2002), 14
De Hirsch, Storm, 170, 195
Departure (Levine; shot 1966–67, finished 1991), 226, 228–29
De Profundis (Brose, 1997), 234
Deren, Maya, 53, 146
Detour (Ulmer, 1946), 52
The Devil's Gonna Get You (Jones and Zane, 1973), 65
DiBenedetto, Barbara, 49, 53, 91–93, 95, 100, 214–17, 218
Dick, Vivienne, 190
Dixon, Sally, 137
Dog Star Man (Brakhage, 1961–64), 60
Doorway (Gottheim, 1971), 141, 204
Don't Expect Too Much (Susan Ray, 2012), 18, 192–93, 224
Dorsky, Nathaniel, 225
Downey, Robert, Sr., 37, 51–52
Dracula (Browning, 1931), 139
Dressed to Kill (De Palma, 1980), 111
Dunham, Cecily, 74

East of Borneo (Melford, 1931), 153
Easy Rider (Hopper, 1969), xiv
Eadweard Muybridge, Zoopraxographer (Andersen, 1975), 158
Eisenberg, Daniel, *see* introductory note on p. 245
Eisenstein, Ken, 93, 220, 243
Elective Affinities series (Gottheim, 1973–80), 14, 71, 178, 206
Emigholz, Heinz, 150, 194
Empire (Solomon, 2008–12), 18
Exit Elena (Silver, 2012), 18
The Experiment (Hocking, 1969), xvii, 210–12, 229
Experimental Televison Center (ETC), xv, 15, 30, 42–43, 61–62, 63–64, 65, 112, 113–14, 131, 153, *164*, 187, 189, 224, 236
The Exquisite Hour (Solomon, 1989, 1994), 18

Faccinto, Victor, 146
Faller, Marion, 93
The Family Album (Berliner, 1986), 11, 202
Family Portrait Sittings (Guzzetti, 1975), 216n23
Farber, Manny, 23, 37
Farrell, Tom, 98, 109, 110
Festival of Independent Avant-Garde Film, 151, 158
Field (Gehr, 1970), 42, 203–04
Field, Simon, 128
Filament (Halpern-Lebrun, 1975), 130
Film Feedback (Conrad, 1974), xvii, 12, 137, 175–76
Film Forum (New York City), 128
Fingeroth, Danny, *see* introductory note on p. 245
Fireworks (Anger, 1947), 24

First Cousin Once Removed (Berliner, 2012), 12
Fisher, Danny, 110
Fisher, Morgan, 157–59, 229–30
Fishing (Hocking, 1971), 212–13, 235
Fitzgibbon, Coleen, 145, 156, 169
The Flaherty. *See* Robert Flaherty Film Seminar
Flaming Creatures (Smith, 1963), xv, 24, 66, 118
The Flicker (Conrad, 1966), 12, 126, 138
Flying Leathernecks (Ray, 1951), 99
Fog Line (Gottheim, 1970), xvii, 9n5, 141, 204–05, 227
Fonda, Jane, 61
Fonoroff, Nina, 148
Forbidden Planet (Wilcox, 1956), 231
Four Shadows (Gottheim, 1978), 71n, 206, 209–10
Frampton, Hollis, 9, 13, 31, 83, 88, 91–96, 214–21, 224
Freaks (Browning, 1932), 24, 108

Gatten, David, 243
Gay Liberation Front (GLF), 74
Gehr, Ernie, *see* introductory note on p. 245
Gersten, Michael, 35, 38, 53, 66–67, 232
The Given Word (Duarte, 1962), 37
Glick, Myrel, 165, 185
Gold Diggers of 1935 (Berkeley, 1935), 56
Goldstein, Mark, *xix*, xx, 14, 194, 243
Gomez, Joseph A., 4
A GOOD NIGHT FOR THE MOVIES (performance; Jacobs, 1972), 57–58
Gorillas in a Can (Fingeroth, 1976), 149
Gottheim, Larry, *see* introductory note on p. 245
Graff, Andrea, 128
Graff, Mark, 119, 127, 128, 129, 151n
The Great Blondino (Nelson, 1967), 31
Great Blondino Preview (Nelson, 1967), 33
Griffith, D. W., 52, 58
Guide to Filmmaking (book; 1969, Ed Pincus), 41
Gunning, Tom, 201
Guttenplan, Howard, 128

Hacha, Jan, 74
Halpern-Lebrun, Amy, *see* introductory note on p. 245
Hammer, Barbara, 186
Hanson, Chris, 243
Hapax Legomena (Frampton, 1971–72), xviii, 9n5, 13, 58, 214
Happy Mother's Day (Chopra and Leacock, 1963), 5
Harlot (Warhol, 1964), 22
Harmonica (Gottheim, 1971), 72, 91, 98, 204–05, 207
Harpur Film Society, 21–26, 28, 31–32, 35, 38, 49, 153, 166, 177–78, 183
Harvey, David, 74
Head against the Walls (*Le tête contre les murs*, Franju, 1958), 24
Hemingway, Ernest, 9
Herskowitz, Richard, *see* introductory note on p. 245
Heymann, Jane, 110
Hills, Henry, 189
History (Gehr, 1970), 40, 72
Hichcock, Alfred, 52
Hoberman, Jim, *see* introductory note on p. 245
Hock, Louis, 145
Hocking, Ralph and Sherry Miller, *see* introductory note on p. 245
Holman, Lloyd Bruce, *see* introductory note on p. 245
Hopper, Dennis, 28, 61, 70, 88
Horizons (Gottheim, 1973), xvii, 14, 42, 47, 71, 116, 141, 150–51,204, 206–07, 208–09, 221, 227

Huge Pupils (part 1 of *The Adventures of the Exquisite Corpse* series, originally known as "Kodak Ghost Poems"; Noren, 1968), 75
Huot, Bob, 91, 158

I-87 (Bode, 1976), 235
Iimura, Taka, 61, 124–25, 209
I'm a Stranger Here Myself: A Portrait of Nicholas Ray (David Helpern, Jr., 1975), 101, 221, 223
In a Lonely Place (Ray, 1950), 17, 91
International Sweethearts of Rhythm (Weiss, 1986), 19
Intimate Stranger (Berliner, 1991), 11
Irwin: A New York Story (Makara, 2011), 149
The Island of Lost Souls (Kenton, 1933), 55
Israel, Bob, 143

Jacobs, Azazel, 15, 45, 86
Jacobs, Flo and Ken, *see* introductory note on p. 245
Jacoby, Roger, 137
Joe (Avildsen, 1970), 51, 59
Johnny Guitar (Ray, 1954), 17, 99
Jones, Bill T., *see* introductory note on p. 245

Kaplan, Daile, *see* introductory note on p. 245
Kaplan, Helene, *see* Helene Kaplan Wright
Karel, Ernst, 219
Karpel, Linda, 49, 53
Kasakove, David, 124, 177
Keller, Marjorie, 145–46, 169, 179
Kesey, Ken, 111
Kessler, Milton, 26, 32, 50
Knife in the Water (Polanski, 1962), 22
Knock on Any Door (Ray, 1949), 17, 91
Korot, Beryl, 64
Krugman, Lee, 135, 143, 151n
Kubelka cooking performance, 119–20, *121*
Kubelka, Peter, *see* introductory note on p. 245
Kubota, Shigeko, 184
Kustom Kar Kommandos (Anger, 1965), xiv

Landow, George, 145
LaPore, Mark, 135, 138, 148, 175
Leacock, Richard, 4, 6, 75
Lecture Hall (Lecture Hall 1 and Lecture Hall 6), 5, 28–29, 35, 160
Lemon (Frampton, 1969), 51, 126
Lennon, John, 58
Levenson, Leslie, 104, 116
Levi, Charlie, 119
Levine, Martin, 74
Levine, Richard, 151, 166
Levine, Saul, *see* introductory note on p. 245
Lightning over Water (Ray and Wenders, 1980), 109, 221
Line Describing a Cone (McCall, 1973), 135
Lippard, Lucy, 145
Little Stabs at Happiness (Jacobs, 1963), 31, 33, 35, 54, 58
Lonesome Cowboys (Warhol, 1967–68), 61
Looking Left (political organization), 163, 172, 173
Los Angeles Independent Film Oasis, 130
Love (Ai) (Iimura, 1963), 33
Lovell, Mike, 232
Loving (Brakhage, 1957), 148

Macao (Ray, 1952) 17
Magellan Cycle (Frampton, 1972–1980), 13
Manning, Nick, 30
The Man with a Movie Camera (Vertov, 1929), 113, 156
Marc, David, *see* introductory note on p. 245
Massachusetts College of Art and Design (MassArt), 11, 17, 143, 146–47, 174–75, 178–79

Matrix Dance (performance; Bode and Blackman, 1975), 131
Maus (graphic novel; Spiegelman), 42n, 124, 125, 240–41
McCall, Anthony, 135
McElhatten, Mark, 91, 154
Meet John Doe (Capra, 1941), 124
Mekas, Jonas, 22, 23, 26, 30, 31, 43, 62, 76, 83, 86, 128, 184, 190, 209
Memoranda for a Dream of Magellan (Frampton, 1972), 220n28
Michaels, Joseph, 244
Michelson, Annette, xiv, 19, 169
Millennium Film Workshop, 30, 36–37, 48, 127–28, 146, 158, 185
Misconception (Keller, 1977), 145–46
Mitchell, Eric, 190
Momma's Man (Azazel Jacobs, 2008), 15
Moritz, Bill, 130
Morning (Gehr, 1967), 31, 40, 204
Murphy, J. J., 243
Museum of Jurassic Technology, 130
Musser, Charles, 201
Mouches Volantes (Gottheim, 1976), 71n, 153, 161, 206, 207–09
Movement as Meaning in Experimental Film (book; Barnett), 11, 144, 148, 225n33, 226
Movements for Video, Dance and Music (Bode and Blackman, 1975), 131
Mr. Radio Man (radio show; Anker and Jacobs, 1960s–70s), 102

New Left Note (Levine, 1968–82), 226
Newman, Frank, 21
New York State Council on the Arts (NYSCA), 124
Night of the Living Dead (Romero, 1968), xiv
Nissan Ariana Window (Jacobs, 1969), 3, 5, 117–18
Nitelite (Solomon, 1975), 18, 231, 232–33
Nitsch, Hermann, 61, 72, 76–82, 102
Nobody's Business (Berliner, 1966), 11
Noren, Andrew, 58, 75
(nostalgia) (Frampton, 1971), 93–96
A Note in a Bottle (Barnett, c. 1974), 225n33
Note to Colleen (Levine, 1974), 226
Notes of an Early Fall (Levine, 1976), 148, 178, 226, 228
Now Voyager (Rapper, 1942), 65
Nygren, Scott, 189

Oberle, Luke, 110
October (Eisenstein, 1928), 156
O'Grady, Gerald, 4, 172, 195, 244
Oh Dem Watermelons (Nelson, 1965), 32
Ondine, 137, 138–39
O'Neill, Beverly, 130
O'Neill, Pat, 130
Ono, Yoko, 58
On the Hill in Johnson City (Zane, 1972), 57
On the Spot (Levine, 1973), 226–27
100 Sec. Lumination (Bode, 1976), 235
Orgien Mysterien Theater (Nitsch, 1962–98), x, 61, 76–82, *78–79*
Orpheus (*Orphée*, Cocteau, 1950), 22
Our Harpur Film (Gottheim, 1969), 43
Our Trip to Africa (*Unsere Afrikareise*, Kubelka, 1966), 17

Paglia, Camille, *see* introductory note on p. 245
Paik, Nam June, 29–30, 42, 153, 175, 176–77, 210, 224
Patent Pending (Berliner, 1975), 160, 231, 233–34
Pawlikowski, Robert, 43
"The Perils of Space" (artshow), 158, 160
Peterson, Sidney, 169
Pictures of the Lost Word (*Bilder vom verlorenen Wort*, Wyborny, 1975), 20, 153, 230–31
Pincus, Ed, 41

Polan, Dana, xiii
Popular Songs (Barnett, c. 1974), 225n33
Portapak, early use of, 29–30, 89, 210, 218–20, 221
Portrait of Jason (Clarke, 1967), x, 33–34
Portrayal: Memorial Day (Levine, 1978), 226
Prenovitz, Bill, 158
The Present (Gottheim, 1968), 31
Pull My Daisy (Frank, 1959), 148
Pull Out/Fallout (Barnett, c. 1974), 225n33
Putney Swope (Downey, 1969), 51–52

Ragona, Melissa, 216n21
Rainer, Yvonne, 179, 188–89, 212
Rambling Notes (Levine, 1977), 226
Ray, Nicholas and Susan, *see* introductory note on p. 245
Rebel without a Cause (Ray, 1955), xv, 17, 99, 111, 115
La Région Centrale (Snow, 1971), 67
Remains to Be Seen (Solomon, 1989, 1994), 18
Reminiscences of a Journey to Lithuania (Mekas, 1972), 62
Renée Is Wonderful (Barnett, c. 1974), 225
Resume (Levine, 1977), 226
Return to the Scene of the Crime (Jacobs, 2008), 201n7
Reverberation (Gehr, 1969), 40
Rich, B. Ruby, 145
Richter, Hans, 38n
Ring Modulation (Bode, 1978), 235
Robert Flaherty Film Seminar, 14, 83–84
Robbins, Karen, 232
Rose Hobart (Cornell, 1936), 153
Ross, Ken, *see* introductory note on p. 245
Røssaak, Eivind, 200
Rowe, Dan, 29, 33, 35
Rubin, Jon, 122

Sacker, Lushe, 128
Salzman, Ben, 244
Sarokin, Stephanie, 75
Saturday Night Fever (Badham, 1977), 111
Scarface (Hawks, 1932), 153
Scheiner, Brandi Dawn, 143
Schenec-Tady (Emigholz, 1973), 150–51, 153
Schilling, Alfons, 61, 137, 154, 157, 164–65, 209
Schneemann, Carolee, 53, 124, 146, 168, 169, 178
Schneider, Bob, 89–90, 151n
School of Advanced Technology, 150
Scorpio Rising (Anger, 1963), xiv, 23, 24, 32
Scrambled Legs (Hocking, 1977), 213–14
Second Bach Dance (Hocking, 1973), 213
The Secret Garden (Solomon, 1988), 18
Self Portrait (performance; Zane, 1973), 134–35
Seltzer, Charles, 74
Serene Velocity (Gehr, 1970), xvii, 3, 5, 6, 8, 13, 40, 42, 179 203, 204, 235–38
Shadow play performance, 48, 56–58, 66, 67
Shadows of Forgotten Ancestors (Parajanov, 1964), 117–18, 170
Shafransky, Renée, 49, 56, 119, 128, 130, 143, 151, 153, 174, 232
Sharits, Paul, 61, 62, 72, 73, 75, 83
Silver, Harvey, *see* introductory note on p. 245
Silver, Nathan, 18, 194
Sitney, P. Adams, 61, 86, 169n, 199, 203–04, 244
Sitting by the Window (Hocking, 1977), xvii, 213–14

Slow Flush (now *Three Preparations*; Halpern-Lebrun, 1972) 129
Slow Scan (Hocking, 1980), 64
Smith, Harry, 177
Smith, Jack, 48, 61, 95, 124, 134, 169
Snow, Michael, 67, 94, 156
Soft Fiction (Strand, 1979), 14
Soft in the Head (Silver, 2013), 18
Soft Rain (Jacobs; 1968), 5, 6, 198
Sokolowski, Linda Robinson, 74, 192
Solomon, Phil, *see* introductory note on p. 245
Spiegelman, Art, 26, 42, 52–53, 125, 151, 240–41
Star Spangled to Death (Jacobs; shot 1957–59, completed 2004), 54, 190–91
State University of New York at Buffalo (SUNY-Buffalo, now University at Buffalo), 171–72, 189–90, 220
Stern, Seymour, 58–*59*
Still (Gehr, 1967), 42, 59, 203
Sykas, Philip, *see* introductory note on p. 245

Tafler, David, 151n
Tambellini, Aldo (Tambellini's Gate theater), 22, 23
Tenant (Barnett, 1977), 225n33
Testa, Bart, 199n1
Theater of Gibberish (Hoberman and Schneider), 89–90, 234
They Live By Night (Ray, 1949), xv, 17, 52, 70, 99, 103, 108
Three (Gehr, 1970), 42
Tom, Tom, the Piper's Son (Biograph; 1905), 198–201
Tom, Tom, the Piper's Son (Jacobs,1969, revised 1971), xvii, 16, 35, 38, 47, 52, 66, 144, 198–201, 203, 205, 215, 223
Touch of Evil (Welles, 1958), 52
Trail of Dreams (Gorman), 149, 231, 234
Transparency (Gehr, 1969), 40
Travelling Matte (Frampton, 1971), 214, 218–21
Tree of Knowledge (Gottheim, 1980), 71n, 206
Turim, Maureen, *see* introductory note on p. 245
Turn On Red (Holman, 1974), 170

Uncertain Terms (Silver, 2014), 18
Unreachable Homeless (Wyborny, 1978), 20
Unsere Afrikareise (*Our Trip to Africa*, Kubelka, 1966), 17
Urban Peasants (Jacobs, 1975), 202

Valentin de las Sierras (Baillie, 1968), 34
Vanderbeek, Stan, 30, 31, 37, 222
Variety (Gordon, 1984), 19
Vasulka, Woody and Steina, 64, 124, 195
Vogel, Amos, 130
Voight, Karen, 74
Vinyl (Warhol, 1965), 232n44
Vivre sa vie (Godard, 1962), 135–37
Vukasin, Peter, 45, 143

Wait (Gehr, 1967), 31, 40
Warhol, Andy, 22, 32, 134, 138, 205
Water and Power (O'Neill, 1990), 14
Wavelength (Snow, 1967), 62, 137
We Can't Go Home Again (Ray, shot and edited 1971–73, released 2011), xvii, 12, 17, 18, 72, 76, 104, 106–07, 108–11, 115–16, 138, 192–93, 221–24
Weinbren, Grahame, 130
Weisberg, Steven, 135, 140, 151n
Weisman, Phil, *see* introductory note on p. 245
Weiss, Andrea, *see* introductory note on p. 245
Welk, Lois, 131, *136*
Wenders, Wim, 109, 221

White Heart (Barnett, 1975), 11, 144, 148, 156, 159, 161, 225–26
The Weir-Falcon Saga (Brakhage, 1970), 50
Wilson, Diana and David, 130
Wind across the Everglades (Ray, 1958), 17
Window (Jacobs, 1964), 31
Window Water Baby Moving (Brakhage, 1959), 33
The Wizard of Oz (many directors, 1929), 91
Women in Art (Zane, c. 1973), 65
Works & Days (Frampton, 1969), 62
Wright, Helene Kaplan, *see* introductory note on p. 245
Wright, Walter, 64

Zane, Arnie, 55, 74–75, 131–*32*, 133–35, *136*, 192
Zorns Lemma (Frampton, 1970), 9n5, 13, 209, 215
Zryd, Michael, xiv, 122

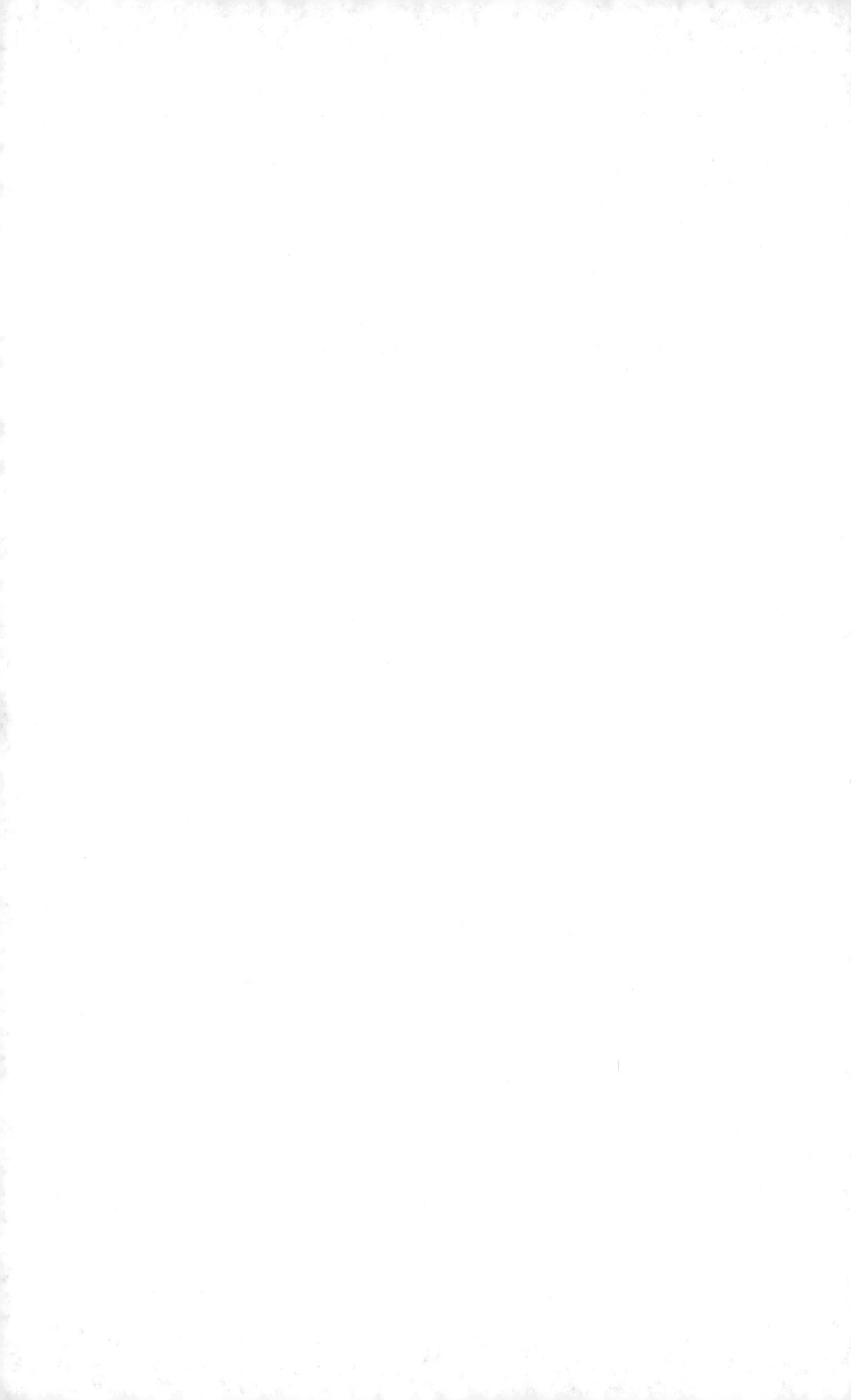

www.ingramcontent.com/pod-product-compliance
Lightning Source LLC
LaVergne TN
LVHW020437080826
844660LV00033B/1314

* 9 7 8 1 4 3 8 4 5 8 8 8 5 *